EUROPEAN IMMIGRANTS AND AMERICAN SOCIETY

•

Edited by
Timothy Walch and
Edward R. Kantowicz

•

A Garland Series

THE BURDEN OF ETHNICITY

•

The German Question in Chicago, 1914–1941

•

Leslie V. Tischauser

GARLAND PUBLISHING • NEW YORK & LONDON • 1990

Library of Congress Cataloging-in-Publication Data

Tischauser, Lelsie V.
The burden of ethnicity: the German question in Chicago,
1914–1941/ Leslie V. Tischauser.
p. cm.—(European immigrants and American society)
Thesis (Ph. D.)—University of Illinois, 1981.
Includes bibliographical references.
ISBN 0-8240-0356-X (alk. paper)
1. German Americans—Illinois—Chicago—History—
20th century. 2. Chicago (Ill.)—History—1875– .
I. Title. II. Series.
F548.9.G3T56   1990
977.3'1100431—dc20   90-3293

●

Printed on acid-free, 250-year-life paper.
Manufactured in the United States of America

Design by
Julie Threlkeld

Preface

*T*he *German Question in Chicago* traces the political history of the German community in the city from 1914 to 1941. It seeks to provide an answer to what it meant to be identified as a German-American in a time of trouble and chaos. Chicago was chosen for the study because it was generally regarded to be "the German capital" of the United States. Since its incorporation in 1837 the city's German population had always been around twenty-five percent of its total, and Germans had made many contributions to Chicago's economic, cultural, and political expansion. No other work covers the time frame established in this book, hence much of the material throws a new light on the events, elections, personalities, issues, and activities of the post-World War I period. Chicago is seen from the perspective of German newspapers, club members, and political leaders.

During much of the period under discussion, German-Americans were viewed as a threat to American society. Most of the residents of the community (and German-American refers to anyone who felt he or she belonged to that ethnic group) knew or cared little about subversive activities designated as Kaiserism, Hitlerism, revolutionary socialism, or "unAmericanism," but few escaped the smear of those epithets. Germans were "Huns," "Nazis," or beer-swilling barbarians, and they never could be trusted to be good Americans since militarism was "in their blood." Individual accomplishments meant little in this atmosphere highly charged with collective guilt and bitter negative stereotyping. Events in Germany created the image, and little that Americans of German descent in Chicago, or anywhere else for that matter, did could change the picture in other people's minds. Much of the rhetoric of German leaders in Chicago was aimed at rejecting that image. But these men too were caught up in an unreal world, one that reflected a false belief in recapturing a "German unity" that had never existed politically or socially. But in response to the extreme criticism German-Americans were subjected to during and after the great war such bombastic projections of greatness and cultural splendor seemed perhaps the best way to sustain some measure of pride. That, after all, was the only thing around which German-Americans could unite in the postwar world, as all other community resources had been destroyed during the anti-Hun crusade in 1917 and 1918. By the time of the debate over intervention in the Second World War began even that pride was gone. This work is the story of the final destruction of the German-American community in Chicago.

I wish to thank Professors Richard Fried, Melvin Holli, Richard Jensen, Marian Miller, and Leo Schelbert for their great help and support while writing this dissertation. Mrs. Gertrude Bolton provided splendid translations of many speeches, newspaper articles, and club minutes. None of this would have been possible without Connie, my wife and main inspiration. The next one will be for Jeffrey and Michael, who were not ready yet when this was written.

Leslie V. Tischauser

TABLE OF CONTENTS

INTRODUCTION

Did German-American culture disappear from the United States after
World War I? If any aspects of culture did survive, what were they and
how did German-Americans react to assertions of ethnic consciousness? What
methods did leaders of the German-American community use to keep the spirit
of ethnicity alive after the devastation of the anti-Hun crusade of 1917-1918?
How did German-Americans react to the reassertion of German power under
Adolf Hitler? And, finally, how did German-Americans view the coming of
another war with their old homeland? These will be the central questions
addressed in this study of German-Americans in Chicago between 1914 and 1941.

Chicago was chosen as the focal point for a study of German-Americans
because of its large German population (426,466, or 19.5 per cent of the
total population in 1910). German-Americans made up 22 per cent of the
city's work force, a higher percentage than that of native-born Americans.
Before World War I, Chicago had two daily German language newspapers with
a combined circulation of approximately 75,000, a German orchestra, theater,
and opera house, as well as over 400 German societies and clubs. Slightly
more than 76,000 German Catholics and 40,000 German Lutherans added to the
religious diversity of the German community. Thousands of Turners, free-
thinkers, and Socialists helped make the Chicago German community a true
cross-section of Teutonic culture in the United States.[1]

Between 1941 and 1919, Germans in the city felt the effects of a
crusade against everything vital to the continuance of their culture.

The anti-Hun campaign led by agents of the American Protective League almost succeeded in annihilating Teutonic culture. The German language almost disappeared, German schools were burned, German-American citizens were arrested, and any sign of allegiance to the old country became a symbol of disloyalty and un-Americanism. Ethnic attachments died hard for some. Militant Germans, or Germanists, vigorously protested American entrance into the war and dreaded the day German culture disappeared from American soil. For then the United States would become a dull, gray replica of England. These Germanists included the editors of German language newspapers, teachers of German in high schools and colleges, ministers who used German in their sermons and church work, leaders of ethnic societies, and such businessmen as restaurant owners, saloon-keepers, and brewers. As leaders of the German community, they depended on the existence of that community for their economic welfare. The anti-Hun campaign turned many less militant German-Americans away from their ethnic heritage and there-fore threatened the existence of the German leadership. When the war ended Germanists found themselves in a precarious position--they were leaders without followers.

Between 1919 and 1941 several attempts were made to rejuvenate an ethnic consciousness among German-Americans. These efforts were divided into two periods, pre- and post-Adolph Hitler. Leaders experienced major problems in the first period because there was little to organize around. No issues existed over which German-Americans could unite. Germany had been devastated by the war and Germanists attempted to use the image of a ravaged homeland to bring together American Germans but few seemed interested. Not even the candidacy and pro-German rhetoric of Robert La Follette in the 1924 presidential campaign fulfilled the hopes of

Germanists. (On the local level, German-American politicians were handed
a series of defeats in various elections, another indication of the weak-
ness of the ethnic bond.)

Some Germanists tried to unite their followers around the prohibition
question but that too failed. For most Germans in the city, as for other
Chicagoans, liquor remained readily available and at most the Eighteenth
Amendment was a minor annoyance. A few leaders tried to raise the war-guilt
question but with little success. "Spokesmen" for the German community
appeared at the 1927-28 school textbook controversy to push for the in-
clusion of German-American heroes in American history books. That incident,
however, devolved into a farce and a ludicrous exhibit of Teutonic thickheadedness. What seemed clear by 1933 was that few German-Americans were
interested in their ethnicity.

The arrival of Adolph Hitler in 1933 led to a renewed effort on the
part of Germanists to increase their influence. The image of an energetic
leader restoring Germany to world power would be used to ignite a consciousness of German ethnicity in America. New groups like the German-
American Bund attracted several thousand members, but the Bundists, for the
most part, were recent immigrants from Germany unable to find satisfaction
in American life. These first-generation German-Americans, some thirty
thousand of whom arrived between 1924 and 1927, had little in common with
the older German-Americans. They had not experienced the "reign of terror"
of 1917-1918, so they were not afraid to display openly their pride in
things German. The recent German immigrants had not shared the dilemma of
divided loyalty during wartime. They had not suffered the consequences of
being considered disloyal merely because of the place of their birth, or
the place of their father's birth. The Bund failed, in other words, because

it had little of importance to say to German-Americans. Hitler's growing power led to an increase of interest in German-American societies but Hitler was never as popular among German-Americans as Mussolini was among Italian-Americans. Most German-Americans still remembered the anti-Hun crusade during World War I and preferred to avoid any displays of ethnic loyalty. It was safer to be an American and forget the hyphen.

Between 1914 and 1941 most German-Americans rejected an ethnic identity. The only members of the group still proclaiming loyalty to the German spirit in 1941 were Nazis and Fascists. The reasons for the dis-appearance were three: First, the German language had vanished from most churches and schools by the end of the First World War; second, Germanists were unable to develop a new ideology stressing the differences between German and American culture (or what was considered "Puritanical" culture); and last, loyalty to the old country, an important factor in keeping alive an ethnic consciousness, became for German-Americans a source of stress and abuse. Twice within a generation the word "German" had become associated with the enemies of the United States. With the loss of all three factors involved in an ethnic identity, the German-American community disappeared from Chicago. The consequences of ethnicity under stress and the unsuccess-ful efforts of German-American leaders to unite their community form the subjects of this dissertation.[2]

NOTES

Introduction.

1. U.S. Department of Commerce and Labor, Bureau of the Census, Special Reports: Occupations at the Twelfth Census, 1900 (Washington: Government Printing Office, 1904), pp 516-523; the number of Catholics comes from an ethnic census of communicant members found in, Report of Archbishop James Quigley to Cardinal de Lai, Rome, March 21, 1913, as quoted in James Sanders, "The Education of Chicago Catholics: An Urban History," (Ph. D. dissertation, University of Chicago, p. 112, 138; number of Lutherans established by a count of members for the Northern Illinois District of the Missouri Synod found in Lutheran Witness, June 29, 1915, p. 13; also, see Sharvy G. Umbeck, "The Social Adaptation of a Selected Group of German-Background Protestant Churches in Chicago," (Ph. D. dissertation, University of Chicago, 1940), p. 121; for German societies and clubs see, Chicago Abendpost March 15, 1915.

2. The major books on German-Americans in the Twentieth Century are: Frederick Luebke, Bonds of Loyalty: German-Americans and World War I (Dekalb: Northern Illinois University Press, 1974); and, Phyllis Keller, States of Belonging: German-American Intellectuals and the First World War (Cambridge, Mass.: Harvard University Press, 1979). Both Luebke and Keller conclude that the war-time anti-Hun crusade in the United States destroyed German-American ethnicity. For the post-war period see; Frederick Luebke, "The Germans," in Ethnic Leadership in America, pp. 64-90, edited by John Higham. (Baltimore: Johns Hopkins University Press, 1978), and Ronald Bayor, Neighbors in Conflict: The Germans, Italians, Irish and Jews of New York City, 1920-1941 (Baltimore: John Hopkins University Press, 1979).

CHAPTER I

"WE TOO ARE AMERICANS": GERMAN-AMERICANS
IN CHICAGO AND THE COMING OF WORLD WAR I, 1914-1917

German-Americans assumed when the war broke out that, with America's
stated policy of neutrality, there was no conflict between their loyalty
to the Fatherland and their allegiance to the United States. This
assumption was to be sorely tested. As the war became the focus of
attention in American politics, they faced cruel dilemmas. Ultimately, no
political leader emerged who offered an answer to the problem of their divided
loyalties and eventually their expressions of dual allegiance would prove
their undoing. Between the outbreak of the war in Europe and America's
entry, German-Americans proclaimed that the United States should avoid
"entangling alliances" with Great Britain and pursue a strictly neutral
policy towards the belligerents. German-American leaders had little doubt
that Germany would win the war if Woodrow Wilson followed such a policy.
Teutonic culture would then triumph over "Anglo-Saxonism" with little
trouble.

Leaders of German-American clubs and societies in 1914 believed in
the superiority of Germanic civilization. English culture, Anglo-Saxonism,
as it was usually referred to, was markedly inferior. Whereas Germans were
hardworking, progressive, practical, liberal, and efficient, the British
were somber and puritanical. Unfortunately, that spirit of fanatic
puritanism was spreading to America. A German victory would help stop the

6

spread of the "shopkeeper" mentality. Such excessive ethnic chauvinism
also formed an important theme of the pre-war debate.

Chicago Germans and the Outbreak of the War

When news reached Chicago that a war in Europe had begun, leaders
of the Germania Club and the German Club, the largest and most influential
German societies in the city, called a large rally to protest "the slanderous
lies spread by the English press" concerning the outbreak of the war. Club
leaders also wanted to demonstrate the loyalty and "undying love" Germans
of Chicago had for "His Imperial Majesty, Kaiser Wilhelm." In the German
neighborhoods of Chicago's north side, a number of the 400,000 German-
Americans in the city listened to orchestras and saloon bands playing end-
less renditions of "Deutschland, Deutschland Uber Alles," and "Wacht am
Rhein." At Sieben's Hall, one of the largest saloons on the "nord seite,"
two thousand young men rushed to enlist in a volunteer regiment to go off
to help the Kaiser. Several thousand dollars were raised to send them to
"the fatherland," and the volunteers received permission from the German
consul to leave for Germany immediately. German flags, red, white and
black, streamed from almost every building along North Avenue, the main
street of Chicago's German belt, as members of Chicago's largest ethnic
group displayed pride in the power and might of their homeland.[1] The
outbreak of war in Europe gave every German Chicagoan an opportunity to
become a Germanist, one who found German culture superior to any other.
A victory for Germany, the Chicago Abendpost explained, would be a great
blessing for German-Americans, for only then would "a strong, true, and
independent Americanism" emerge, only with the defeat of Britain would
Americans be saved from Anglo-Saxonism.[2]

In analyzing the war German leaders in the city emphasized first,
that the war was a continuation of the age-old racial conflict between
Teutons and Slavs; second, that the war would determine whether the
civilization of Germany or the barbarism of Russia would prevail; and
third, that the English language press in the United States had already
shown a distinct prejudice in favor of the Slavs. This last point particularly
disturbed Ernest J. Kruetgen, vice-president of the Germania Club, and a
future postmaster of Chicago, because in his view "the United States had
gained practically nothing" from the Slavs while the Germans had contributed much in the way of culture and history. Michael Girten, president
of the German Aid Society, supported Kruetgen's view and emphasized that
the United States had no role to play in the conflict. The Teutons were
fighting for the improvement of the human race and, therefore, it was
"absurd for the American newspapers to take a pro-Slavic attitude . . . ."[3]
Other German leaders, including Dr. Otto Schmidt, prominent physician and
historian; Charles Wacker, head of the Chicago Plan Commission; former
congressman Julius Goldzier; Karl Eitel, owner of the Bismarck Hotel;
Oscar Mayer, "the sausage maker"; and newspaper publishers Horace Brand
(Illinois Staats-Zeitung) and Paul Mueller, (Chicagoer Abendpost)
publicly declared their views in a petition presented to a mass-meeting
called to protest biased news coverage. The petition declared that
German-American loyalty "to our adopted country does not prevent us from
extending sympathy and affection to the people of Germany and Austria-
Hungary." Four thousand Germans attended the meeting which also passed
a resolution deploring the spread of "racial prejudice" against Germans in
the United States and another which implored Woodrow Wilson to delay any

verdict on going to war on the side of England, since Americans who were not getting an accurate picture of wartime events in the press, could not make a proper choice. After the rally, a large portion of the crowd took to the streets and marched through Grant Park and Chicago's Loop singing patriotic German songs as they waved numerous German flags. The marchers went to the headquarters of the Chicago Tribune for a few minutes of booing and hissing, then advanced to the Hearst building where they carried on in a similar manner.[4]

Some Germanists wanted to go beyond petition campaigns and street demonstrations to show their feelings. Despite being prohibited from participating in politics by its charter, the German American National Alliance urged its branches to become politically active in the fall of 1914. Several members of the Chicago branch urged such a course but a majority, led by Ferdinand Walther, refused to go along. Walther, branch president, felt that support for political candidates would eventually lead to a take-over of the organization by politicians who would then lead it away from the ideals and aims for which the Alliance had always stood. Thus, the Chicago Alliance voted to endorse only candidates for non-controversial posts such as state university trustees.[5] Not until 1916 would Walther change his mind.

The senatorial election of 1914 offered no clue as to the attitudes of German-Americans toward the policies of the Wilson administration. The Republican incumbent Lawrence Y. Sherman, denounced the Democrats for war-mongering and for creating a depression by lowering the tariff. "Any sane president could keep us out of war," he told a predominantly German-American audience in the Lakeview section of Chicago, expressing his own support for neutrality.[6] His Democratic opponent, Roger Sullivan, campaigned as a firm supporter of the president's program to keep the United States out of war. Some German Lutheran ministers aided the Sullivan campaign by issuing an open letter which declared that only Sullivan had "a truly neutral attitude," while his opponents were supported by "anglo-maniacs" who were "steeped in hatred for the alien." Sherman made no open denunciation of Germans or aliens, and neither did the Progressive party candidate Raymond Robbins, who was quick to point out that his wife attended the same church as the ministers.[7] The incident probably had little effect on the outcome of the election but illustrates an attitude prevalent among many German ministers, editors, club leaders, and politicians. They felt that German culture was under attack and that German contributions to American history would be lost in a pro-British crusade. Republican Sherman won the election but ran behind Sullivan in German wards in Chicago and in German areas in the state. Sullivan defeated his rivals with 54 per cent to 24 per cent for Sherman and 22 per cent for Robbins, the Progressive, in German precincts in the city. Sherman carried the state with 57 per cent of the vote.[8]

Supporters of a pro-German position realized they had no chance to persuade Americans of the justice of their cause; thus they demanded strict neutrality on the part of the United States. Late in 1914, these Germanists began to build support for the embargo proposal of Richard Bartholdt, a Republican congressman from Missouri. Bartholdt's legislation, introduced into the House on December 7, gave the president the power to stop the export of arms to any country at his discretion. To drum up support for the measure, Congressman Henry Vollmer, (Dem., Iowa) explained to a crowd in Chicago that the embargo would help Germany win the war. "If we just refrain from helping the Allies," he predicted, "Germany will defeat [that] motley gang within three months."[9]

MAP 1

CHICAGO WARD MAP, 1901-1921

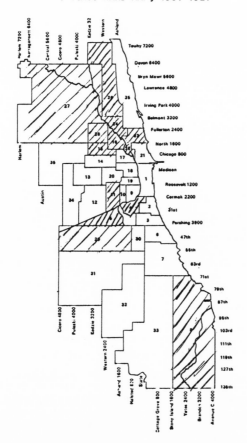

Wards over 20% German shaded in red.

On December 11, over five thousand German Chicagoans attended a
meeting at the Medinah Temple dedicated to the theme of "Germany Forever!"
Speakers included Dr. Bernhard Dernburg of the German Red Cross, who was
touring the United States raising funds, and Professor George Scherger of
the Armour Institute. Scherger was a prominent Germanist and would one day
become a Lutheran minister and eventually president of the Germania Club in
1938. Participants in the rally shouted approval of a call for a complete
German victory over the Allies and applauded the great victories the German
army had already won. Why should German-Americans, Scherger asked, "hide
their satisfaction over the glorious victories the German people had won
over a world of enemies?" Germany was not an enemy of the United States,
only of England. Dr. Dernburg began his speech in English but had to
switch to German after his opening words were lost in a chorus of whistles
and boos. "When your culture, your native land, and your forefathers are
defamed and insulted," Dernburg told his American audience, "by the
application of the term 'Hun' it is up to you to hurl back this obscene
lie." "There is a limit to patience," he concluded. The meeting concluded
with a rousing cheer in support of an embargo law. As participants headed
out the door several thousand gathered in the street and paraded through
the German section singing "Wacht am Rhein," and other patriotic songs.
Dernburg had spoken for many Germans in the city as had Scherger; the
feeling was growing among Germanists that their culture was under attack
and that they, along with Germans in the "old homeland," were indeed
surrounded by a world of enemies.[10]

One example of the attack on everything German was the showing of
the motion picture "The Ordeal," which told the story of how the German
Army had executed an entire family in an effort to get a French soldier to

talk. The movie had no basis in fact, according to the Abendpost, and was merely a piece of French propaganda. It had already been banned in New York and other cities and German leaders asked Mayor Carter Harrison II to take similar action in Chicago. The Chicago Board of Censors allowed "The Ordeal" to be shown, however, a move that led to a call for German-Americans to vote against Harrison in the coming primary.[11]

Harrison, who had been traditionally a friend of the Germans, had angered other German voters and anti-prohibitionists with a campaign to close some of Chicago's more notorious saloons. In the Democratic primary Harrison managed to get only 34% of the German vote, a fact he attributed to the effects of "the European war" and the fact that his opponent, Robert Sweitzer, had a German name.[12] Many Germanists in the city agreed and were proud of the role German voters had played in defeating Harrison.[13]

With a German candidate running for mayor in the second largest city in the United States, German-American leaders saw an opportunity to let Washington know how German-Americans felt about American involvement in the European war. Sweitzer's victory, the editor of the Abendpost commented, showed the world that "Chicago is manifestly 'pro-German,' and a city of German spirit in the best sense of the word."[14] Anti-war and anti-prohibition both revealed that of "German spirit" since both movements stood in opposition to the Anglo-Saxonization of America.

In the mayoral election Germanists in the city jumped on "Smiling Bob" Sweitzer's bandwagon. The candidate himself had little to say concerning the war of the aspirations of German-Americans. Most of his campaign rhetoric concerned holding down spending, cutting taxes, and keeping the saloons open, even on Sundays. For Germanists, however, the name of the candidate stood as the most important and only issue. When Sweitzer's ethnicity was challenged by his opponent, William Hale Thompson, the German American Citizens League for Sweitzer appointed a committee headed by Dr. Otto Schmidt, future president of the Chicago Historical Society, to look into the matter. Thompson had charged that Sweitzer's father had actually been an Irishman who had adopted the name of his German stepfather, Martin Sweitzer. The committee launched a full scale investigation and ascertained that Sweitzer's father had indeed been adopted but that he had been born in Germany whence he and his step-parents had emigrated when Martin Sweitzer was 7 years old. Though Sweitzer would deny this version of the story in 1919, when being German was a political handicap, in 1915 he made no attempt to refute Dr. Schmidt.[15] Sweitzer's true ancestry seems irrelevant; what was important was the fact that so much was made of the issue--Germanists needed Sweitzer in 1915 as much as he needed them.

William Hale Thompson was not a favorite of Germanists in 1915. During the campaign the Abendpost revealed that Thompson and his campaign manager had openly sided with England at the beginning of the war. At that time Thompson had offered the British the use of a $50,000 motorboat for reconnaissance purposes whenever they should need it. The English had turned down the offer, but simply by making it Thompson, in the German paper's view, had offended German-Americans and thus deserved to be defeated.[16]

Thompson, like his opponent, avoided talking about the war. Instead he stressed local issues like fixing streets and improving the schools. Early in the campaign, however, he and his advisors raised the issue of Sweitzer's Catholicism. With the election of "Smiling Bob," a pro-Thompson circular warned, the public schools would be turned over to followers of the Pope. Sweitzer's religion divided the German-American community, since Missouri Synod Lutherans feared the power of the Church of Rome. For them religion was a far more important factor in their lives than ethnicity.

German-American leaders tried to bridge divisions in their community by appealing to love of the Old Homeland. That strategy failed as on election day Sweitzer, the "German candidate," got only 34 per cent of German votes.[17] That percentage represented a seventeen-point drop from the German Democratic vote for Carter Harrison in 1911 and a twenty-two point decline from the percentage given to the last German-American candidate, "Fat Freddie" Busse, in 1907. Religion had not been an issue in the Busse campaign. Chicago Germans actually cast a smaller percentage of votes for "their" candidate than did the rest of the city, which gave Sweitzer 38 per cent. Both candidates were "wet" enough on the prohibition issue so that the United Societies for Local Self-Government, the voice of the anti-prohibition forces in the city, did not have to issue a recommendation. What seems apparent from the results is that religion played a stronger role in the campaign than did any other issue.[18] The war and feelings about German pride were not enough to bring German-Americans together despite the pleas of German-American leaders. The fight for the maintenance of German-Americanism would have to continue on other fronts.

In February, 1915, a nationwide campaign for "True Neutrality" had commenced under the leadership of several national pacifist, Irish-American, and German-American groups. In Chicago, several thousand Germans attended a mass meeting to help organize a League for Neutrality. Horace Brand, publisher of the Illinois Staats-Zeitung, chaired the meeting, which quickly turned into a anti-British demonstration. After Jeremiah O'Leary, president of the violently anti-British American Truth Society made a loud attack on John Bull, several pacifists showed their feelings by walking out of the meeting. The representative of the Swedish League for Peace denounced O'Leary for his diatribe and declared that he was ashamed to be on the same platform with such pro-German spokesmen. Jenkin Lloyd Jones, an old-line Chicago radical and pacifist, attempted to restore order to the peace rally when he shouted to the audience not to be "pro-German or pro-British," but to act instead as "citizens of the world." Jones plea led to a new outbreak of booing and hissing as the audience refused to take a nonpartisan position.

After the rally, more militant pro-Germans took to the streets and marched behind a German band to the Loop and then to the North Side, as Chicago streets again echoed to the sounds of "<u>Deutschland, Ueber Alles</u>." Signs carried by the demonstrators spoke of the feelings of German-Americans who had participated in the League for Neutrality meeting: "Be Neutral-- Remember We Too Are Americans."[19]

The Bismarck Centenial on April 2, 1915, gave Germanists another opportunity to celebrate their heritage and plead their case for neutrality. Four thousand Chicago Germans gathered at the Auditorium Theater to hear Congressman Henry Vollmer of Iowa and other defenders of German culture denounce those Americans who "in the name of patriotism, destroy the good name of our race . . . in our country." If loyalty was the measure of Americanism, Vollmer asserted, "there is and never will be greater or purer loyalty to the government of the United States than that given by citizens of German birth or descent." Contrast German-American actions with those of the "other side," Vollmer enjoined. "Was it really being neutral and loyal to America "to sell tools of murder" to the side which had "seven fold numerical superiority, and whose perfidious diplomacy had engineered the whole [war] by years of international plotting?" A policy of support for such a government, the government of England, "outrages our most profound convictions of loyalty and decency."

The Bismarck Centennial was the last celebration Germans held before the sinking of the Lusitania. After that disaster, public opinion turned sharply against Germany, and the activities of American pro-Germans became more suspect. The loss of 128 American lives was the first occurrence in a process which led to the creation of the "Hun" image in American newspapers and popular thought.[20]

The sinking of the Lusitania did not dampen the enthusiasm of Germanists. The Abendpost found the sinking "justified" on the grounds of self-defense and blamed England for initiating "warfare against innocent women and children" with the imposition of its blockade. Those passengers who had not paid attention to Germany's warnings not to sail on the pride of the English fleet were "now at the mercy of the waves or sleep their eternal sleep in a watery grave."[21] A smaller circulation newspaper, the Chicagoer Frei Presse agreed with the conclusions of Secretary of State William Jennings Bryan, who believed that "England lured Americans to their death, and that therefore it was illogical for the United States "to tolerate and submit to all actions of England simply because she rules the waves."[22] Germanists insisted that Germany had not acted like a barbarian nation. As Horace Brand of the Staats-Zeitung told the Tribune, "Americans who took passage upon the Lusitania did so at their own risk"; therefore,

Germany was not solely responsible for their deaths. Several Lutheran
ministers expressed their feelings in a open letter to their fellow
clergymen: German pastors . . . had to explain in their next Sunday's
sermons "that the German government had been forced by England to this
horrible step." German pastors would have a special obligation to inform
their congregations of the true circumstances of the sinking to counter
"the pro-English press," which was making capital out of the affair, and
to counter the "hundreds of English speaking ministers" who "will support
this hostile press from their pulpits."[23] The minister of Trinity Lutheran
Church told an interviewer he deeply regretted the loss of life but then
explained that the "German government" could not be "held to blame. As sons
of the fatherland," all German-Americans had to defend Germany in "a just
cause." The Tribune interviewed five Lutheran pastors and all agreed with
the view that Germany had not acted wantonly in the Lusitania sinking.[24]

Traditional American pacifist organizations tried to avoid too close
an association with pro-German anti-war efforts. Germanists attempted to
become active in the Friends of Peace and the Chicago Peace Society but
were rebuffed by the leaders and members of these anti-war groups. The
Friends of Peace had been founded in New York City in 1915 and originally
contained several prominent German-American citizens in high level positions.
Henry Weisemann, presiding officer of the group, was head of the United
German American Societies of the State of New York. Other members included
Henry Vollmer and Jeremiah O'Leary. At the first meeting in New York City,
attended by 25,000, William Jennings Bryan spoke. Weisemann welcomed the
recently resigned Secretary of State to "this German atmosphere" in Madison
Square Garden, and Bryan outlined a program for neutrality. Vollmer made
the most sensational speech at the rally, however, when he excused the

sinking of the _Lusitania_ because, as had recently been revealed, the ship had been carrying "instruments of murder" to the Allies.[25] The pro-German tenor of Vollmer's speech alienated many of the pacifist groups who might otherwise have joined the Friends of Peace.

Early in September the group held a national convention in Chicago to which all peace groups in the country were invited. The official proclamation called for an isolationist position on the part of the United States and declared belief in "the existence of a preconceived plot," formulated by the British and their friends in the White House, "to involve the United States in the war." In order to defend the United States from such subversion, the chairman of the executive committee of the Chicago branch, Chancellor J. J. Tobias of the Chicago Law School announced that the "five million voters of Teutonic blood" would have to "raise hell" with any political party opposed to their views. Such pronouncements so angered Samuel Gompers and other labor leaders invited to the convention that they urged union men to stay away, as most did. The Chicago Peace Society also refused to attend, for as it explained: "We say simply that the Friends of Peace is not an organization that opposes the principles of war, as do we, but is an organization working in favor of peace for one set of belligerents." Too many pro-Germans were in positions of power, the Society charged.[26]

Ex-congressman Richard Barthold of St. Louis gave voice to the feelings of many participants when he wrote that a victory for the "Teutonic-Turkish powers" would lead to a world of disarmament and peace. "Europe is exhausted and America is threatened as never before with the same militarism which has cursed and bloodied all the nations of the

Old World." In order to avoid that threat, the United States would have
to avoid war and allow Germany to bring peace to Europe. It would be a
difficult assignment to keep the United States out of war because of the
existence "of all the Security Leagues and Naval Leagues and ammunition
rings," but Bartholdt implied that German-Americans could play a leading
role in fulfilling that task.

German-American involvement in leadership positions gave the Friends
of Peace a pro-Kaiser image in the press. The activities of some of the
participants did nothing to change this view. On September 7, 1915 the opening day of the Friends Chicago convention, the announcement of the sinking of
the Hesperian by a German submarine brought a sustained round of cheers and
applause from the audience. Only after cries of "Shame, shame," from
pacifist delegates did the audience quiet down. After that incident it was
difficult to avoid the notion that the Friends of Peace might be "the agent
of the German Empire" as the Chicago Peace Society had charged.[28]

A majority of the speakers at the Friends of Peace convention bore
German names. Speakers like the Reverend G. C. Berkheimer and Dr. Phillip
Vollmer placed the blame for the war on the British, the French, and the
Russians. America seemed to favor the Allies only because of "the jingo
American press; the money and war munitions trusts, and the rowdy type of
American politicians." German-Americans stood as the true defenders of
American constitutional traditions; to those who argued just "Let the
president do it, and we will stand back of him," Dr. Vollmer argued German-
Americans were to say "that is the Russian doctrine, not an American
doctrine." Congressman Henry Vollmer addressed the proceedings with an
attack on Woodrow Wilson who, in his view, had unfortunately shown a
preference for Mexican "kultur" over that of the Germans. As evidence for

this charge, Vollmer pointed out that Wilson had placed an embargo on the shipment of arms to Mexico but not on shipments to the Allies. William Jennings Bryan concluded the proceedings by defending his neutral position but he got the greatest response when he defended his reaction to the Lusitania sinking. "When the danger of war was talked of," he told a cheering crowd, "I wasn't willing to sacrifice 100,000 men because a little more than 100 Americans took a ship they ought not to have taken."

Despite the urging of some delegates that resolutions favoring an arms embargo be passed, leaders prevailed upon the group not to take such a "pro-German" stance. Instead a resolution condemning the growth of the war spirit in the United States was passed, as well as a "New Declaration of Independence" which called for "freedom of the seas" and the prohibition of the manufacture and sale of arms and ammunition in the United States for any purpose other than national defense.[29] Despite attempts by leaders of the Friends of Peace to avoid the appearance of a pro-German position, the rhetoric of the participants and the major speakers made such an effort futile.

Another gorup which had difficulty proving to the public that it was supporting neutrality rather than the Kaiser was the American Embargo Conference. Though its declaration of principles clearly stated that the group stood for "an Americanism which unqualifididly supports the Constitution of the United States" the group was immediately branded by the press as "pro-German."[30] The Conference was founded early in 1915 by Gustave H. Jacobson, a Chicago real estate developer, and was headed by Colonel Jasper P. Darling, also of Chicago. Darling acknowledged the group would be perceived as pro-German but denied that it had anything to do with the German government. Its aim was simply to keep the United States out of war.[31]

The Embargo Conference organized as a pressure group to get Congress to approve an arms embargo to all nations. By late 1915 its leaders announced the formation of over 1000 local organizations and estimated its membership at over 500,000. The local committees were urged to work for the defeat of any Congressmen, regardless of party, who refused to support embargo legislation. National headquarters proudly announced that over 100,000 letters urging passage of an embargo had been received by Congressmen within the first weeks of the campaign.[32]

Conference leaders decided to take an active role in the presidential campaign of 1916 and to support the candidate most "pro-American" in his views, and that meant the candidate most likely to support an arms embargo. The arms embargo, of course, would greatly affect the course of the war in favor of Germany. Thus, "pro-American" would actually mean "pro-German," and few Germanists saw any contradiction in that definition. That German-Americans had great power in the Embargo Conference is evident from the names of the executive committee which met in Detroit to discuss tactics for the presidential campaign. Thirteen names listed on the sixteen member committee were distinctly German. Eight members of the nine-member finance committee were German.[33] Despite this ethnic preponderance, the Conference insisted that its goal was the election of a "pro-American Congress so that its real American members can stand in the way of any Tory president who might be taking orders from either United States or Bethlehem Steel."[34] Comments of participants at the Detroit meeting indicate that in the campaign for neutrality and an embargo law neither presidential candidate in 1916, Woodrow Wilson or Charles Evans Hughes, could be trusted.

The Election of 1916 and German-Americanism

Before the election Germanists in Chicago celebrated the 57th
birthday of their beloved leader, Kaiser Wilhelm. The crowd at the celebration was so large that police had to be called to keep those unable to
enter the hall from rioting in the street. The principal speaker of the
evening, Professor Eugen Kuehnemann, who was travelling through the United
States under the auspices of the German government, expressed the view that
"in the titanic conflict between the Anglo-Saxon and Germanistic thought, a
world Germanism will be born." German-Americans had a great task to perform,
that of disseminating German thought in the United States. Thus, the war
had served a useful purpose, it had re-awakened a love for "the old fatherland" in the hearts of Germans everywhere. That the professor was not just
engaging in wishful thinking was evident from the opinion voiced by another
speaker, American-born businessman and future Chicago postmaster Ernest
J. Kruetgen, and the reaction of Chicago's leading German newspaper, Kruetgen
warned that Germanism was endangered by the concerted attack on it in
Europe and the United States. German-Americans were duty bound to "proclaim the importance of their origins" because the German nation represented the "noblest elements of humanity" while the Allies represented only
"narrowmindedness, conceit, and slavery." Germany had as its war aim the
alleviation of "sorrow and suffering" and a victory for Germany would be a
triumph for civilization. Germans in America could share in that triumph
by helping to stop the shipments of "death" to the Allies.[35] German-
Americans, according to the Abendpost, had a duty "here at the outposts
to disseminate German ideals, morals, and customs."[36] Germanists in the
city took the challenge seriously.

The spirit of Germanism was kept alive through rallies and celebrations and by the publication of Michael Singer's Jahrbuch der Deutschen in Chicago für das Jahr 1915, which was followed by yearbooks for 1916 and 1917. The books were compilations of articles and speeches by prominent Chicago Germans describing German contributions to culture and history. Singer saw the war as an opportunity to re-awaken the German spirit, "The war has become a purgatory for German-Americans in which they were stripped of all weaknesses" and past sins. The war crisis enabled them to rediscover their heritage. The "baseless charges of disloyalty" had forced German-Americans to "shake off indifference" and rejoin the battle against the chief enemies Germanism, Puritanism and Anglo-Saxon culture.[37]

The newly organized, militant, Germanistic Society, published anti-war pamphlets and argued that "if the Americans get to know our thoughts, they will appreciate them" and reject English propaganda.[38] Germanists shared a belief that American society had not yet achieved its full maturity, and never would do so so long as it only wanted to become a pale replica of England. "There is still a groping in the dark, a seeking for a final destiny" in America, wrote J. P. Schroeter, president of the Technical Society of Chicago. Part of that destiny, Schroeter explained, would include a recognition of German achievements and contributions to American society. Language did not matter as much as the maintenance of German ideals such as "an insistence on discipline and a renewed study of German science and pedagogical methods." What was essential was that the "German spirit be kept alive in American life."[39] Edward Goldbeck, a columnist for the Sunday Tribune, in late 1916, gave a clear explanation of what Germanists wanted in an essay on "Germanizing America." "Most of the deficiencies in the American character," Goldbeck explained, such as exaggerated individualism, ruthless brutality in business life, and base adoration of the rich man" resulted from the fact that "this country has been Anglicized through centuries. . . ." Now was the time "to do some Germanizing." By that Goldbeck meant that it was up to German-Americans to show other Americans that "independence is a fiction; it does not exist. . . . The right word is interdependence, the knowledge that we all depend on each other and that every act, every word of ours has never ending consequences." German-Americans had to teach that "American individualism" threatened to become "ruthless selfishness," unless it acquired the leavening force of German culture. German-Americans could best go about Germanizing the United States by participating in American politics and popularizing German ideals.[40] Germanists agreed with Horace Brand who pointed out that German-Americans "want to be Americans . . . but they decline to become English."[41] Many Germanists agreed with Professor Julius Goebel of the University of Illinois, who had once told the German-American Alliance that Germans had to refute all attempts to submerge German "racial individuality . . . in the slop kitchen of a national Melting Pot."[42] Preservation of the "German soul" became the primary task of this group of intellectuals, editors, and religious leaders.

The appointment of George Mundelein, a third generation German-American, as archbishop of Chicago raised the hopes of some Germanists in the city that the new prelate would give their community another spokesman. But any notion that Mundelein would speak as a German Catholic was quickly dispelled. Asked by an Abendpost reporter whether he had any special message for German Catholics, Mundelein replied that he had "none other than the message to all Catholics of Chicago. I have no separate message for any particular nationality. I shall not speak to the Germans as Germans, or

the Italians as Italians, or any other class of our people. My simple
message will be to call Catholics of whatever nationality."[43] Mundelein
retained that policy throughout his career as he became a leading force for
Americanization.[44]

Issues involving the ethnic identity and the loyalty of German-
Americans arose in the election of 1916. German-Americans faced a dilemma.
President Wilson had kept the peace, but he had hardly kept the country
strictly neutral, by which Germanists meant embargoing shipments of arms to
England. The Republican candidate, Charles Evans Hughes, made some friendly
statements concerning German-Americans early in the campaign, but right behind him stood the leading proponent of war against Germany, Theodore
Roosevelt. The Democratic party appeared uninterested in German voters;
its platform condemned as subversive of this nation's unity and integrity
the activities and designs of every group or organization. . . that has
for its object the advancement of the interest of a foreign power. . . ."
To Germanists, that seemed like a direct attack on their activities.[45] The
Democrats had to walk a narrow line in order to attract ethnic voters.
Wilson was a minority president, having received only 43 per cent of the vote
in 1912. And, as William Jennings Bryan pointed out, he could only be re-
elected by retaining the support of the peace movement, which included many
German-Americans.[46]

In an effort to retain some part of the German vote, the Democrats
hired Charles Boerchenstein, national committeeman from Illinois, to head a
special German language bureau which published large quantities of material.
Boerchenstein spread the word through German areas of the midwest that if
Charles Evans Hughes was elected he would name Theodore Roosevelt secretary

of state. The German bureau stressed the issues of "America First" and
patriotism, pointing out that German-Americans had exhibited the highest
qualities of loyalty during the neutrality debate.[47]

Questions concerning the true meaning of loyalty and patriotism
troubled some German-American leaders. The eighty-five delegates at the
meeting of the German-American National Alliance in Chicago resolved to
oppose any candidate who did not "treat England with as much severity as
the dual monarchies." The Alliance endorsed "freedom of the seas" but
explained that this phrase did not mean "British controlled seas." The
general mood of the delegates was summarized by a spokesman who told the
Tribune that though "German-Americans might be hyphenated Americans, there is
nothing hyphenated about their patriotism," so they supported adequate
preparedness for war and equal treatment for Germany. Another delegate
expressed a more militant view, declaring that he would "rather cut off his
hands than vote for Wilson."[48]

So loudly were some German-American groups campaigning for Charles
Evans Hughes that the Republicans had a difficult time in answering
Democratic charges that German-Americans controlled their candidate. "Can
the Kaiser defeat the President?" Democratic advertisements asked.[49] But
a major change in campaign strategy and rhetoric occurred late in August
after Theodore Roosevelt began making anti-hyphenate speeches. Roosevelt
condemned the "professional" German-Americans who acted as "servants and
allies of Germany" and accused these spokesmen of treason to the Republic.[50]
Hughes, who had been courting German-Americans, ended the courtship quickly
with a telegram congratulating Roosevelt for his remarks. Hughes's
reversal did not surprise the German-American leader Carl E. Schmidt of
Detroit, a leader in the American Embargo Conference who had recently

concluded a series of conversations with the Republican candidate. These convinced him that Hughes was likely to be just as anti-German and "even more un-American in his administration than Mr. Wilson is accused of being."[5]

Both parties adopted German-baiting as a tactic in the closing days of the campaign. German Republicans in Chicago journeyed to Iowa to talk with Theodore Roosevelt before his scheduled appearance in Illinois in a attempt to encourage him to tone down his anti-German remarks, but with little success. Roosevelt continued to attack hyphenates and to question the loyalty of German-Americans. Coming from a former admirer of Germany and a candidate whom many Germans had supported in 1912, these assaults seemed especially painful to Germanists.[52]

Wilson did not let Roosevelt monopolize the anti-German issue. After Jeremiah O'Leary, president of the anti-British American Truth Society and a director of the American Embargo Conference, sent a telegram to the President denouncing his favoritism toward Britain, Wilson responded with an attack on all "pro-Germans." "Your telegram received," Wilson wired O'Leary, "I would feel deeply mortified to have you or anybody like you vote for me. Since you have access to many disloyal Americans and I have not, I will ask you to convey this message to them."[53] Yet, Wilson balanced his attack on allegedly disloyal elements with constant reminders that he had done all he could do to keep the peace. Thus, German-Americans were left with a choice between a candidate who appeared to be heavily influenced by the most dynamic crusader for war, Theodore Roosevelt, and a sitting president who had kept the United States out of a shooting war but who had also made loud attacks upon the patriotism of Germanists.

Chicago Democrats made peace rather than preparedness or hyphenism the major issue. A "peace day" was declared the week before the election

and speakers at several different rallies reminded voters of the horrors
of war, and of the fact that Woodrow Wilson had preserved the country from
this. "You Are Working Not Fighting! Alive and Happy--Not Cannon Fodder!"
Democratic campaign posters read. The Abendpost, which supported Wilson
because of his foreign policy, carried an advertisement which asked: "Wilson
and Peace with Honor or Hughes with Roosevelt and War? Which Will it be?"
The Republicans campaigned on the theme that keeping the United States out
of war was not enough: Wilson and his economic policies would ruin the
country if the war ended, party campaign literature suggested.[54]

Germans in Chicago had traditionally supported Republican presidential
candidates, and 1916 was no exception. Only once since 1896 (in 1900) had the
Democratic candidate received more than 42 per cent of the vote. In 1912,
Woodrow Wilson received only 26 per cent of the German vote compared to
the 41 per cent for the Bull Moose Party. In 1916, Wilson managed to get 41
per cent of German votes while Hughes increased the Republican total to 56
per cent. The Socialist vote almost disappeared from German areas of the
city as Alan Benson, the party's presidential candidate in 1916, mustered
less than 2 per cent of the vote, a 14 per cent drop from Eugene Debs'
total in 1912. The fact was that either major party choice in 1916 was
safe for German-Americans. Both major candidates had made anti-war statements, a German-American could vote for either of them and remain within
the American consensus. Woodrow Wilson's anti-German rhetoric was matched
by that of Theodore Roosevelt. There still was no conflict between loyalty
to the Old Homeland and allegiance to the United States.[55]

Circumstances changed swiftly, however, especially after Germany
announced it was reopening unlimited submarine warfare on February 1, 1917.

Still, the fervently pro-German _Illinois Staats-Zeitung_ found little cause
for Americans to be overly alarmed. Germany was striking back at England
with "the only weapon which guaranteed success against its treacherous and
cunning foe." England would "die within six months," the paper confidently
predicted, and could only save itself by "coming to terms" with the Kaiser.
Horace Brand, publisher of the _Staats-Zeitung_, warned Chicagoans in an
interview with the _Tribune_ that if the United States took sides in the conflict it would lead to a "war of races" in the West; by that he meant that
Teutons would have to fight Anglo-Saxons and Slavs. Brand's solution was for
the country to unite and think of "America first, last, and at all times."
Ironically, Wilson wanted the same result _via war_.[56]

With the threat of war approaching ever closer, German-American
leaders rallied to the call of Americanism and isolationism. Harry Rubens,
former secretary to Carl Schurz and a vice-president of the _Germania_ Club,
assured Chicagoans that German-Americans would always stand by the stars-and-
stripes. Rubens recalled a conversation with Schurz when the latter had
termed a war between the United States and Germany "unthinkable." "The
unthinkable" was about to happen, Rubens felt, but Germans would never forget their true loyalty. Judge Theodore Brentano echoed Rubens' remarks when
he declared his deep regret at the turn of events in Europe but re-empha-
sized the view that every German would put loyalty "to their country ahead
of every other consideration or tie."[57]

The war against Germany would lead to a campaign against everything
German in America, Germanists feared. Already a bitter hatred of everything
Teutonic in Chicago was growing, a group of Lutheran ministers lamented.
Even before the declaration of war thousands of Chicagoans had joined the
American Protective League, which looked upon all German-Americans as

potential spies and saboteurs. The A.P.L., Horace Brand and Paul Mueller feared, witnessed the rebirth of "know-nothingism" and stood as a reminder of the American Protective Association, which had engaged in anti-German and anti-immigrant activities in the 1890s.[58]

The A.P.L., organized by a group of Chicago businessmen in March, 1917, quickly became a nationwide organization of 200,000 volunteers who gathered information for the United States Justice Department on aliens and allegedly disloyal citizens. The Chicago branch of the League had over 13,000 members who watched their neighbors and their fellow-workers for potential trouble makers. At the behest of the Justice Department, the Investigation Bureau of the A.P.L. conducted surveillance of citizens suspected of disloyalty. Over 300 reports on disloyalty were filed daily with district and branch offices after the United States entered the war. This "web" of ultrapatriots had little success, however, in Chicago or anywhere else in the United States, finding dangerous saboteurs in the German-American community. Not a single spy or saboteur of German origin was convicted on evidence raised by League operatives. The A.P.L. did, however, do a great deal of harm to the reputations of many loyal German-Americans and succeeded in conveying the impression that large numbers of German-Americans were disloyal.[59]

Until the outbreak of war German-Americans conducted themselves in what they considered a loyal manner. Few Germanist leaders believed that hostilities with the Fatherland would change that situation. As Horace Brand acknowledged, "if Congress declares war . . . German-Americans will support war," reluctantly, perhaps, but the support would be there "because German-Americans have never been traitors." It would be up to other Americans to understand the difficult position of German-Americans, but the attempt had to be made, otherwise German culture in the United States would die. German-Americans had lost the neutrality debate but retained their heritage. Patriotism had never been an issue. During the war, Brand hoped, the non-German majority would remember the ethnic ties of German-Americans and treat with "kindly forbearance the unguarded but otherwise unintentionall unfortunate remarks that a German-American might be guilty of." Americans had the responsibility "to help ease fear among German-Americans that spies surround them ever ready to misinterpret innocent acts."[60] The war would offer an opportunity to see how both sides, Germanists and A.P.L.'ers would respond to loyalty under pressure.

NOTES

Chapter I.

1. Chicagoer Abendpost, August 2, 1914; Chicago Tribune, April 2,3, 1914.

2. Abendpost, August 30, 1914.

3. Chicago Tribune, April 2, 1914.

4. Abendpost, August 6, 1914; Tribune, August 6, 1914.

5. Abendpost, October 20, 1914.

6. Chicago Tribune, October 28, 1914.

7. Abendpost, October 27, 1914.

8. Election results from Chicago Tribune, November 4, 1914. The German population of Chicago's 35 wards averaged 19.5%. Those wards over 20% German were: Fourth (25.6%); Fifth (25.7%); Eighth (21.3%); Eleventh (24.0%); Fifteenth (30.3%); Sixteenth (47.4%); Twenty-second (20.1%); Twenty-third (40.6%); Twenty-fourth (46.8%); Twenty-sixth (33.6%); Twenty-seventh (32.1%); Twenty-eighth (35.6%); Twenty-ninth (25.7%). In the three wards over 40% German, Sullivan defeated Sherman 55%-27% (Sixteenth); 40%-27% (Twenty-third); and 38%-28% (Twenty-fourth).

9. Abendpost, December 2, 1914.

10. Abendpost, December 11, 1914; Chicago Tribune, December 11, 1914.

11. Abendpost, December 28, 1914.

12. Chicago Tribune, February 22, 1915; Harrison's primary vote derived from ward percentages listed in Abendpost, February 24, 1915.

13. Abendpost, February 22, 23, 1915.

14. Abendpost, February 24, 1915.

15. Abendpost, March 28, 1915.

16. Abendpost, March 30, 1915.

17. Chicago Tribune, March 19, 30, 1915.

18. Chicago Tribune, March 27, April 6, 7, 1915; Abendpost, March 30, 31, April 4, 5, 1915; John Allswang, A House for All Peoples: Ethnic Politics in Chicago, 1890-1936 (Lexington, Ky.; University of Kentucky Press, 1971), p. 220.

19. Chicago *Tribune*, February 8, 1915; *Abendpost* February 8, 1915.

20. Chicago *Tribune*, April 2, 1915.

21. *Abendpost*, May 8, 1915.

22. Chicago *Freie Presse*, May 9, 1915.

23. Chicago *Tribune*, May 9, 1915.

24. Chicago *Tribune*, May 10, 1915.

25. *New York Times*, June 25, 1915.

26. *New York Times*, July 19, September 5, 1915.

27. *New York Times*, September 5, 1915.

28. Chicago *Tribune*, September 5, 6, 1915.

29. *New York Times*, September 8, 1915.

30. "Declaration of Principles of the American Embargo Conference," Dr. Otto Schmidt Papers, Chicago Historical Society, Box 2, Folder 11; Chicago *Tribune*, April 26, 1916.

31. Chicago *Tribune*, April 26, 1916.

32. W.R. McDonald to Otto Schmidt, November 3, 1915, Schmidt Papers, CHS.

33. "Report of the Proceedings of the National Campaign Committee . . . September 6th and 7th, 1916," Schmidt Papers, Box 2, Folder 11, CHS.

34. W. R. McDonald to Otto Schmidt, August 17, 1916, Schmidt Papers, CHS.

35. *Abendpost*, January 28, 1916.

36. *Abendpost*, February 9, 1916.

37. Illinois *Staats-Zeitung*, October 24, 1915. (Hereinafter cited as *ISZ*.)

38. *ISZ*, October 24, 25, 1915.

39. *Abendpost*, February 14, 1915.

40. Chicago *Tribune*, November 5, 1916.

41. *ISZ*, September 27, 1915.

42. U.S. Congress, Senate, Committee on the Judiciary, *Hearings on the National German-American Alliance*, 65th Cong., 2d sess., 1918, p. 695.

43. Chicago Tribune, February 9, 1916; Abendpost, February 9, 1916.

44. For Cardinal Mundelein's Americanization program, see the discussion in James Sanders, "The Education of Chicago Catholics: An Urban History" (Ph.D. dissertation, University of Chicago, 1970), pp. 112, 138-140.

45. NYT, June 15, 17, 1916.

46. NYT, May 13, 1916.

47. Meyer, J. Nathan, "The Presidential Election of 1916 in the Middle West," (Ph. D. dissertation, Princeton University, 1966), p. 232.

48. Michael Singer, ed., Jahrbuch der Deutschamerikaner for das Jahr 1917 Chicago: German Yearbook Publishing Company, 1916), pp. 148-49; 194-95; the yearbooks contained speeches and historical sketches of German leaders and contributions to American history. Similar type yearbooks were published by Negro defense groups, especially in times of distress. Chicago Tribune, May 29, 1916.

49. NYT, June 14, 1916.

50. NYT, Sept. 1, 1916.

51. Carl Schmidt to Otto Schmidt, August 17, 1916, Schmidt Papers, CHS.

52. Chicago Tribune, Oct. 26, 27, 1916.

53. NYT, Sept. 30, 1916.

54. Abendpost, Nov. 3, 1916; Chicago Tribune, Nov. 3, 1916.

55. Allswang, A House for All Peoples, pp. 219-220; David Burner, The Politics of Provincialism: The Democratic Party in Transition, 1916-1932 (New York: W.W. Norton Co., 1968), p. 241.

56. ISZ, Jan. 31, 1917, Chicago Tribune, Feb. 4, 1917.

57. Chicago Tribune, Feb. 5, 1917.

58. Abendpost, Feb. 5, 1917.

59. Jean Jensen, The Price of Vigilence (Chicago: Rand, McNally Co., 1969), p. 98, 124-132; for a highly biased, anti-German, contemporary account see, Emmerson Hough, The Web: The Authorized History of the American Protective League (Chicago: Reilly & Lee, 1919).

60. Chicago Tribune, March 20, 1917, ISZ, April 1, 1917; Chicago Daily News, April 2, 1917.

CHAPTER II

"A DEEP SENSE OF UNFAIRNESS": GERMAN-AMERICANS
IN CHICAGO AND THE FIRST WORLD WAR

After Congress declared war against Germany on April 6, 1917,
"loyalty" became the major issue for German-Americans. In Chicago, some
German-Americans were spied on, terrorized, investigated, jailed, and discharged from their jobs in an effort to produce "100% Americanism."
German-Americans responded to this wave of hysteria in a number of ways:
militant Germanists became silent for the most part, as many were
imprisoned or sent to camps in Georgia or North Carolina. The "church
Germans" professed loyalty once war was declared, though many Missouri
Synod Lutherans continued to hold services in German, much to the conster-
nation of the American Protective League. The "stomach Germans" were
drafted, bought Liberty Bonds, and avoided open displays of their ethnic
identity. German-Americans who protested the war did so by voting for anti-
war Socialists in city elections.

The one hope about which all German-Americans could coalesce was the
political career of William Hale Thompson, the leading pro-German politician
and foe of the war in the state. Thompson allowed the city to become the
center of anti-war activity in the entire nation in 1917 and won the
admiration of many militant Germanists for his conduct. The mayor did little
however, about the activities of the 13,000 volunteer operatives of the
American Protective League working in Chicago. Chicago boasted the largest

organization of amateur spies in the United States and they, at times, made
life miserable for the city's German population.

Origins of the Anti-German Campaign in Chicago

With the coming of war, most German-American leaders called for a
suspension of the activities of German societies. The militant German-
American National Alliance cancelled a meeting scheduled for Chicago, and
other cultural and social clubs followed suit. Horace Brand, who had
recently returned from Washington after a futile attempt to lobby Illinois
congressmen into voting against a declaration of war, was one of the few
German-American leaders opposed to cancelling activities. Cancellation,
he explained, would give "the enemies of German-Americans" the impression
"that their contention that these societies are not American but German" was
correct. So, Brand's newspaper, the Illinois Staats Zeitung, urged its
readers to continue attending and participating in their traditional cultural
activities. Most German-Americans, though, saw withdrawal rather than the
assertion of ethnicity, as the proper course to follow.

On April 7, hundreds of German Chicagoans were secretly taken into
custody and held for questioning. One south-side German-American physician
remained in custody for several days before relatives were informed of his
whereabouts; others of those arrested by federal agents of the Bureau of
Investigation for alleged "pro-Germanism" found themselves in similar
circumstances. Hinton S. Clabaugh, chief of the Bureau in Chicago, explained
the purpose of the arrests: whereas "partisanship" for Germany had been
nothing more than a violation of neutrality before the declaration of war,
pro-Germanism was now classified as "treason." The question most German-
Americans were interested in was how "pro-Germanism" would be defined.

In the first few days of war the definition was broadly drawn as was
illustrated by the activities of Bureau of Investigation agents and
volunteer operatives in the American Protective League. Clabaugh announced
that undercover agents were working in Chicago factories and offices
looking for persons who might make pro-German comments. Agents had also
been on the trail of "pro-Germanists" for several weeks. Anyone caught
making comments favorable to Germany could be subject to arrest under the
Alien and Sedition laws of 1798.[2]

Among those arrested in the first week of the war were several
German-Americans allegedly involved in a conspiracy to transport arms and
money to India to help bring about a revolt against British rule. The so-
called "Hindu plot" involved former officers of the American Embargo
Conference, the group which had been actively opposed to American involvement in the war in 1915-1916.[3] Two days later, 14 German Chicagoans employed
at the Deering Works of International Harvester were arrested and charged
with conspiring to blow up that large factory. Hundreds of other arrests
were reported, including that of a Catholic priest turned in by his parishio-
ners for a "pro-German" sermon; a high school teacher of German extraction
who had written a pamphlet critical of American involvement in the war; a
doctor who expressed pro-German sentiments to some of his patients; and
others, who in the words of a Chicago policeman, had simply "talked their
way into jail" by making known their pro-German views.[4] The message for
Chicago Germans was perfectly clear: do not express publicly any sentiments
on the war unless such sentiments are 100% pro-American. "Hundreds of loyal
Americans," a spokesman for the A.P.L. boasted, were "combing the city for
enemies, and reporting on acts of violence."[5]

The experience of Otto Heyne, a 26-year-old downtown office clerk, gave Chicago Germans a good idea of what to expect for public expressions of less than perfect loyalty. Heyne was asked by fellow employees to demonstrate his patriotic fervor by wearing an American flag in his lapel. He refused, offering a denigrating remark as to the flag's worth. For this response he was chased from his office to a bridge over the Chicago River. There he was grabbed by a mob of about 30 loyal citizens, hoisted over the side of the bridge, and threatened with drowning unless he pledged true loyalty, which he quickly did. When police arrived Heyne was arrested, charged with disorderly conduct, and fined $50.00.[6]

Publicly Germans were under pressure to display perfect loyalty; in the privacy of the voting booth however, German-Americans were free to express other feelings. The clearest indication of the anti-war attitudes of many Chicago Germans came in the aldermanic election of April 4, 1917, only two days after President Wilson asked for a declaration of war against Germany. In the campaign the Socialist party in Chicago adopted a staunch anti-war position and asked Chicagoans to demonstrate their feelings toward war by returning a Socialist majority to City Hall. The Socialists fell far short of their goal, managing to win seats in only three wards, but the party reported that it did exceptionally well in German areas of the city. Two of the three Socialists elected came from wards with large numbers of German voters.[7]

Public expressions of loyalty along with private privately held doubts was the pattern for many Chicago German-Americans. Leaders of the Chicago Branch of the German-American Alliance stressed the need to collect data demonstrating German-American loyalty during the war. Service records, Red Cross contributions, and Liberty Bond sales figures had to be

maintained in order to fight the "false propaganda" being spread against
the loyalty of German-Americans. Statistical material demonstrating
patriotism would be valuable after the war should any charges of disloyalty
arise. Loyalty to the United States during the war, members were urged to
keep in mind, would be the best means of protecting Germanism in the future.
For as the Chicago branch president observed, "the German Empire might cease
to exist" if the war "turned out wrong," but "the German people would never
vanish." Germans in the United States would see to that last provision.
Thus, the Chicago branch of the Alliance made the Germanist position in the
United States clear: Germanists would support the United States in order to
preserve "the spiritual possessions" of the German people.[8] Loyal Americans
could also be loyal supporters of German culture.

Less militant German organizations such as the German Club of Chicago
felt the pressure toward true loyalty and quickly took measures to demonstrate
that the Club was 100 per cent American. German-Americans were even more
patriotic than other Americans. Members cheered loud and long after Henry
Vollmer suggested that German-Americans "should not only do their share, but
even more. Send your sons into the fight with the admonition to sacrifice
more than the next man," he exclaimed. That extra patriotism would prove
that German culture truly was supreme; it would help offset propaganda
alleging German "atrocities and barbarism" in Belgium.[9] German-Americans had
a double burden; first they had to prove their loyalty to the United States,
second they had to show by their bravery that Germans were not "Huns."
In order to demonstrate its loyalty, the German Club voted to hold future
meetings in English and to change its name to the American Unity Club.[10]
The Germania Club, a businessman's club with about 350 members, cancelled

choir rehearsals for the duration of the war, and changed its name to the Lincoln Club of Chicago.[11]

German churches like the Lutheran Church-Missouri Synod and the Evangelical Synod were aware that many people considered them unpatriotic. The idea that the Missouri Synod was "totally out of touch and harmony with genuine Americanism," a minister explained, was "absolutely untrue." Lutherans had an obligation to demonstrate that they were bound to no European country.[12] The fact that many Lutheran churches continued to hold German language services disturbed non-German speaking Americans. One survey showed that in 1915 79% of the services in Evangelical Synod churches were in German: by 1919 that percentage had only dropped to 59%.[13] Early in January, 1918, Lutheran churches were attacked as agencies of subversion in a newspaper article published nationwide. Lutherans, the article written by a Syracuse University professor insisted, were intent on spreading German propaganda.[14] A Missouri Synod pastor answered this charge by pointing to the history of the Synod. Any implication that the Missouri Synod, which had been founded in Chicago in 1843, was connected "with the Prussian State Church" was totally false. The history of the Synod had always been one of opposition to any connection between church and state—that had been the reason the founding fathers had left Germany in the first place.

One of the younger leaders of the Missouri Synod, Theodore Graebner, for a short time pastor of Jehovah Lutheran Church in Chicago, argued that Lutherans supported the American government but only because that government had not attempted to hinder the "free preaching of the Law and the Gospel." Graebner urged Lutherans to show the spirit of patriotism by supporting the American war effort. His church was one of the first to fly the American

flag.[15] Graebner's position did not reflect the view of other church
leaders. Synod president Frederick Pfotenhauer, also pastor of a Chicago
church, expressed his disappointment with the "pro-war" faction.
Pfotenhauer did not want to drag the war into church affairs lest it
severely divide the membership. Pfotenhauser felt that a majority of his
congregation opposed the war; he emphasized that they did not wish to create
a split inside the church while it was under attack from without.[16]
Graebner responded to his critics by arguing that the United States cause
was just; he joined with other German-Americans who argued that "the ruling
class of Germany was corrupt and militaristic," so, therefore, a victory
for the United States would represent a victory for the German people.[17]

German Catholics had an easier time proving their loyalty because
of the early patriotic response of their leaders. Cardinal Mundelein
announced on April 10, 1917, that "one thing is certain . . . the moment the
President of the United States affixed his signature to the resolutions of
Congress, all differences of opinion ceased. We stand seriously, solidly,
and loyally behind our President and his congress."[18] The Archbishop even
increased his effort to break up ethnic parishes and to "Americanize" his
diocese. The war offered a wonderful opportunity for such a task. "One of
the benefits of the war, that has accrued to Catholics," he told members
of the Associated Catholic Charities, "is that the eyes of the American
people have been opened to their loyalty." Robert Sweitzer, a prominent
German Catholic layman and Chicago mayoral candidate in 1915 and 1919,
praised the Archbishop for his work in guarding the image of German Catholics.
"Not a single act of sedition or disloyalty" involving a "Chicago German
Catholic" had been reported. Part of the credit for that achievement,

Sweitzer proclaimed, lay with Cardinal Mundelein who represented "the greatest Americanizing force in Chicago."[19] The difference between Lutheran Germans and Catholic Germans was illustrated by a meeting of German Lutheran school teachers. The teachers voted unanimously against a proposal that they teach "undefiled Americanism" in their classrooms.[20]

One German Jewish leader, Rabbi Emil G. Hirsch, had a difficult time establishing that he was not "pro-German." In the Spring of 1918 a petition was circulated among members of the Sinai Temple asking Dr. Hirsch to resign for allegedly making a "pro-German" statement during a sermon. The Rabbi admitted his love for the German people and German culture, a love he had attained during his student days, but denied being a supporter of the Central Powers' cause. The fact that Dr. Hirsch had nine relatives serving in the German army may have made his love for Germany more understandable. After the Rabbi announced he opposed "Prussianism," the petition was withdrawn. The incident dramatically pointed out the difficulty many German-Americans had in giving undivided support to the Allied cause.[21]

German Freemasons also felt obliged to demonstrate their loyalty. State leaders ordered all meetings to be conducted in English. The three largest German lodges in Chicago at first refused to comply with that order. Members argued that loyalty to the United States could be expressed as well in German as it could be in English. "Patriotism does not manifest itself in words, but in deeds," the Freemason's argued, but to no avail. The English language was ultimately used by all the lodges.[22]

This sampling of statements by leaders of Chicago Germans indicates that in their view German-American loyalty to their adopted nation was beyond question. "Why shouldn't we be loyal?" Henry Vollmer asked. "Here

are our homes and firesides; here are our graves and our loved ones."
Most German-Americans were ready to be as loyal as any other Americans.[23]

Leaders of the A.P.L. rejected this idea, however. After the
arrests of "pro-Germans," the A.P.L. announced its view that all citizens
of Germany residing in the United States would be considered "alien enemies"
subject to internment. Attorney General Thomas Gregory issued a proclamation on April 18, 1917, which ordered "all alien enemies residing within
one-half mile of a fort, camp, aircraft station, navy yard, factory, or
workshop for manufacturing of munitions" to move before June 1 "or be
subject to arrest." This order effected all Germans in the United States
who had not taken out "first papers." In Chicago, the order was interpreted as meaning that German aliens were excluded from living, working, or
travelling through the Loop without a permit. Germans were also excluded
from the steel mill area of the South side, the Stockyards district, and
the Lakefront area. Any German caught within these areas was subject to
arrest, Hinton Clabaugh announced. That the ultra-loyalists took Clabaugh
at his word was indicated by the fact that an average of sixty persons a
day were detained during the course of the war. The order on aliens had
tragic results in one instance when Frederick Studer, a former mental
patient "in the habit of taking night walks," was shot and killed by a
guard in the steel mill district after failing to produce proper identification.[24]

About 6,500 alien Germans lived in the city and they became the
focus of the anti-German hysteria in the city. In January 1918, the United
States Marshal for Chicago warned that "internment in prison camps of the
barbed-wire-fence and armed-guard variety copied from the Prussian original"
awaited all "Chicago Germans and other alien enemies" if they were caught

in the "barred zones without permits." At the same time it was announced
that the "alien express" would begin running on a regular basis to internment
camps in Georgia. Eventually four trains left Chicago carrying some 200
Chicago Germans to their new homes.[25]

Late in November, 1917, President Wilson had ordered all male German
aliens, age 14 and over, to register with their local police. February 4,
1918 was registration day in Chicago and thousands of Germans, many of whom
admitted to having lived in the United States for years without becoming
citizens, were fingerprinted and interrogated. Then each alien was given a
certificate, which he was required to carry with him at all times, and sent
on his way.[26] The police kept photographs, addresses, and interrogation
reports on each registrant. Women aliens were not ordered to register
until April but the same procedure was followed: everyone who was not a
naturalized citizen, including those who had taken out first papers, had to
appear at a police station or be subject to arrest.[27]

Along with the fear of aliens, rumors of spy plots and murder
conspiracies involving large numbers of "agents of the Kaiser" fostered
suspicions of Germans in America. Between April 7, 1917, and November 10,
1918, twenty-five such plots were revealed in the pages of Chicago newspapers. These schemes of German agents ranged from allegations that pro-
Germans led a wildcat strike of coal miners in Southern Illinois to charges
that other followers of Wilhelm II dressed as women had taken jobs as
maids in the homes of several Chicago industrial leaders with intentions of
assassinating them. These "counterfeit women," a federal agent explained,
had been arrested just in time to foil their plot. A few weeks later
German agents were charged with infecting bandages with tetanus germs
while others were allegedly attempting to poison Chicago's meat supply.

Though dozens of people were arrested in connection with these incidents, all were released after investigation and not one German-American in the city was sent to prison in connection with these alleged acts of subversion.[28]

In a Flag Day address on June 14, 1917, Woodrow Wilson denounced "the sinister intrigue" being conducted by agents of the Kaiser's government, thus giving an element of respectability to the wild charges being made. A few weeks later, in a letter to a Missouri congressman which received wide circulation in the press, Wilson attempted to reassure German-Americans that he did not view them all as disloyal. He was aware, he wrote, of the unfortunate position of German-Americans, and he expressed his "confidence in the entire integrity and loyalty of the great body of our citizens of German blood." The ambivalence of the opinions expressed in these two statements did little to help the position of German-Americans.[29]

Hostility to things German was on the increase and reached its peak in the Spring of 1918. On March 25, federal agents in Chicago swept through German neighborhoods arresting hundreds of citizens who were reportedly celebrating a German victory over French forces. For a week an average of 200 persons a day were arrested; groups foolish enough to be singing German songs were especially vulnerable, as were those who touched beer steins together--an action interpreted by federal agents as a salute to the German army. A Lutheran church on the North Side was invaded, two members were dragged out and beaten, and then the church was desecrated. Two days later a Lutheran school was set ablaze.[30]

Throughout the United States the demand that German spies be found and dealt with grew louder. Senator Warren Harding demanded death for spies in a Baltimore speech, and in Muskogee, Oklahoma, on April 3,

William Howard Taft urged that spies be shot. On April 4, a mob in Collinsville, Illinois, lynched Robert Prager, a German socialist. The response to the Prager incident among German-Americans, at least in public, was silence. The lynching was denounced by Governor Frank Lowden and other state officials, but German-Americans apparently felt it best not to say anything.[31] Privately, however, some leaders were very angry and bitter. Otto Butz, president of the pro-war Friends of German Democracy in Chicago, vigorously protested the incident in a letter to Woodrow Wilson. The President assured Butz that his administration would "cooperate with every effort to see to it that the loyal residents of the United States of German birth or descent are given genuine proof of the sincerity of our constitutions."[32] But many Germans were beginning to doubt whether the Constitution really protected them. One correspondent wrote Jane Addams that German-Americans had a sense of "bewilderment. It is not a question of loyalty they have a very real loyalty, [sic] it is more a pain and a deep sense of unfairness." German-Americans had tried to demonstrate their loyalty with apparently little influence on public perceptions.[33]

After the Prager lynching, Paul Mueller wrote Senator James Hamilton Lewis decrying the "war of injustice and hatred against citizens of German stock. . . . It is a war of destruction," Mueller continued:

> Annihilation is its aim. . . . Under the plea that it is necessary to defeat the Kaiser, that the interests of the U. S. and the patriotism of its citizens demand it, the German language is to be tabooed, every man and woman of German stock and name is to be made a despised pariah, and left to the tender mercies of any bloodthirsty mob, or any scoundrel, who uses the Stars and Stripes to hide behind, so as to be enabled to safely carry out his plans of private vengeance or greed or mere ordinary cussedness.

Mueller was most concerned about the "coming destruction of the German language Press . . ." embodied in a resolution introduced by Senator King of Utah which would have prohibited "the distribution of anything printed in the German language after July 1st." Mueller pleaded with Senator Lewis to vote against the measure. German-Americans did not deserve to be robbed of their language for they had been nothing but loyal since the outbreak of war.[34]

The lynching of Robert Prager most dramatically illustrated the attitude of nativist Americans toward German citizens; the hanging demonstrated vividly the hatred engendered for things German among citizens of the United States. In Chicago, however, German leaders looked to one man, Mayor William Hale Thompson, to protect them from the excesses of patriotism. The survival of German culture in the city seemed to depend on his actions.

Loyalty Under Pressure

Elected in 1915 over a German-American opponent, Thompson had initially made some enemies in the German community in 1916 by ordering enforcement of a state law requiring saloons to be closed on Sundays--this despite the fact that during the campaign he had promised he would never enforce such a law. Shortly after the declaration of war Thompson and his political advisor Fred "Swede" Lundin had decided the conflict would be politically unpopular and that opposition to the war would help Thompson get to the United States Senate. Soon under "Big Bill" Chicago became the center of anti-war activities in the United States.

Two national peace groups met in the city in 1917. A rally held by pacifists in May ended in a riot as police attacked and clubbed the

war-protesters. Later in the year, eighty anti-war leaders, barred from
holding their convention in several other midwestern cities from Milwaukee
to Fargo were invited to Chicago by the mayor. Thompson guaranteed their
safety but showed that he could do little to protect them. Governor
Frank Lowden ordered out the National Guard to prevent the peace meeting
from opening and the opponents of the war were sent on their way. German-
Americans played no part in either of the anti-war assemblies afraid to
trigger attacks on their loyalty.[35]

Schools became another battleground after the Thompson-appointed
Board of Education voted to allow high school students to continue to study
the German language if they wished; only in grammar schools was the teaching
of German and all other modern foreign languages banned. The board decided
it was better to bar all languages than single out only German.

The major anti-German incident in the schools involved an English
language story found in an eighth-grade speller. In August, 1917, Board
member Clement Czarnicki led a move to get a story on the good deeds of the
Kaiser removed from eighth grade spelling books. "What I ask is the
elimination of praise for the worst despot the world has ever seen,"
Czarnicki explained. Thompson supporter Mrs. E.S. Snodgrass opposed the
removal, "If we were to take action that would cause the children to tear
out this page we would have a lot of anarchists in the making," she reasoned.
"I do not understand that we have declared war against German citizens in
this country." The School Board took no immediate action on the matter but
the Tribune urged Chicago children to show their support of the war effort
by tearing out the offensive page, which contained a little story on what
a "good pupil" Kaiser Wilhelm had been as a boy--"There is in him a
fundamental bent toward what is clean, manly and aboveboard," the passage,

published in 1910, read, offering a stereotypical view of the German character. Over the next few days the _Tribune_ reported receiving "numerous" pages in the mail.[36]

Few non-Germans in Chicago spoke out in behalf of the rights of German-Americans. Jane Addams spoke on "Patriotism and Pacifism" before an Evanston church group on June 10, 1917. Addams opined that the feelings of German-born American citizens should have been considered before war was declared. For expressing that sentiment Addams was publicly denounced before the church group by Justice Orrin N. Carter of the Illinois Supreme Court. It was no time for such consideration, the Judge implied. "We are in the war and it is our business to get behind the government." The Judge became an overnight hero in the press and Addams was denigrated frequently for her "uncommonly silly outburst of pro-German twaddle." For the remainder of the war she said little more about the plight of German-Americans.[37]

Thompson said little about German-Americans until he launched his campaign for the United States Senate in August, 1918. Then, during the Republican primary, he spoke throughout the state attacking the Wilson administration and defending German-American loyalty. He condemnded the Deomcratic party for getting the United States involved in the war through its "inability and inefficiency." As for his chief Republican opponent in the primary, Medill McCormick, Thompson said that he was hiding behind "the subterfuge of loyalty" and was an active supporter of the war. No one had been more loyal, on the other hand, than "Big Bill" Thompson. "I am an American," he told a German-American audience, "I was born and live as an American . . . I love only one flag--Old Glory." Upholding the constitutional rights of citizens was not treasonable, he claimed. Despite his

super-patriotic rhetoric and his appeal to German-American voters,
Thompson was swamped by Medill McCormick on election day, though the mayor
did carry Chicago.[38]

Another politician with an interest in the German vote and the
attitude of German-Americans toward the war was Frederick Britten,
Representative from Chicago's heavily German 9th District. Britten, a
second generation German-American, had voted against going to war and had
sponsored legislation that would have exempted German-American draftees from
fighting in Europe. Britten was challenged for the Republican nomination
by Fletcher Dobyns, a Progressive and fervent supporter of America's entry
into the war. Dobyns campaigned on the theme that Britten had been far
too friendly toward Germany and that it was necessary for a 100% American
to replace him. Britten responded by arguing that Dobyns was a tool of
the rich men on the Gold Coast of Chicago, which formed part of the 9th
District. "A small number of rich men," Britten claimed, "are determined
to buy my defeat." Any aspersions concerning loyalty and patriotism were
brought into the campaign by these rich men to cover-up the Congressman's
charges that these rich men and others of their ilk had actually conspired
to get the United States into the War. As for his own patriotism, Britten
announced, "the flag my father fought for under Lincoln has been my guiding
star." His vote against the war, he explained, was a patriotic vote based
on sound constitutional principles: no one could claim it was a disloyal
act. Republicans in Britten's district responded to his campaign by
giving him over 70% of the vote in the primary.[39]

In the general election, Britten's Democratic opponent echoed many
of Dobyns' charges, but Britten received 56 per cent of the vote. In the
same election, only one week before the Armistice, German voters helped

defeat a candidate for sheriff, Anton Cermak, who engaged in a violently
"anti-Hun" campaign against the incumbent, the German-American Republican,
Charles Peters. Peters won by a narrow margin due to the support of
German voters. German-Americans continued to support ethnic candidates.
They had little to lose by doing that; their loyalty could not be questioned
simply for voting, unless it was for a Socialist.[40]

Chicago Germans made efforts, under pressure, to demonstrate
loyalty by purchasing Liberty bonds. The English speaking press would not
recognize the true loyalty of German-Americans, a leader of the bond drive
among Chicago Germans declared, unless they bought more bonds than any
other ethnic group, and a major effort was made to reach that goal. At
bond rallies in German areas of Chicago, speakers from various German
societies pressed the point that contributions would serve a double purpose:
they would prove German-American loyalty, while at the same time they
would save Germany from the despotism of Prussian rule. Cardinal Mundelein
ordered every parish in the city to buy bonds, and appeals were made from
the pulpits of all 350 parishes. Even Mayor Thompson indicated that he
would purchase some Liberty bonds and urged all Chicagoans to follow his
example.[41] About 400 volunteers visited the homes of Chicago Germans
during the Third Liberty Loan drive in April, 1918. "The average German
citizen is all right," Harold L. Ickes, director of the neighborhood
committees conducting the drive declared, as he reported bond sales
averaging $20,000 a day in German neighborhoods. Karl Matthie, a second
generation German-American, reported little difficulty getting his share
of contributions. Matthie said he just told the German-Americans he and
his volunteers visited that they had to buy bonds. "Lukewarm loyalty or

passive patriotism today is out of the question," he would explain. "Neutrality is treason. You are either American or German now. . . .There is no fence to sit on. There is nothing but a trench into [sic] which will be buried every man who refuses to take sides." With such inspiration, Germans contributed over $5,085,000 to the third loan, a figure exceeded only by the Bohemians and the Poles in the city.[42]

Those German-Americans wishing to go beyond buying bonds to prove their loyalty could join a group called the Friends of German Democracy. Established with the assistance of George Creel's Committee of Public Information, the Friends organized rallies in New York, Chicago, Milwaukee, and other cities with large German populations. The message the group presented was simple and familiar: Germany had been taken over by war-mongering Prussians; therefore, it was in the interest of Germans everywhere to overthrow the military dictatorship in their old homeland. As New York banker Otto Kahn told readers of the Abendpost, "Germany today is no longer the Germany of my youth. . . . The apirit of Prussianism and Americanism cannot live together in the same world. One must die." Kahn urged German-Americans to unite in liberating "the soul of the German people" from the chains of Prussian slavery so that "the German people again speak the language of humanity, freedom, and justice.[43] Another member of the Friends told the Chicago Association of Commerce and Industry that the German army had to be defeated quickly, and the scourge of Prussianism had to be removed as quickly as possible; otherwise the scourge of Bolshevism would overtake the country. A victory "for the German people then would be far more difficult."[44] Otto Butz, head of the Chicago Friends, claimed that his group was fighting for the same principles as "the '48ers,'" those liberals who had escaped from Germany after the aborted revolution of 1848.

Butz felt all Germans should join the fight against "the frightfulness of autocracy." Participants at the group's only Chicago meeting during the war heard Butz and others describe the difficult position under which German-Americans were placed in the war against the home of their fathers. Pastor Thomas Dornblauer recounted the struggle of divided consciences but concluded that "Martin Luther would have fought the Kaiser" because, according to his own principles Luther "was an American." Professor Max Meyer of the University of Missouri gave German-Americans additional justifications for fighting when he explained that the United States made war against "the ideal of the ruling class" and the enlargement of state power. Meyer said he had been a member of various peace groups before the United States entered the war but had since become convinced that only an American victory could bring Germany "to its senses."[45]

Total membership in the Friends was not reported but the message conveyed at its meetings and in its propaganda echoed the explanations and feelings expressed by other groups in German Chicago. The war was not against Germany but against Prussian militarism; German-Americans could therefore join in the crusade and not feel like they were betraying the home of their forefathers; and, because of the difficulty of their position in the United States, German-Americans had earned the admiration of fellow Americans for their patriotic endeavors which were above and beyond those asked of other Americans. On the latter point Germanists felt that they never got the recognition they deserved, and this feeling added to a general view that German contributions to American history had never been adequately recognized, despite the size of the German-American population and the importance of the German-American legacy.[46]

The loyalty of German-Americans was challenged, however, in two congressional hearings. In February 1918, the Senate held hearings on revoking the national charter of the German-American Alliance. In November of that year, a special committee of Senators looked into "German and Bolshevik propaganda" which allegedly had subverted the war effort. The Alliance hearings opened with a charge that the group constituted a "potent agent of Pan-Germanism" and had worked in the interests of the German cause. The Alliance, Gustave Ohlinger, a Toledo lawyer, charged, had worked to elect a "pro-German" president in 1916. Other witnesses portrayed a picture of widespread subversion and disloyalty on the part of large numbers of German-Americans. German-American leaders brought to testify demonstrated a great deal of naivete about American politics and the power of German-Americans as a voting bloc but revealed little that was outrightly treasonable or even subversive of the war effort. The hearings, held by the Senate Judiciary Committee, produced evidence showing that the Alliance received money from American brewers to use in a campaign against prohibition and that this cause, actually, had occupied most of the group's time. The bombastic rhetoric of Alliance spokesmen did little to reassure the committee members of the patriotism of the group.[47]

The hearings linking brewing and liquor interests with the dissemination of German and Bolshevik propaganda did not open until a week after the war ended. Testimony by government investigators did little to improve the image of German-Americans. Lutheran churches came in for especially heavy criticism. "We have found," an Army intelligence officer testified, that "from the period of August, 1914 down to April 6, 1917, in hundreds of the Lutheran churches the continuous preaching was in favor and hope of German victory." The witness did not indicate whether the content of the sermons changed after the United States entered the war.[48]

The propaganda hearings continued on into 1919 but the major emphasis shifted to an investigation of Bolshevism. The Hearings established that there had been an attempt by the German government to buy English language newspaper before the war, and that the German Counsul in Chicago had been interested in the activities of the American Embargo Conference, mainly making sure the group avoided becoming too German. Little else was uncovered by investigators but the very fact of a Congressional investigation helped create a feeling that many German-Americans had not been loyal.[49]

Other incidents in Chicago itself added to a negative image of German-Americans. An investigation by the United States Attorney's office into charges of alleged disloyalty in the Chicago Symphony Orchestra turned up the fact that a cellist had informed another member that if Germany lost the war he would commit suicide; for this statement the cellist was threatened with imprisonment. A second incident involved a cornet player who had shouted at one of his students for standing up when the "Marseillaise" was played. In response to this charge, made by one Leo Jaworski, the cornet player sued his accuser for $10,000 charging defamation of character. A few weeks later Frederick Stock, orchestra conductor, resigned from his position, which he had held since 1905. Stock expressed concern over the fact that he had never taken out final citizenship papers might injure the reputation of the Chicago Symphony; he would rather resign than do that.[50]

The explosion of a "death bomb" outside the Federal Building September 5, 1918, which killed four Chicagoans and injured thirty, led to a sweep of German areas in the city in a search for the bombers. Ten

men were arrested, seven of whom had German names, and the manufacture of
the bomb was traced to the shop of Leo Kreutzinger, a machinist whose two
children had already been sent to jail for "aiding the enemy" in time of
war. The bombing and arrests heightened the feeling among Americans that
agents of the Kaiser were still active in the city, according to the Tribune.[51]

With the ending of the war, one German-American leader asked for a
return of understanding and a recognition of German loyalty. The "supreme
test" of loyalty had been passed magnificently, Ernest Kruetgen told members
of the Lincoln Club. German-Americans had proven their "sincere, decent"
citizenship. Any "bitter recollections of disloyalty by the few during the
bitter days of the war" would best be forgotten and German-Americans would
have little difficulty returning to their pre-war position of high
prestige in American society.[52]

Most Chicago Germans came away from the war with the feeling that
they had behaved quite patriotically. But as members of the German Roman
Catholic Alliance pointed out, "We cannot but express our feeling of utmost
contempt for the suspicions and insults to which we have been exposed."[53]
Members of openly identified German groups had been investigated and jailed.
German-born citizens who had failed to take out American citizenship papers
had also suffered harassment and abuse. The American Protective League had
raided German neighborhoods and reported on any open displays of affection
for the Old Country. Yet no wide-scale subversive activities had been uncovered and no massive arrests of German-Americans had taken place. The
German language disappeared from Chicago elementary schools and the German
theater closed down. The loss of the theater, however, may have stemmed
as much from the popularity of silent films as from any hatred of things
German.

Chicago escaped much of the anti-German hysteria which possessed other parts of the country. William Hale Thompson had little to do with that fact as he spent much of the time out of the city on trips and vacations. Probably the principal reason Chicago Germans were spared a fervent anti-Hun crusade was the large size of the German population. "Hun" hunters made life difficult for Germanists and supporters of the Kaiser but good logic would indicate to most German-Americans that if they wanted to avoid trouble they merely would have to refrain from supporting the declared enemie of the United States. Except for militant defenders of German culture most Chicago Germans followed this safer, more sensible course. Ethnicity simply did not have enough to offer in terms of security and pride to risk going to jail.[54]

Only the Germanists emerged from the wartime experience with a feeling that their culture and identity had to be preserved. Michael Singer, in his last _Jahrbuch_, made his case for the necessity of preserving the German heritage in the United States. "American Germanism should and must free American democracy from the most hateful and dangerous . . . aristo cracy, the annihilating aristocracy of Anglo-Saxonism." Defenders of German culture had to remain steadfast in their goal of preserving German concepts of liberality and open-mindedness. "We must either cultivate with a gardener's love our ideals . . . or we must let the fragrant blossom of cultural and social life die under the frosty breath of English domination," Singer concluded. The prohibition amendment, added to the Constitution after the termination of the war, symbolized the aims of the Puritanical forces dominating American life. These "fanatics," as Germanists usually referred to the Anglo-Saxons and Puritans responsible

for the Nineteenth Amendment, had forgotten the true meaning of American
traditions of individual conscience. Germanists, since the German heritage
was more in line with the true meaning of Americanism, had the task preserving those ideals.[55] The problem for leaders of the German community
would be to arouse enough interest in a revival of the ethnic spirit among
their followers to make Singer's goal a genuine possibility.

Other groups to which an ethnic identity remained important, like
the Missouri Synod, the Turnverein, and various singing societies and clubs,
had less lofty aims. For the Missouri Synod, the German heritage was not
as important as the protection of Lutheran theology. The war had not
affected the Synod's goal of separating itself as much as possible from
the mainstream of American society. It made little difference whether
avoidance of the world was taught in English or German. German Turners
turned increasingly to gymnastics and athletic events as their inducement
to membership, abjuring politics for the most part. The German vereine
had little difficulty re-establishing themselves, singing in German and
dancing to Strauss' waltzes with little interference after November 11, 1918.
And those clubs smart enough to lay in a supply of liquor before prohibition
went into effect did not even have to do without schnapps and beer until
supplies ran out. (At the Germania Club that did not happen until 1923.)[56]

NOTES

Chapter II.

1. Chicago Tribune, April 1,2,3, 1917; ISZ, June 25, 1917.

2. Chicago Daily News, April 7, 1917.

3. Chicago Daily News, October 16, 1917. The "India Plotters" were tried before Judge Keenesaw Mountain Landis and sentenced to 3 years in prison, and fined $13,000. Among the "plotters" were Chicago business-man and former supporter of the American Embargo Conference, Gustave Jacobsen; Albert Wehrde and George Paul Boehm, as well as Heramba La Gupta. The German consul in Chicago, Curt von Reiswitz, was indicted but had returned to Germany. Chicago Daily News, October 29, 19

4. Chicago Daily News, April 10, 11, 13, 1917; Chicago Tribune, April 12, 19

5. Chicago Daily News, April 14, 1917.

6. Chicago Daily News, April 20, 1917; Chicago Abendpost, April 20, 1917.

7. Chicago Tribune, April 4, 1917; Socialists were elected in the Fifteenth Ward, 31% German; the Twenty-seventh Ward, 32% German; and the Ninth Ward, which was only 9% German. In other wards with high percentages of German voters, such as the 24th, 25th, and 26th, German candidates headed the ballots and these ethnic candidates were sent to the City Council, usually without mentioning the war.

8. Abendpost,January 29, February 10, 1918; ISZ, February 12, 1918.

9. ISZ, December 31, 1917.

10. Abendpost, April 21, 1918.

11. Germania Club of Chicago, Minutes of Meeting of Board of Directors, March 17, 1918. In another name change the German State Bank became the Cosmopolitan State Bank, February 1, 1918. Germania Club minutes are in a vault in the clubhouse. Permission to use them granted by George Felbinger, Club President.

12. English District of the Missouri Synod for Northern Illinois, Report of District Meeting, July, 1916, pp. 43-44. Klinck Library, Concordia College, River Forest, Illinois.

13. As quoted in Sharvy G. Umbeck, "The Social Adaptation of a Select Group of German Background Protestant Churches in Chicago," (Ph.D. dissertation, University of Chicago, 1940), p. 60.

14. Chicago Tribune, January 13, 1918.

15. _Lutheran Witness_, December 25, 1917, p. 45; _Abendpost_, January 21, 1918.

16. _Lutheran Witness_, January 13, 1918.

17. _Abendpost_, Oct. 3, 1918.

18. George Cardinal Mundelein, _Two Crowded Years_ (Chicago, 1918), pp. 146-47.

19. _Chicago Tribune_, April 2, 1918.

20. _Chicago Tribune_, Dec. 2, 1918.

21. _Chicago Tribune_, April 2, 1918.

22. _Abendpost,_ Sept. 9, 1917.

23. _Chicago Daily News_, April 14, 1917.

24. _Chicago Daily News_, April 18, 19, May 31, 1917; March 26, 1918;
    Abendpost, April 18, 1917.

25. _Chicago Daily News,_ Nov. 19, 23, 27, 1917.

26. _Chicago Daily News_, Jan. 3, May 10, 23, 1918.

27. _Chicago Daily News_, Feb. 4, 1918.

28. _Chicago Daily News_, June 18, 1918; Margaret Jenisen, _Illinois in the
    World War: The Wartime Organization of Illinois_ (Springfield: Illinois
    State Historical Library, 1923). p. 42. Jenisen reports that 40,234
    aliens registered in Illinois. No German-American in the state was
    convicted of seditious activity.

29. _Chicago Daily News_, May 8, July 28, Sept. 22, 1917; _Chicago Tribune_,
    June 15, 1917.

30. _Chicago Daily News_, March 26, 28, 1918; _Chicago Tribune_, Aug. 3, 1918.

31. _Chicago Daily News_, April 3, 4, 5, 1918; Donald Hickey, "The Prager
    Affair: A Study in Wartime Hysteria," _Journal of the Illionis State
    Historical Society_ 62 (Summer 1969), pp. 117-134; _NYT_, April 5, 1918.

32. Woodrow Wilson to Otto Butz, April 12, 1918, CHS.

33. Alfred Booth to Jane Addams, June 11, 1918, Jane Addams Collection,
    Chronological File of Correspondence, University of Illinois at
    Chicago Circle.

34. Paul Mueller to Senator James H. Lewis, April 6, 1918, Arthur Cole
    Notes on First World War, Illinois Historical Survey, University of
    Illinois Library, Urbana.

35. Chicago Tribune, May 28, 1917.

36. Chicago Tribune, Sept. 4, 7, 1918. Attendance fell drastically in German language classes: from 17,674 in 1916 to 1,246 in 1918.

37. Chicago Tribune, June 11, 12, 1917.

38. Abendpost, May 28, Aug. 7, 1918; Chicago Tribune, Sept. 11, Nov. 6, 1918 Seward W. Livermore, Politics is Adjourned: Woodrow Wilson and the War Congress, 1916-1918 (Middletown, Conn.: Wesleyan University Press, 1966) p. 167-68.

39. Abendpost, July 13, 24, Aug. 15, 16, Oct. 22, Nov. 6, 1918.

40. Chicago Tribune, Nov. 6, 1918; Alex Gottfired, Boss Cermak of Chicago: A Study in Political Leadership (Seattle: University of Washington Press 1962), pp. 42-43.

41. Abendpost, March 26, 1918.

42. Chicago Tribune, May 29, 1918; Abendpost, May 8, 1918. The following table lists the results from the Third Liberty Loan drive:

LIBERTY LOAN SALES

	Subscribers	Amount	Average Subscription
Germans	50,000	$5,085,000	$101.70
Bohemians	60,610	5,578,000	92.00
Italians	39,000	3,300,000	84,61
Norwegians	20,000	1,250,000	62.50
Polish	70,000	5,600,000	80.00
Cook County	716,794	$142,446,350	$19.87

43. Chicago Daily News, April 12, May 8, 1918.

44. Abendpost, Jan. 17, 1918.

45. Abendpost, April 18, 1918.

46. Abendpost, March 6, 1918.

47. NYT, Feb. 24, 1916; U.S. Congress, Senate, Committee on the Judiciary, Hearings on the National German-American Alliance, 65th Cong., 2d sess. p. 8, 95, 333, 449.

48. U.S. Congress, Senate, Committee on the Judiciary, Hearings on Brewing and Liquor Interests and German Propaganda, 65th Cong., 2d sess., I: pp. 618-619.

49. <u>NYT</u>, Nov. 18, 1918; Jan. 15, 1919.

50. <u>Chicago Daily News</u>, Oct. 7, 1918.

51. <u>Chicago Tribune</u>, Sept. 5, 1918; <u>Chicago Daily News</u>, Sept. 23, 1918.

52. <u>Chicago Tribune</u>, Nov. 11, 1918.

53. <u>Abendpost</u>, July 1, 1919.

54. <u>NYT</u>, Dec. 17, 1918.

55. Michael Singer, ed., <u>German-American Yearbook for 1918</u> (Chicago: German-American Publishing Co., 1917), p. 3.

56. Germania Club of Chicago, Minutes of Meeting of Board of Directors, Jan. 1919 through Dec. 1923. The minutes reflect a constant interest in the state of the club's liquor supply.

CHAPTER III

"A NEW UNITY": EFFORTS TOWARDS A
NEW DEFINITION OF GERMAN-AMERICANISM, 1919-1922

The problem for German-American civic leaders, intellectuals,
editors, and businessmen in 1919 was how to redefine the German part of
their heritage. The war had devastated the old homeland and practically
destroyed everything German in the United States. The most important
protector of German customs and traditions in America, the German language,
had been banned from public schools. Public use of that language had largely
disappeared from Chicago. Two issues on which German-American leaders tried
to rebuild an ethnic consciousness remained. They hoped to use the image of
a violated and abused homeland to maintain loyalty among their followers,
and they wanted to keep alive the memory of the contempt, slander, and injustice suffered during the war.

German-American leaders were determined not to allow their community
to disappear. The economic survival of the leadership depended on it.
Also, the passing away of their group would mean the victory of the
Puritanical forces in American society. The United States, without German-
American contributions, would become a pale copy of England--another nation
of shopkeepers. The passage of the Nineteenth Amendment witnessed the power
of the Puritan fanatics.

The rebuilding of German-Americanism required that other Americans
would have to be shown the significance of German contributions to American

64

history. The wartime experience of German-Americans would have to serve
as a reminder to group members of what could happen if they did not stand
together to defend their cultural heritage. Germany would have to be
resurrected. The accomplishment of these tasks would assure the survival
of the German-American community.

I

For German-American leaders the war-time experience had demonstrated
that German-Americans were the true "100% Americans." "If actual tests can
be taken into consideration," Paul Mueller, publisher of the Abendpost,
commented, "Then American citizens of German perentage can claim to be the
most loyal and patriotic of all Americans, because their patriotism and
loyalty have been subjected to the severest tests that men can desire;
tests which no other so-called foreign element has been forced to undergo."[1]
Ernest J. Kruetgen, who had participated in several anti-war demonstrations
before 1917, supported Mueller's view. Only a few German-Americans had been
arrested for overt acts of disloyalty during the war, he told a Lincoln
Club gathering, while most German-American parents had loyally and eagerly
sent their sons to fight for the new homeland. Such patriotism demonstrated
that it was time for all Americans "to eradicate all hyphens and to kindle
the fires under the melting-pot." German-Americans had shown they were
ready "to fight for American ideals," so other citizens had an obligation
to "efface any bitter recollections of disloyalty by the few during the
bitter days of the war."[2]

The American Unity Club, formerly the German Club, held a "victory"
celebration for the German people who had been freed from "militarism and
autocracy" by the Allied victory. The principal speaker at the affair,

Senator-elect Medill McCormick, called for a return to "mutual understanding" among all Americans. The Great War, he said, had been fought for the same reasons as the Civil War, to free people from slavery and German-Americans had fought valiantly in both struggles. No one, he concluded, could doubt their loyalty or that German-Americans were charged with the same spirit that guided Washington and Lincoln.[3]

The Friends of German Democracy, a group formed by the Creel Committee to generate support for the war among German-Americans, also celebrated the victory over autocracy. To help restore friendly relations between all groups in the United States, Otto Butz, the group's president, called for an increased number of Americanization classes for "the German element." Another member explained the Friends' criticism of previous organizations which claimed to represent German-Americans by asserting that the German American Alliance had made a great mistake by isolating itself from American society. "The National Alliance went bankrupt because it attempted to segregate the so-called German element . . . in the interest of protecting German ideals." Instead of standing "as a thing apart," however, it was the duty of German organizations to make German ideals "part of the American soil," and that could only be done through active participation in all areas of American life.[4] The Friends's solution to the problems suffered by German-Americans was to ask for more Americanization classes.[5]

The assimilationist view espoused by the Friends contained several themes: one could become an American yet still retain the best ideals of "Germanism"; racial and ethnic antagonisms had to be overcome, but not at the price of losing the sense of order, personal liberty, and opposition to regimentation best associated with the German character. "We must stick with

America," national president Franz Sigel told a Milwaukee chapter of the Friends, "but we do not have to change our characters. America is a diverse country . . . and Americanism has to do with a state of mind rather than with blood," so the best chance to maintain German culture lay in fighting the notion that Americanism meant "uniformity of opinion"; what it really meant, Sigel explained, was "diversity and growth." The best hope for the retention of German ideals in their battle against "Puritanism," in other words, was in the creation of a pluralist society.[6]

The assimilationist argument was rejected by members of the German-American Citizens League. Founded on June 9, 1918, in Chicago, the League did not hold its first public meeting until January 30, 1919. At that meeting, several hundred delegates from over fifty German societies re-solved to build "a better understanding among German-Americans" by keeping alive "the culture, the beauty, and the honor of the motherland." League members decided to take an active role in American politics; Michael Girten, American-born president of the German Aid Society, explained that "German-Americans had sinned by hiding their lights under a bushel" in the years before the war, but that they could not allow that to happen again. The charges of disoloyalty and the anti-German hysteria of the war years had perhaps been just "punishment for this pre-war isolation," Girten suggested, but it was time to make sure nothing resembling the war experience ever happened again and to make sure "that German cultural and political contributions to America received due recognition." The only way that recognition could be achieved was by gaining political power "at all levels of involvement." A second speaker, Washington University trained theologian Pastor Alfred Meyer, also chastised German-Americans for their pre-war behavior. If German-Americans really loved their country, Meyer shouted, "they must see to it that German culture does not perish here." The preservation of German culture involved more than saving beer and pretzels; it involved German music, art, science, theater, and gymnastics. But culture could only be protected by some semblance of political respect- ability and power. Therefore, the Evangelical minister urged the Citizens League to promote actively the political careers of "men who understand and respect German ideas and German character.[7] The German-American Citizens League became the principal voice in the city for the point of view that, far from being defensive, German-Americans should be aggressivly pro- German in their attempts to rebuild a broken community. A less than militant stance, it was feared, would lead to complete "Anglo-Saxonization" of American culture. Pro-Germanists would have to assert their power, politically and culturally.

Thus, two major attitudes towards political action had emerged. The Friend's of German Democracy eschewed political action but the Citizens league did not, and the latter view prevailed. German-Americans organized the Independent Voters Association of Chicago in February, 1919. The Association, made up of delegates from over seventy German clubs, and its eye on the coming mayoral election and the chance to support "Big Bill" Thompson. The Association hoped to unite all German voters behind Thompson as a demonstration of the power of "the German vote," and also as a way of thanking the mayor for protecting the rights of German-Americans during the war.[10]

Thompson first had to face Captain Charles Merriam in the Republican primary. "Captain" Merriam ran against the Kaiser in his campaign and suggested Thompson had been Wilhelm the Second's "best friend during the war." Merriam, who had fought in Italy suggested that "Kaiser Bill" join his "best friend" in exile where he might one day find out that "the red, white, and blue of the American flag" had not become a "yellow streak. It was only the mayor's jaundiced eye which saw yellow."[10] George Pretzel, German-American alderman of the 24th ward, served as Merriam's campaign manager. "I know personally the sentiments of thousands of American citizens of German descent," he claimed. "They feel themselves insulted by the apparent belief of the mayor and his advisors that they are not loyal Americans." Germans, he suggested, should show the falsity of the belief of supporting the "100 per cent American candidate," Charles Merriam. "The hyphen was shot out of Americanism" by the war, Pretzel proclaimed, and "Thompsonism" deserved to be refuted.[11] Most German-Americans did not agree with this position, however, and Merriam received less than 3% of the vote in Pretzel's own ward, the most heavily Germanic in the city.[12] Pretzel himself was defeated in the aldermanic election of 1920 when he received less than 35% of the vote.

The Democrats chose Robert Sweitzer to head their ticket, so voters had the opportunity to replay the 1915 election. Sweitzer made loyalty one of the chief issues of the campaign, and vigorously attacked "Kaiser Bill's" war record. Thompson had "blemished" Chicago's good name by his conduct and every step he took, from denouncing the draft to refusing to greet a French general, and "was an obstacle to successful prosecution of the war." "Smiling Bob" proudly contrasted the "disloyalty" of Thompson with his own patriotic service on the Illinois State Defense Council and with the American Red Cross; and at the same time he denied being of German ancestry. He actually was Irish, he explained; his real father had died when he was only six years old and his mother had then married a German.[14] Although in 1915 a committee of German-Americans had verified Sweitzer's claims to German ancestry, in 1919 no such effort was made.

German-American organizations rushed to the support of Mayor Thompson. As the president of the Citizens League pointed out, "Chicago was the only city in America during the Great War in which German-Americans were spared from the mob and able to hold their meetings." Thompson deserved full credit for protecting German-American rights. Thompson had represented "true Americanism" during the war because only he among politicians had the courage "to maintain the rule of the Constitution." Therefore, a vote for Thompson was not a "pro-German" vote, as the opposition charged, but truly "pro-American."[15]

The Democrats reminded Chicagoans that Thompson had, despite his pledges, closed all saloons on Sundays. The Citizens League defended the mayor on this breach of "personal liberty," however, and explained that Thompson had no choice; he was obligated to uphold the law as a public official, no matter how onerous it might be.[16] Besides, some Germans found the "beer issue" embarrassing, according to Ferdinand Walther. "Germans have been accused of becoming politically involved only over the beer question"; this accusation was "demeaning" to the grander goals of German culture and deserved to be refuted. "Do not set your sights only of the 'beer question,'" the Independent Voters Association warned, "but vote as a 100% American for law and the Constitution" and "Big Bill" Thompson.

The prohibition issue symbolized far more than simply the denial of a glass of beer, as one minister pointed out. Prohibition was only the first step in a plot by Puritanical "fanatics" who wanted to "Anglicize" thoroughly the United States. If the fanatics were unopposed they would soon turn the United States into a "pale, graying copy of England." During the war "lack of vigilance" on the part of German-Americans had permitted the victory of the prohibitionists; unless German-Americans woke up quickly the Eighteenth Amendment would be only the first of a series of "fanatical laws" added to the Constitution.[17] The United German Male Chorus of Chicago responded to the call for an awakened German America by urgently appealing to its members to vote down a referendum proposal that would have led to the early introduction of prohibition into Cook County. The proposal would have made the county dry as of July 1, 1919 rather than waiting until January 16, 1920 when the Volstead Act was scheduled to go into effect nationwide. "The Whole Country is looking to Chicago," the appeal read. "If we vote against prohibition, then the gentlemen in Washington will hear the real voice of the people" and begin a movement toward repeal. German women had an especially important role to play because "every German woman's vote will render that of a prohibitionist harmless."[18] As for the mayoral candidates, the leaders of the Choruses offered no choice; both Sweitzer and Thompson favored a "wet" city, so the choice would have to be made on other issues.

The election became a three-way race after State's Attorney Maclay Hoyne entered on a platform which stressed reform and good government. Hoyne signed an Anti-Saloon League petition and further angered German-American leaders by "waving the bloody shirt," as the Abendpost called it.[19] The Tribune called it a drive for "pure Americanism" as Hoyne denounced the "racial appeals" of his opponents. Hoyne welcomed the votes of "those men of German blood who are first and foremost American citizens." Those who supported disloyalty, he implied, probably would vote for Thompson of the "Sweitzer-Stuckart ticket." (Henry Stuckart, a German-American, was the

Democratic candidate for City Treasurer.) Hoyne reminded voters that in 1915 Sweitzer's supporters had described their man as "the German candidate" and had urged his victory as a message to Woodrow Wilson that Chicagoans did not want to go to war.[21]

A week before the election the Chicago _Tribune_ filed suit against Mayor Thompson, charging him with seditious activity during the war. The action came in response to a libel suit filed by the mayor which charged that war-time articles in the newspaper had severely damaged his reputation. The seditious activity on the part of the mayor, the _Tribune_ claimed, included statements such as Thompson's charge that "the closer you get to Wall Street the more flags you see." It was also charged that the Germans had published some of Thompson's speeches and had showered them from airplanes over Allied trenches. As a Hoyne supporter said after the suit was filed, "Chicago is on trial before the world. The shame of Chicago should be wiped out."[22] In response to this suit, leaders of German-American societies became more determined to support Thompson. "Thompson's foes are our foes," the Citizens League declared; his battles are our battles."[23]

Thompson made his war record a principal issue of his campaign. He struck out at the National Security League, calling it "a dangerous parasite" which threatened free government. He also attacked the "capitalists" who had been responsible for the war and warned of the dangers of "a false patriotism" which had led to wartime persecution of many loyal Americans.[24] Democratic campaign material distributed in German areas of the city warned that Thompson's true friends were "the Negroes," while Sweitzer's supporters in Polish and Lithuanian neighborhoods warned against voting for Thompson and "the disloyal dachschund element."[25]

On election day Thompson carried the city 39% to 36% for Sweitzer, and 17% for Hoyne. Thomas Fitzpatrick, a Socialist, received 8% of the vote. In German areas of the city the vote was extremely close: Sweitzer received 47% of the vote in selected precincts (at least 80% German), while Thompson got 46%. A precinct-by-precinct analysis based on social class, computed on the basis of annual rent, shows that Sweitzer did far better, 65%, among "lower-middle class" voters than he did among "middle-class" voters where he received only 34% of the vote.[27] Religious differences in voting cannot be computed since evidence is lacking; "Lutheran" and "Catholic" areas in the city cannot be defined, as both religious groups were well established in all German areas of the city. Class differences appeared as the major obstacle to German unity in the 1919 city mayoral election.[28] Despite Robert Sweitzer's loss, Henry Stuckart managed to win the post of City Treasurer by a narrow 14,000-vote margin. He attributed his success to his showing in the German wards, where he did somewhat better than Sweitzer. He received 57% of the vote in the two heaviest German wards, where Sweitzer received only 51%.[29] On only one issue could German-Americans agree; on the question "Shall Chicago become Anti-Saloon or Dry?" they voted 86% "No," compared with 74% for the entire city.[30]

German-American analysts at the time attributed Thompson's victory to his anti-war stance, and to the united strength of the German vote. The Abendpost claimed he won because "he had the courage to respect the American ideal of liberty" and pledged future support. George Sylvester Viereck's staunchly pro-German, nationally distributed, American Monthly lauded Thompson's victory and agreed with the New York Evening Post that both parties had a lesson to learn for 1920: "it pays to cultivate the German

vote."[31] In reality, however, the German vote remained as divided as it
had been before the war; class and religious differences prevented any
unified "German vote."[32]

II

On November 12, 1918, an Appeal from the Women of Germany to the
Women of America appeared in several American newspapers. Without immediate
assistance, Americans were warned, thousands of children and women would soon
die of starvation. Though the war was over the Allies continued their
blockade of German ports and were not allowing any food to get through.[33]
German-American leaders such as Harry Rubens, a vice-president of the
Germania Club, Charles Wacker, head of the Chicago Plan Commission, Ernest
Kruetgen, and Judge A. K. Nippert of Cincinnati led the call for German-
Americans to take action. "We have shown we could work for America,"
Nippert said, "now it is time to show we can also work for the Fatherland."
At a meeting in New York City, delegates from across the country discussed
means to raise money. Harry Rubens, one-time secretary to Carl Schurz, made
an emotional plea for relief, "Germany will never die," he shouted to the
audience "Never, never." German-Americans had to do everything possible to
"save the German spirit" and to educate other Americans about the necessity
of saving the German nation. Politicians must be made to understand.[34]

The United States Congress appropriated $100,000,000 for European
relief in 1919, but an amendment added by Senator Henry Cabot Lodge prohibited the use of any of this money in "ex-enemy countries." The Allies
did give Germany permission to import food as of April, 1919, but by that
time, according to Herbert Hoover, in charge of Red Cross efforts to

distribute food in Europe, the situation in Germany was "to a large degree one of complete abandonment of hope."[35]

At a relief rally in Chicago, thousands of German-Americans heard Jane Addams describe the starvation and hunger she had witnessed in Germany and Austria during her recent European tour. German children lacked milk, food, and hospital facilities and were on the verge of mass starvation, she reported. A representative of the Chicago Archdiocese read a plea from Cardinal Mundelein offering his full support for relief efforts, and Harry Rubens warned that Germany would not survive the winter without massive relief. As a result of the rally, a committee to coordinate fund-raising was created with the respected Charles Wacker, a former leader of the pre-war German and Austro-Hungarian Aid Society, as chairman. Wacker hoped to duplicate the efforts of his old group, which had raised over $700,000 between 1915 and 1917; during the first month of its existence the German-American Aid Society raised over $50,000 in the city.[36]

Several German-Americans from Chicago visited Germany in the aftermath of war and reported on its plight. Congressman Frederick Britten was shocked "by the hundreds of thousands of wasted, hungry, cold, tubercular children" he saw, and was angered that "nobody was trying to help them." He pledged to lead an effort in Congress to provide relief money for all areas of Europe. "Hate against militarism and autocracy does not have to be directed against children," he explained.[37] Another visitor told an audience at a "Relief Concert" sponsored by the Chicago _Singeverein_ that he came away from Germany feeling German-Americans had a special duty to give to relief projects because they had been partially responsible for causing the devastation and defeat of "the Old Homeland."[38] Professor George Scherger, a historian at the Armour Institute, warned of the possibilities

of "a Bolshevik revolution" in a speech at the Germania Club, and blamed
the French and British for the appalling conditions he found in Germany.
"There is no trace of humanity, no wish for peace, no sense of justice among
them. Only blind hate, and exploitation, and the desire for revenge."
Britten expanded on these observations in a speech to the German Club and
pointed to the Versailles Treaty, "the most reprehensible document of all
time," as the chief cause of Germany's difficulties.[40] The Abendpost also
found the Treaty an insult to the German people; it was a "brutal injustice
aimed at a helpless and starving country," but there was little anyone could
do about it. Germany, however, would never forget the "brutal rape of
right and good faith."[41]

Robert La Follette led the fight in the Senate for German relief.
He warned his colleagues that their denial of food for German children would
eventually make them "writhe and cringe in shame."[42] But most Senators
found more to agree with in the statement of Henry Myers of Montana who said
that Germany deserved nothing; it had "violated every principle of international law, of civilized warfare, of humanity and decency," and, therefore,
deserved no relief.[43] The Senate remained adamant; there would be no
American relief for the Germans. Private relief was allowed and most of
it was administered by the American Friends Service Committee and Herbert
Hoover's American Relief Committee for German Children. (The Lutheran
Church--Missouri Synod had its own relief project, as did the Catholic
Church.) The AFSC and the Hoover Committee raised over $29,000,000 in
their first two years; of this total it was estimated that between $600,000
and $850,000 came from German-Americans, about one-half of the total collecte
was spent in Germany and Austria. Harry Rubens and Charles Wacker expressed
disappointment over the amount collected among Chicago Germans, but Rubens

offered an explanation for the poor showing. Many German-Americans, in his view, felt they were paying twice for the war--once to purchase Liberty Bonds to win the war, and now again to help pay for rebuilding what had been destroyed. Other potential contributors were simply resentful toward the United States for warring against the Fatherland and were refusing to contribute to any programs sponsored by the American government. A Lutheran minister pointed to another reason for the limited contributions of German-Americans; in his view "it would be better for German children to starve than to give aid through the Quakers." He charged that the relief funds were actually being used for "religious proselytizing," and denounced efforts to raise any more funds.[44] Private donations continued to dwindle: a campaign to raise $250,000 in the city late in 1921 managed to raise only $70,000. Leaders of the German-American community turned increasingly to Congress to provide aid.[45]

Events had somewhat softened congressional opposition to German relief. Congress showed a renewed interest in the issue after receiving thousands of letters complaining about the alleged rape and molestation of thousands of German women and children by the African troops France had stationed on German soil. Congressmen began receiving letters regarding the issue after an "Appeal from the Women of Germany Regarding the Black Terror" appeared in German-American newspapers across the country in August, 1920. The Appeal described in lurid terms the alleged degenerate activities of the Africans and urged "all women's groups in the United States to write and present an appeal to the Secretary of the League of Nations to remove the black terror from German soil."[46]

Congressman Britten confirmed the charges of criminal behavior against the African troops. He had observed "the colored troops" in the

Rhineland and, in his view, the German women's appeal "contained nothing but the truth." Britten headed the cast of speakers at a protest rally held on October 24, just one week before the presidential election. The main theme of the meeting was a denunciation of France for the humiliation it heaped upon Germany be stationing "uncivilized savages" in the Rhineland. "We are met here in the name of humanity to ask for protection for the women of the Rhineland," German Aid Society president Michael Girten announced. Britten told of how he delivered a petition asking President Wilson to pressure the French government to remove the black troops, but he had "received no answer from the sick old man in the White House" and expected to get none.

Alfred Meyer began his speech in English but switched to German after loud protests from the crowd, but his message was the same no matter what the language. "The watch on the Rhine has now changed," he proclaimed, "Revenge is now the watch on the Rhine. The fury of war and naked revenge hold the watch on the Rhine. For the carrying-out of revenge the Tiger [France] was not brave enough, for that it required hyenas, the animal-like Senegalese, products of the Sahara desert." The purpose of "the black outrage" was very clear, "the French laugh at 'the Huns'; they want to destroy the genius of the German people," and the best way to do that was to destroy German pride. "We must not remain silent," Meyer concluded. German-Americans would have to work together to save the honor of their Old Homeland. The rally decrying the "Black Horror on the Rhine" demonstrated that some German-Americans could be aroused to action against abuse of the Old Country.[47]

III

The election of 1920 showed that the issue of a violated homeland could be used to win German-American votes.[48] Attitudes toward Germany and the war played a major role in campaign rhetoric at both the state and national level. The race for Illinois governor saw Len Small, a close associate of William Hale Thompson, attack his opponent, James Hamilton Lewis, for the latter's staunch support of Woodrow Wilson in 1917 and 1918. Small reminded his listeners that Lewis had said that "only Woodrow Wilson could bring about a just peace" and that Lewis had "helped fool the American people" in 1916 into re-electing Wilson on the false promise "to the mothers of America that Wilson would keep us out of war."[49] Thompson, in a talk at the Northside Turner Hall, attacked the League of Nations and asked for votes "against the Wilson dynasty." As to charges that Small had embezzled thousands of dollars while state treasurer, Thompson insisted that Democratic "mismanagement" during the war was a far more important issue. "Ham" Lewis, in several speeches to German-American audiences, attempted to explain his support for the war and his support for the League of Nations. Before the American Unity Club, formerly the German Club, Lewis said that the League would help "save Germany from destruction." The war had been "a fight against kings and for freedom in the tradition of Washington, Jefferson, and Lincoln." America was a friend of the German people, and Germans could be sure "that America will not crush those people, but will help raise them up," if followers of Woodrow Wilson were given the chance to do so.[51] In a speech to a German veterans group Lewis asked for "peace, protection, and shoes for Germany." The League of Nations, he insisted, would free Germany from "the oppressive yoke" of Allied control.

Germany could present its complaints to an international commission of the League which could then begin to erase the "oppressive conditions" imposed by the Allies.[52]

In the closing days of the campaign, Lewis appealed directly to those "Germans, who in great numbers . . . are being used by candidate Small to your eternal dishonor. . . . He says you should support him for governor because he was against the United States when it was fighting in the great war." Yet "this man" had been charged with being an embezzler "and will betray you after you have given him your hopes as he would betray his own land for the votes."[53] A few days later, Lewis attacked Small and Thompson for threatening Chicago "with criminal Negro domination."[54] "So long as I have breath to speak," he told another audience, "I shall raise my voice to prevent criminal Negroes from lording it over Christian white men."[55]

Small was an outspoken proponent of Prohibition and Lewis attacked him vigorously for that position. Nevertheless, both the German-American Citizens League and the Independent Voters Association supported Len Small. The League argued that Thompson's candidate deserved the support of German-Americans because of the mayor's "support of citizens of German extraction at a time when the tides of hate were against them"[56] Wet groups like the United Societies for Local Self Government supported Lewis, arguing that "a vote for Lewis would be a vote against prohibition." However, the thoroughly "wet" Abendpost urged a vote for the candidate supported by "Unser Bill," the mayor who had "stood by us when German-American was a dirty word."[57]

In the presidential election of 1920, German-Americans were presented with an easy choice. "A vote for Harding," the Citizens League declared "is a vote against the unjust persecution of Americans of German extraction during the War."[58] Democratic presidential candidate James Cox offended German-Americans on several occasions with statements like "Every mother's son of the enemies of America during the war will vote for Harding."[59] He also accused German-Americans of supporting Harding only because the Republicans would be more lenient towards Germany.[60] In a speech in Columbus, Ohio, Cox listed the various groups opposed to him, groups such as "the reactionary party, the party friendly towards Germany whose members fought the successful prosecution of the war; the Italian party, . . . the isolationist party, and the party which sets the colored people against the other races like in Chicago, the fortress of William Hale Thompson."[61] In Democratic campaign rhetoric German-Americans became identified with the enemies of America. In Chicago, Secretary of State Bainbridge Colby led the Democratic attack on German-American loyalty. "Everyone who was suspected of being a German-lover during the war is supporting the Republican ticket," he announced on one occasion. Republicans were pro-moting "pro-Germanism" in a desperate appeal for votes, and Germans were supporting Harding out of hatred for Woodrow Wilson, "the president who pulled the mask aside from Prussian arrogance."[62]

During the last days of the campaign, rumors spread through German areas of the city which claimed that Democratic headquarters were "plastered with signs" which declared "No Separate Peace with Germany." These signs, the Abendpost declared, were additional evidence that the war was not yet over in the minds of the Democratic candidates.[63] James Hamilton Lewis had the last words for the Democrats when he declared that it was a voter's "duty to those boys who lie in France to carry on the fight they began for Americanism," by electing the Democratic ticket.[64]

Not surprisingly, German-American voters in Chicago gave 82% of their votes to Warren G. Harding. In the race for the governorship, Len Small the Republican candidate, received 69% of the German-American vote. In the city as a whole the Republicans managed 75% of the vote.[66] The dissatisfaction with Democratic rule was general, but the German-Americans had special reasons for voting against the party of Woodrow Wilson. They had been singled out for attack during the campaign and had been charged with disloyalty. Perhaps this factor and the general feeling of "revenge" for war-time treatment accounts for the unity in the German-American vote.[67]

IV

After emotions quieted down over the "black horror," a stream of visitors returned from the Old Country with stories of other dangers and disasters. Alderman John Haederlein reported that "if no help comes from Americans, the children of Germany and the middle classes will be offered-up to destruction." The theme of the imminent destruction of the middle class reverberated through many reports on Germany. Senator Medill McCormick pictured a devastated landscape and people to members of the German Club. He pledged to do his best to get a program of aid for Germany through Congress.[68] A visitor to the Munich Turnfest was struck by the fatigue and apathy of the German people; the old German spirit had simply evaporated, he told Chicago Turners.[69] At a mass-meeting called by the German Aid Society, several thousand German-Americans heard pleas to do something "for those in the homeland who are hungry and cold." Germany's middle classes were suffering beyond belief, one speaker reported, and he warned that with the destruction of the middle-class the Bolsheviks would have a free road to power.[70]

Such warnings were also heard at the "German Day" celebration of 1921. Organized by the German-American Citizens League, German Day festivities were meant to celebrate German culture in the United States. The proceedings were the first such celebration since 1914 and would, the sponsors hoped, help revive the ailing spirit of Germanism. Ten thousand people gathered for the concert, the folk dancing, and the gymnastic exhibitions. The crowd shouted its approval of a proposal to declare the Versailles Treaty "null and void," and called for the suspension of "all German reparations for all time." The main speaker, Professor George Scherger, warned German-Americans that "if we wait only a year" to help the people of Germany "it will be too late." Without immediate American assistance Germany would soon be completely destitute, and then "whole cities will be destroyed and the yellow race will conclude its triumph over the white. The danger at this moment is very great." Pastor Alfred Meyer denounced the Harding administration for its cowardice in refusing to talk with the French about the "black horror," and attacked an American foreign policy which supported "French and English imperialism and the League of Nations." Americans were prepared to fight "for their own shores and for their own land" but not for France and England. Ernest Kruetgen, chairman of the German Day Committee called for an end "to the enslavement of Germany" and called for German-Americans to unite in demanding fair treatment for Germans everywhere. If feelings for the Old Country were not enough to unite all German-Americans, he declared, they should also join in a crusade to save America from becoming "a new England." Perhaps, he hoped, a campaign emphasizing both themes would unite German-Americans.[71]

German Day organizers felt so enthusiastic by the attendance at their festival that they issued a call for a meeting to unite all German societies,

churches, and women's groups in Chicago. Delegates from over seventy clubs
and organizations were invited to a meeting in May, 1922 to discuss the
possibility of unification. They emerged with a plan for the German
Federation of Chicago. The new group would devote itself "to the promotion
of German culture and ideals" and would work to maintain "ties with Germans
in Europe through cultural exchange programs." The Federation would be
strictly "non-political" and "non-religious" with its chief emphasis being
the maintenance of German music, literature, and festivals. By emphasizing
a non-political approach, the delegates hoped to restore "that which was
destroyed by the War."[72]

The first "non-political event" sponsored by the Federation would
be the Mai Fest of 1921. Several thousand German-Americans attended and
saw displays of handicrafts and cultural artifacts, and heard German songs
sung by several dozen choruses. The orators at the Festival went far beyond
culture, though, and called for the organization of a united German-American
political movement. The keynote speaker, Reverend Julius Hoffmann of
Baltimore, asked a critical question: he wanted to know, "How can we of
German origin become true Americans and still retain that which is good
and noble?" He answered that Germans "must become more active in public
life--not as servants but as equals. We must not lose faith in ourselves."
The atmosphere of "vicious nativism" that ran through the country during
the war had not yet dissipated, and he asked for understanding from other
Americans. German-Americans, Hoffmann insisted, wanted nothing more than
"to create a home here for ourselves and our children." The best way to do
that was "to participate in public life, at all levels" and "help build a
new American nation." German-Americans had displayed a true spirit of

"Americanism" during the war, truer than any other group. German-Americans could be proud of their record and proud of their contributions to America; if they only recognized this, Hoffmann concluded, "they could achieve a new unity" not as Germans but as German-Americans.[73]

The search for a "new unity" was also the theme of a speech delivered by George Sylvester Viereck, who was in Chicago for the German-American Citizens League's third annual convention. Viereck said he was speaking as a "100 percent American" to "100 percent Americans." Unlike other immigrant groups, he claimed, Germans could say that because they had been on the continent for almost as long as the English. German-Americans, being one-fifth of the population, had a just claim to one-fifth of the membership in Congress, and only because German-Americans failed to recognize their own power had they become second-class citizens. At the Citizens League convention the delegates adopted a program calling for the withdrawal of all troops from Germany and the adoption of a constitutional amendment requiring a national referendum before any declaration of war. The League also called on school boards to remove all "foreign propaganda" from elementary and high school history texts: an "American" not an "English" history should be taught. Ferdinand Walther had died in April, 1922 so he was replaced by Heinrich Heine, also of Chicago, as League president. Twenty delegates attended the three-day convention and vowed support for a renewed effort to unite all German-Americans into a solid political bloc.

The League issued a proclamation declaring its alienation from American life. The time had come, the League asserted, for German-Americans to see that either "we are trodden underfoot as individuals, or we accomplish our purpose as a united organization." It was time for German-Americans

to unite and instil into American life "that characteristically German
probity and sense of justice for which there is a place and a need." It
was time to declare war on the "fanatical reformers" who were striking a
death blow to "German congeniality and conviviality." The time had come
to join with Schiller and:

> Hold fast together--firm and forever!
> Let the universal tongue be "Freedom"!
>
> Build watch towers high upon your mountain-tops
> So that alliance quickly join alliance!
> United be! United, all united![74]

The Steuben Society adopted a "political program for national action"
at a convention in Milwaukee. Written by Otto Stiefel of Newark, it called
for a "new Americanism" based on principles of One Country, "a country so
fair, tolerant and just that all who live in it may love it"; One Flag,
"An American flag for American purposes only"; and One Language, "The
language of Truth spoken in any tongue in which one chooses to speak it."
The Steuben platform also called for the referendum and recall on a national
level to prevent the breach of campaign pledges made by presidential
candidates as in 1916; the adoption of an amendment to the Constitution
"which shall assure, beyond the powers of even our Federal courts to destroy,
Safety of Speech in America"; the adoption of an amendment which would
allow "enforced enlistment" in the Army of the United States, but only in
the case of "actual invasion of American soil"; and "a change in our
fundamental law so as to prohibit the employment of the proceeds of any
Income Tax in support of any extraterritorial war at any time hereafter,
either directly during the course of such war or indirectly thereafter."
The platform attacked the teaching of "imperialism" in the public schools
by those "who have succumbed to the influence of the pernicious propaganda

now ascendant," and urged retention of local control of schools as a means of protection against "European views of the origin, nature and mission of the United States." The final portion of the platform denounced the Versailles Treaty, "the Treaty of Broken Faith," as an "intolerable measure" and called on President Harding to "make good" on the promises Woodrow Wilson made in his Fourteen Points; only then would "the honor" of the United States be restored.[75]

The political goals expressed by the Steuben Society and the German-American Citizens League represented both a call for typical "progressive reforms," such as referendum and recall, as well as a recognition of German-Americanism as a legitimate form of Americanism. The militant Germanists in each group were calling for a right to exist, as pro-Germans, in a society rapidly becoming, in their eyes, repressive and puritanical.

More moderate leaders among German-Americans could find reasons for hope in the events of 1921-1922. The peace treaty signed by the United States and Germany on August 25, 1921 appeared far less oppressive than the Treaty of Versailles. The Abendpost was pleased that the United States did not demand the surrender and trial of the former Kaiser and that the League of Nations was not a part of the new treaty. It also agreed with Senator Medill McCormick's contention that under the new treaty America "true to her tradition, assumes no political obligations in Europe."[76] A return to respectability on the part of the Old Homeland would lead to a renewed respect on the part of other Americans for German-American citizens. The treaty officially ending hostilities between Germany and the United States emboldened members of the American Unity Club to vote to return to their old name, the German Club of Chicago, and stimulated a movement to have the Chicago Lincoln Club revert to being called the Germania Club.

Anti-German hysteria was on the wane, the Abendpost claimed. The
black troops were being removed from Germany and the election of 1920
demonstrated that German-Americans could vote together. Thus, more
moderate German-American leaders found some reason for hope--their
community seemed to be coming together again.[77]

"Holy Indifference": The
Revolt of the Missouri Synod

However, leaders of one large group of German-Americans appeared jus
as alienated from American society as did leaders of the German-American
Citizens League and the Steuben Society. Leaders of the Missouri Synod
rejected calls for German-American unity and for full participation in
American life. For Synod leaders the only important issue was the
preservation of the faith. The war had dealt a blow to efforts to retain
doctrinal purity through the preservation of the German language. By
1921, fewer than 25% of the churches in Chicago retained strictly German
services, although about 40% had both English and German services.
The mission of the church fathers became one of preserving "our father's
faith" in "our children's language." Thus, the Synod continued its attacks
on dancing, movies, drinking, and the faults of liberalism, but now in
English. The Synod acted to protect its members "from the world," and
especially the American world of sin and seduction.[78]

Synod leaders saw the war as God's punishment for the world of
sinners. "The proper attitude of Christains toward all political affairs,"
Carl Walther, the Synod's major voice in the 19th century, proclaimed "is
one of holy indifference. Let those cut each other's throats who have no
treasures in heaven, the state is but a hostelry, the Christian is but a

guest to whom it cannot occur to overthrow the ruler of the house."[79]
Obedience was the rule even for something as obnoxious as the Eighteenth
Amendment. "According to the teachings of our church," Theodore Graebner,
editor of the Lutheran Witness explained, "every one who transgresses
these liquor regulations is guilty of a sin against the Fourth Commandment.
No matter how ill-considered legislation may be, no matter by what rotten
methods its enactment may have been secured, the Christian has no choice
but to obey the law."[80]

Lutherans, Synod leaders proclaimed, were surrounded by a world of
enemies. The greatest enemy was the Church of Rome, the only true victor
to emerge from the war. Roman Catholics, the Witness pointed out, controlled 24 of the 45 votes in the League of Nations, and that would be the
best reason for the United States to keep out of the League; Rome had the
votes and would use them for its own purposes.[81] Other enemies included
"the international Jew" whom Synod President Pfotenhauer held responsible
for the conditions in Germany.[82] Walter Maier, the young Harvard-educated
leader of the Walther League, laid the blame for much of the "immorality"
prevalent in American society on Jewish financing of the motion picture
industry.[83] Theodore Graebner found an even grander conspiracy; in his
view "the international Jew" had aligned himself with "the Jesuits" in a
scheme to share "control of national destinies."[84] Under these circumstances,
Synod leaders taught, it was best for Missouri to remain unassimilated in
the world, and to stand as the last bastion of truth against the onslaughts
of the modern world. The message the Synod conveyed was simple: the
world was an evil place and had to be avoided, and it made little difference
whether the message was expressed in German or in English; the meaning
was abundantly clear.

Conclusion

Despite the Missouri Synod's rejection of politics, other leaders
of German-Americans kept the dream of a new unity alive. At the 1922 German
Day celebration 10,000 people heard Mayor William Hale Thompson praise the
efforts towards unity and reaffirm his own belief that German-Americans were
the true practitioners of "Americanism." "My enemies were your enemies,"
he proclaimed. He urged a solid show of support for Frederick Britten in
the coming congressional election. "If others had joined Fred Britten in
his vote against the war, 100,000 lives would have been saved." The
president of the German Day Committee, Louis Link, then raised an issue
he hoped his audience would long remember. "We German-Americans have given
our strength and blood for this country, yet we have never received the
recognition and respect we deserve." But one day, Link hoped, "America
will come to its senses and will call us again her finest children."[85]

The message conveyed by leaders of Germanist groups such as the
Steuben Society, the German-American Citizens League, and the German Day
Association was clear: German-Americans could only become America's
"finest children" again by retaining their culture. The best defense
against any future anti-German hysteria would be an assertion of the glories
of German culture and of German contributions to American history. The
reassertion of German-American unity and power depended on the rebuilding
of Germany, for a powerful Germany would add to the prestige of Germans in
America, as well as continued demonstrations of German-American voting
strength. The activities and rhetoric of German-American leaders in
Chicago in the first three years after the World War demonstrate that the
anti-Hun hysteria had not destroyed their dreams of ethnic unity and their

hopes for saving the United States from "Puritan fanatics." The presidential vote of 1920 showed these leaders that German-Americans could vote together; but continued unity would require a concerted effort. German-Americans had not disappeared from American society, the election returns indicated, as did attendance at German Day festivities; they had simply been frightened away by wartime abuse and were awaiting a call to reassert their ethnic consciousness.

NOTES

Chapter 3

1. Chicago Abendpost, April 21, 1919.

2. Chicago Tribune, November 10, 1918.

3. Abendpost, December 8, 1918.

4. Abendpost, November 16, 1918.

5. Abendpost, January 13, 21, 1919.

6. Abendpost, January 23, 1919.

7. Abendpost, February 3, 1919.

8. Chicago und sein Deutschtum (Cleveland: German-American Biographical Publishing Company, 1901), p. 353.

9. Abendpost, February 19, March 7, 1919.

10. Chicago Tribune, February 17, 1919.

11. Statement by George Pretzel, February 19, 1919, Charles Merriam Papers, Box LXXV, Folder 5, Department of Special Collections, University of Chicago Library.

12. Chicago Tribune, February 26, 1919.

13. Abendpost, April 7, 1920.

14. Abendpost, March 8, 16, 1919; Chicago Tribune, March 20, 1919; Dziennick Chicagoski, March 18, 1919.

15. Abendpost, March 28, 1919.

16. Abendpost, March 28, 1919.

17. Abendpost, March 4, 1919.

18. Abendpost, March 7, 1919.

19. Abendpost, February 24, 1919.

20. Abendpost, March 17, 1919.

21. Chicago Tribune, March 24, 1919.

22. Chicago Tribune, March 23, 27, 1919.

23. _Abendpost_, March 28, 1919.

24. _Abendpost_, March 9, 16, 1919.

25. _Abendpost_, March 31, 1919.

26. _Chicago Daily News Almanac For 1920_, (Chicago: Almanac Publishing Company, 1920), p. 838.

27. Allswang, _A House For All Peoples_, p. 194. I have included the votes for Hoyne in my figures, thus they differ slightly from Allswang's.

28. For studies showing the split between German Lutheran and German Catholic voting see: Frederick Luebke, _Immigrants and Politics_ (Lincoln, Nebraska: University of Nebraska Press, 1969); Leslie Tischauser, "Theology and Politics: Lutherans versus Catholics in Chicago, 1888-1898," unpublished seminar paper, University of Illinois at Chicago Circle, 1975, documents the war between Lutherans and Catholics in voting practices in the 1890s.

29. _Chicago Daily News Almanac for 1920_, pp. 835-36.

30. "Referendum Voting in Chicago," unpublished manuscript, Charles Merriam Papers, Box LXXXIX, Folder 18, Department of Special Collections, University of Chicago Library.

31. _Abendpost_, April 3, 1919; _American Monthly_, April, 1919, p. 59.

32. Paul Mueller, "Reflections on the War," Cole Notes, Illinois State Historical Survey, University of Illinois Library, Urbana. Mueller, publisher of the _Abendpost_, decried the fact that German-Americans were not considered good Americans. The experience of the Great War, he wrote a friend proved that German-Americans had "offered their sons, their money, and their efforts" for the cause. What more could be asked of them, he mused.

33. Jane Addams Papers, November 12, 1918, University of Illinois at Chicago Circle.

34. _New York Times_, July 24, 1919.

35. Sidney Brooks, _America and Germany, 1918-1925_ (New York: Macmillan and Co., 1928), pp. 33-40, 122.

36. _Abendpost_, October 11, November 7, 8, 1919.

37. _Abendpost_, December 10, 1919.

38. _Abendpost_, January 29, 1920.

39. _Abendpost_, November 23, 1919.

40. _Abendpost_, February 13, 1919.

41. <u>Abendpost</u>, November 7, 1919.

42. U.S. Congress, Senate, 66th Cong., 1st sess., January 18, 1919, <u>Congressional Record</u>, pp. 1654-1655.

43. Ibid., p. 1869.

44. <u>Abendpost</u>, September 24, 1921.

45. <u>Abendpost</u>, November 19, 1921.

46. <u>Abendpost</u>, August 28, 1920.

47. <u>Abendpost</u>, October 25, 1920. The rally also witnessed a brief alliance between Irish-American groups pressuring Britain to remove the "Black and Tans" from Ireland and the German-Americans pushing for removal of the "Black Horror on the Rhine." The alliance apparently lasted for this meeting only.

48. For the election of 1920 see: Wesley Bagby, <u>The Road to Normalcy</u> (Baltimore: Johns Hopkins University Press, 1962), and, David Burner, <u>The Politics of Provincialism: The Democratic Party in Transition, 1916-1932</u> (New York: W.W. Norton Co., 1968), pp. 78-120. Neither Bagby nor Burner reflect the extent of anti-German rhetoric in the campaign.

49. <u>Chicago Tribune</u>, October 18, 1920.

50. <u>Abendpost</u>, October 27, 1920.

51. <u>Abendpost</u>, February 22, 1920.

52. <u>Abendpost</u>, September 11, 1920.

53. <u>Chicago Tribune</u>, October 22, 1920.

54. <u>Chicago Tribune</u>, November 1, 1920.

55. <u>Chicago Tribune</u>, October 26, 1920.

56. <u>Abendpost</u>, September 12, 1920.

57. <u>Abendpost</u>, November 1, 1920.

58. <u>Abendpost</u>, October 14, 1920.

59. <u>Chicago Tribune</u>, October 17, 1920.

60. <u>Abendpost</u>, September 26, October 15, 1920.

61. <u>Abendpost</u>, October 15, 1920.

62. Abendpost, October 16, 1920; Chicago Tribune October 17, 1920.

63. Abendpost, October 31, 1920.

64. Chicago Tribune, November 3, 1920.

65. Literary Digest, September 18, 1920, p. 11.

66. Allswang, House For All Peoples, p. 194.

67. Clifford Nelson, German-American Political Behavior in Nebraska and Wisconsin, 1916-1920 (Lincoln, Neb.: University of Nebraska Press, 1972), p. 87. Germans in Chicago differed little from the behavior of voters in these two states in 1920.

68. Abendpost, October 9, 1921.

69. Abendpost, February 23, 1921.

70. Abendpost, January 27, 1921.

71. Abendpost, September 24, October 17, 1921.

72. Abendpost, December 5, 1921; New York Times, December 5, 1921.

73. Abendpost, May 29, 1922.

74. Abendpost, July 17, 1922.

75. Abendpost, July 19, 20, 1922; New York Times, July 19, 20, 1922; American Monthly, August, 1922.

76. Abendpost, November 15, 1921; Literary Digest, September 10, 1921, pp. 10-11.

77. Abendpost, October 29, 1921; Minutes, Germania Club of Chicago, September 15, 1921.

78. Lutheran Witness, June 21, 1921, p. 78.

79. Der Lutheraner, February 3, 1852, pp. 90-96.

80. Lutheran Witness, December 6, 1921, p. 25.

81. Lutheran Witness, July 8, 1919, pp. 214-215.

82. Lehre and Wehre, August-September 1922, p. 282.

83. Walther League Messenger, August-September 1921, pp. 58-59.

84. Lutheran Witness, November 22, 1921.

85. Abendpost, October 9, 1922.

CHAPTER IV

"A RELEASE FROM BONDAGE":

German-Americans and the Search for Recognition,

1923-1926

Beyond efforts to bring unity to the German community in Chicago,
leaders of the group also sought means to inform the rest of American
society about the various contributions of German-Americans to history.
Other ethnic groups, such as the Italians and Poles, were also seeking such
recognition but from the point of view of German-American leaders these
recently arrived groups had little to show in terms of contributions to
American society. Germans, on the other hand, had been on American soil
since long before the Revolutionary War and had contributed greatly to
American politics, history, and government. The search for documentation
of such contributions would consume much of the time of leaders of groups
like the Steuben Society and the American Turnerbund. In all efforts,
however, the leadership continued to face an apathetic and unresponsive
public. German-Americans did not seem interested in ethnic issues.

Yet, leaders continued to evoke wartime memories in speeches and
editorials, hoping to arouse a spirit of indignation among their followers.
Robert La Follette offered not only a relief program for Germany, but
vindication for those who had opposed American entrance into the war. Thus,
in 1924, many German-American leaders flocked to his support. Between 1923
and 1926 German-Americans had numerous political choices to make bound up

with the question of the future of their homeland and with the status
of American Germans.

I

The failure of Congress to act in approving aid for Germany in
1920 and 1921 did not end attempts by German-American leaders in Chicago,
Washington, D.C., and other places to seek such aid. Chaos, inflation,
and violence in the old homeland inspired these leaders to work harder to
get what they considered a semblance of justice for Germany. In January,
1923 French troops marched into the Ruhr Valley after Germany refused to
make further reparations payments. In the United States, 14,000 German-
Americans met in New York to protest the new French outrage, while in
Chicago over 8,000 protestors gathered to denounce "the enslavement of
Germany." "Germany Shall Not Wear Chains" was the theme of the Chicago
rally and the audience shouted its approval of resolutions which demanded
the immediate removal of all French troops from German soil and the
abrogation of the treaty of Versailles. The assembly, called at the behest
of the German-American Citizens League, the German Club, and 33 other German-
American organizations, also celebrated the birthday of George Washington,
who, according to rally chairman Ernest J. Kruetgen, represented the true
spirit of Americanism. Woodrow Wilson and American diplomats in the Harding
administration had betrayed that spirit, Patrick O'Donnell, a leader of
Irish nationalists in Chicago, pointed out, by coming under the influence of
English and French ministers. It was time, former judge Michael Girten
explained, for a renewal of traditional American policy--non-alignment with
European nations, including England and France. That message was taken to

President Harding by Congressman Britten in the form of a petition signed
by thousands of Chicago Germans.[1]

Chaotic economic conditions in Germany where, the Abendpost reported, a pair of shoes cost half-a-million marks, added to the feeling among
German-American leaders that the Harding administration had to do something
to save Germany from total collapse.[2] Some leaders expressed bitter despair
at American treatment of the Old Homeland. "Had the German people guessed
in 1918 how much the promises of the United States were worth," a speaker at
the Germania Club declared, "they would never have surrendered; they would
have fought to the last man." American-Germans were told again they had a
special duty to perform since they had been partially responsible for the
defeat of their homeland. "Thousands" of Germans, a Lutheran minister report
were being "driven to starvation by unfeeling enemies," thus, German-
Americans had to rally to urge the American government to take action "to
put an end to the unbearable conditions in Germany."[3] "When the bells
sounded the end of the murderous war," another minister asserted, "we
were led to believe that the suffering would cease. But it did not because
the French spirit of revenge demanded that Germans be made into serfs."
This "senseless rage" of the French made peace impossible.[4] "Millions of
German-American Catholics," the annual convention of the Roman Catholic
Central Verein asserted, demanded the withdrawal of French troops and
called for a massive program of relief for Germany.[5] The pastor of St.
Paul's Lutheran Church, Jacob Pfister, accompanied Victor Berger, the
Milwaukee Socialist, to Germany and reported to his congregation that "we
Americans who fought against the cultures of Austria and Germany have much
to make-up for." The devastation and chaos he saw could only be alleviated
by large amounts of government aid.[6] Members of the Chicago Turnverein

declared that German-Americans "have the holy duty to support our brothers in their desperate battle for existence," and joined in the call for American aid.[7] At the third annual German Day, twelve thousand participants voiced their approval of a proposal to "stand by the German people in their hour of need" and resolved to "wake up American citizens and remind them that Americans have a debt to pay to the German people."[8] Thus, German-American leaders in Chicago were united in a demand that the American government come to the assistance of the defeated homeland.

Several proposals had been made in Congress to aid Germany but none had gotten through the Senate Foreign Relations Committee chaired by Henry Cabot Lodge. Lodge refused to consider proposals of aid to the "Huns."[9] Nevertheless, a group of German-Americans led by former congressman Richard Barthold of St. Louis and Dr. Otto Schmidt of Chicago met late in 1922 and organized a committee which would maintain a Washington office to pressure for a German relief measure. Delegates from the Steuben Society, the Concord Society, a newly formed group dedicated to the study of German-American history, and the German-American Citizens League attended the conference and authorized Barthold to speak for the group and to talk directly with President Harding concerning the matter of German relief. Barthold outlined a plan for $50 million in credit for Germany to enable it to buy foodstuffs before the coming of Winter. The best method of selling that program to Congress, Barthold explained, was to point out that Germany had been one of America's best customers before the war and could be again if she could avoid total collapse. "If the Germans, deserted by God and all the world," collapsed into bankruptcy, the outcome would be predictable: Germany "would reach in desperation for Bolshevism and that would open the doors of the whole world to the Bolshevik menace."[10]

Republican representative Cleveland Newton of Missouri introduced the legislation proposed by Barthold, increasing the appropriation to $70 million. Barthold met with President Harding and came away convinced that the Administration would support the Newton Bill.[11] Barthold reported that in order to secure passage the group had to downplay its German-American connections because of continued hostility toward Germany among many members of Congress. If some non-German names could be listed among sponsors of the bill, he advised, it would look less like a special interest measure and have a better chance of passage. Another task was to speak to the "present generation of German blood in the United States nearly 90%" of whom are "already native born." If these second generation German-Americans coul be involved in a petition and letter writing campaign, Barthold believed, chances for a relief bill would greatly improve.

Congressman Newton reported that many members of Congress were stopping him in the hall every day asking where all the petitions supporting his bill were coming from and "what all the noise is about."[13] Yet he was not very optimistic about the future of his proposal. Talks with colleagues on the Foreign Affairs Committee that convinced him that anti-German sentime remained so strong that the bill faced certain death. In an effort to salvage something for German relief, Newton cut the appropriation he sought to $10 million, the amount Herbert Hoover said would be enough to prevent outright starvation.

The so-called "Flag Incident" dimmed hopes for even the minimal sum. On February 3, 1924, Woodrow Wilson died and the flags of all embassies in Washington, except for the German, were at half-mast. The German action resulted from a "misunderstanding" between Berlin and its American legation and the situation was quickly rectified but not before a mob nailed an

American flag to the door of the German embassy and several Congressman
denounced German arrogance.[14]

Barthold's committee decided that no aid bill supported by a
representative from a district with a large German-American population, like
Newton's, had a chance in Congress, so it urged Hamilton Fish, Republican
of New York, to introduce the next attempt at German aid. Fish's district,
Newton advised, had few German voters and the congressman was a leader of
the American Legion; in no way could he be accused of harboring pro-German
sympathies.[15] The Fish Bill repeated Newton's call for $10 million in
credits for Germany. The House passed the Fish Bill during the turmoil
over the French occupation of the Ruhr, but Henry Cabot Lodge refused to
allow the bill out of the Foreign Relations Committee in the Senate, Robert
La Follette attempted to bring the measure to the floor anyway but was
rebuffed by his colleagues. Senator Thomas Harris of Georgia led the
opposition to La Follette, arguing that:

> the real purpose of this bill is made apparent by
> a study of the census reports from which it will
> be seen that at least 4,500,000 of our men and
> women of voting age are German born or of German
> parentage, and there are millions more whose grand-
> parents were born in Germany. Most of these voters
> converse in German, they get their news from papers
> printed in German; in fact, many of them are still
> German to the core.

For that reason, Harris concluded, Americans had to oppose the bill.[16]

La Follette, who had been closely associated with opposition to the
war and with efforts to get relief for Germany, was not a presidential
candidate who expected to get much support from German-American voters.
These considerations may also have played a part in the Senate's refusal to
pass a German relief bill. The Coolidge administration was aware of the

importance of the issue to German-American voters and was developing a
plan of its own to deal with the crisis in Germany, the Dawes Plan. The
administration remained neutral on the Newton and Fish bills, though
the President indicated that if a German relief bill crossed his desk he
would give it "his most careful consideration."[18] Beyond that promise,
however, the administration refused to make any public statements of support.
The whole issue of German relief would be vigorously debated during the 1924
campaign as the administration attempted to get around Senate opposition
to German relief through the voluntary and privately financed proposals
of the Dawes Plan.

The support given the Newton and Fish bills by German-Americans, in
the form of petitions, letters, and speeches, demonstrated that issues
involving the Old Homeland still interested some of the diverse elements of
German-American society. The response to the invasion of the Ruhr showed
that thousands of German-Americans could still gather to protest mistreatment of the Fatherland. The petitions, letters, and denunciations had
little effect on American policy, however. Secretary of State Charles Evans
Hughes announced that American policy towards French occupation of the Ruhr
would be "dealt with purely as a question of fact irrespective of any
consideration as to the legality or the propriety of the action taken by
France, and without manifesting any criticism or approval of such action."
Hughes's announcement convinced some German-American leaders that an anti-
German conspiracy existed in Washington, London, and Paris, dedicated to a
policy whereby "millions of our German kin across the sea are being
exterminated by a ruthless warfare not only against men who surrendered their
armor, but against defenseless women and children by starving them to death."

Charles Nagel, former Secretary of Commerce, told a New York audience "the treatment of the citizens of German ancestry in this country has been unfair, ignorant, and destructive of the very idea of unity of our people, . . ." The debates in Congress over the German relief bill illustrated a profound dislike for everything German. "[T]his position of race hatred must not outlast pressures from without. It will take a generation to destroy the seeds of discord. . . . The test of understanding and union is not speech or promise or slogan but conduct." Only when the "destitute of Germany and Austria" were treated "on the same basis with the sufferers of other countries" would the test be met. Until such a time, Nagel feared, German-Americans would have to stand alone in support of "the peace and honor and standing of our country" and of Germany.[21]

General Henry T. Allen, former commander of American troops in Germany, entered the campaign for German relief in order to save the German nation from the threat of revolution and Bolshevism. He was not, however, very successful because of the feelings of hatred towards Germany he encountered in his travels across the United States. The argument against Allen's appeal was that wealthy people in Germany had deposited their money in other countries in order to evade their own responsibilities toward the German poor. Charles Gates Dawes, who headed the Chicago Committee for the Starving German Children, a group organized by several Protestant churches in the city, rejected that argument; the problem was too great for Germany itself to solve and required the help of all Americans. "There is no question that the German children are starving," he told Chicagoans. His efforts to raise $1,000,000 in Chicago proved unsuccessful, however; only $355,149 was raised, $100,000 of that amount coming from Julius Rosenwald.

One reason for the failure of the fund-raising effort was the intense bitterness felt toward Germany. Another reason was that many German-Americans did not care to contribute further to the rescue of their homeland, not even five dollars worth. Some German-Americans told the Abendpost that since the American government caused the destruction of Germany, that government should be responsible for rescuing Germany from its turmoil (Others in the interviews conducted by the Abendpost simply felt they had contributed enough in past years and could afford no more.) Private sources of contributions thus apparently had dried up and it would be up to the American Congress to act to save the old homeland.[22]

II

Chicago Germans had an opportunity to demonstrate their level of ethnic consciousness in the mayoral election of 1923. William Hale Thompson decided not to seek re-nomination that year; a series of scandals involving men closely associated with the mayor had led to an upswell of public indignation against the Thompson regime. In the judicial election of 1922 the "Thompson slate" of judges had been soundly defeated. This defeat apparently convinced "Big Bill" that he would have to wait a few years before seeking office again. Thus, Arthur Lueder, a German Lutheran and treasurer of Chicago's German Club, was chosen to head the Republican primary ticket by the voters. The Democrats chose Judge William Dever, an Irish Catholic with close connections to the Progressive wing of the party.[23]

Leaders of German organizations in the city, including church groups, singing societies, and political clubs saw the Lueder candidacy as a test for their members. "If Lueder loses," the German-American Lueder Club, representing 140 German organizations, warned, "then the Germans of the future will always take a subordinate position in American politics."[24] The United Singers of Chicago, an umbrella group representing over 70 German male choruses, advised its members that they had a duty to support "the German candidate" not only for the good of Chicago but for the good of Germans everywhere; "even Germans in Germany" would be delighted with a Lueder victory "in the second city of America."[25] The Abendpost saw the campaign as beyond mere politics. "It is not a Republican battle which is being waged, but a German battle. If Lueder loses German-Americans will never regain the recognition they deserve."[26]

During the campaign, Lueder emphasized that he never had been a member of the German-American National Alliance, and pointed out that the German Club had been patriotic during the war. He concentrated on the issues of honesty in government and his support of the municipal ownership of public transportation. "As the son of immigrant parents," he told a Republican sponsored "Citizens of All Nations" dinner, he would never forget "the foreign element" in the city. Among German-Americans, the principal charge raised by the Democrats was that Lueder was a "reformer," and possibly a "prohibitionist." "I am called a reformer but I am not a reformer," he told a German audience. "I am a restorer. I will restore things as they were and as they should be."[27] Lueder had attended an Anti-Saloon League Luncheon early in the campaign and never publicly attacked prohibition, a move which would have cost him thousands of Republican votes. He explained, however, that "vice was thousands of years old" and would not be abolished during one campaign.[28]

The German-American Citizens League raised a new issue during the campaign, one it considered far more important than "the beer question."

The League argued that Lueder could be better trusted than Dever to guard
the city's schools from the further intrusion of "British propaganda" into
textbooks. Because of lies about the origins of the Great War "outstanding
accomplishments of citizens of German origin have disappeared from
American textbooks because of British interference." Only a German-American
like Arthur Lueder would be able to correct the situation and make sure
that a "proper persepctive" concerning the role of Germany in the world, and
the contributions of German Americans to American history would be returned
to the educational process.[29] The League campaign for a fairer treatment
of Germany in school textbooks coincided with a campaign in New York City
which led to the banning of David Muzzey's History of America because of its
"pro-British" attitude.[30]

As in 1915 and 1919, religion played a major role in the campaign.
Leaflets were handed out which warned that if a Catholic became mayor the
school board would soon be taken over by Catholics. Another circular ex-
plained that "the one outstanding issue" in the campaign was: "Arthur
Lueder, Republican, Protestant. William Dever, Democrat, CATHOLIC."[31]
The Catholic weekly, Our Sunday Visitor, Republicans charged, had urged
Catholics to help make "America dominantly Catholic by voting for Wm.
E. Dever for mayor." The paper also reminded Catholics that "nationalities
must be subordinated to religion and we must learn that we are Catholics
first and citizens next."[32]

The Democrats accused Lueder of being closely connected with the
Ku Klux Klan, which had thousands of members in the city in the early 1920s.
In the closing days of the campaign, Dever's supporters raised the issue
of Lueder's ethnicity. Raymond Robbins, a Dever supporter, told a rally
that the Republicans "wanted a man who could get the vote of the German

people away from Thompson so they picked Lueder, who for twelve years has been secretary of the Germania [sic] Club." Judge Dever explained to another group of voters that Lueder "was picked because of his name. If it had been Brown or Jones he would not have been nominated."[33] J. Hamilton Lewis, former senator, urged voters not to vote for a candidate simply because of his nationality. Lueder, from the Democratic point of view, represented prohibition, the K.K.K., and, by implication, "the Hun."[34]

A poll in the Chicago Tribune indicated that German voters would give 67% of their vote to Arthur Lueder, with Dever doing only slightly better than the Socialist candidate, 17.6% to 15.4%.[35] Actually, the poll only showed how German Turners and club members would vote; the pollsters canvassed 1183 persons at various meetings at the three Chicago Turnhalle. On election day, Lueder received 55% of the German vote, with middle-class Germans giving the Republican candidate 71% and the working class 40%. Both percentages were 5% above the vote William Hale Thompson received in 1919. Among the nine major ethnic groups in the city, Germans voted with the widest diversity along class lines. Lueder's emphasis on honesty in government may have had a greater effect on the results among middle-class Germans than did any ethnic appeal. If ethnicity was a decisive factor, it should have attracted German voters regardless of class differences. Whatever, Dever defeated Lueder decisively in the city, 60 per cent to 35 per cent.[36]

A study by Charles Merriam and Harold Gosnell, Non-Voting: Causes and Methods of Control (1924), measured the ethnic factor in voter apathy, The survey of non-voters found that a large percentage of them were German-Americans. One precinct captain reported that "many" of those who

did not register in his precinct were "of German blood." "I know that
in some cases," he continued, the Germans were "resentful of what they
regard as America's condonation of Britain's highhandedness on the seas,
1914-17, and America's alertness to opportunities for quarrel with
Germany at that time; resentful of the accusatory attitude observed toward
those of German blood by so many of our people during . . . the war with
the Central Powers."[37]

In a "typical" German precinct, the interviewer found that
60% of the eligible voters were registered. However, "the proportion of
the adult female citizens," he reported, was "smaller than in any precinct...
except the colored precinct." The interviewer found that the women who
failed to register "explained their abstention on the grounds of general
indifference, illness, disbelief in women's voting, or ignorance regarding
elections. . . ."[38] One elderly German woman explained that "a woman is a
flower for the man to look after. She should not spoil it and mingle in his
affairs." Another German woman said she did not vote because women should
not "stick their noses in politics." Women did not understand politics and
therefore should not "butt in men's work." The preponderance of such views
in German areas of the city cut the Lueder vote by a significant margin.
The 60% German registration compared with 77 per cent for the rest of the
city. Memories of the war and traditional attitudes towards women accounted
for much of that disparity.[39]

Despite Lueder's weak showing, the president of the German-American
Citizens League felt that the election "had proven that the German-American
vote could never be ignored."[40] The fight for unification of the German vote
in his view, was being won. A similar view was expressed by leaders of
the Teutonic Americans, a society founded in 1915 to fight "hostility and

defamation against the German race." In 1923, the Teutonic Americans began
a new campaign for membership and for the promotion of "the German language,
and the great achievements of German culture."[41] Both groups reported an
increase in membership and activities during the year.

Visitors to the German Day festivities also heard praise for the
growing unity of German-Americans along with a plea to retain that unity.[42]
Even the lectures by Professor George Scherger on German-American contributions to American history, held at the Germania Club, were attracting large
crowds.[43] The Club itself began to consider a change from Lincoln Club to
its original name of Germania Club.[44] Such activities the German societies
to conclude that local Germans were really beginning to reassert their power.

Three events in 1923; the Ruhr protest, the mayoral election, and the
Supreme Court decision in the case of Meyer v. Nebraska, Louis Link,
president of the Citizens League reported, had made it a very successful
year for German-Americans. In the Supreme Court case a Nebraska law banning
foreign language instruction in all elementary schools was declared unconstitutional. The decision represented "a victory for those of us who
want to uphold German culture," according to Link. The Court had reaffirmed
the view among German-Americans that the Constitution was meant for their
protection too. The presidential election of 1924, Link asserted, would
provide an opportunity for another demonstration of German political power.[45]

III

In the presidential election of 1924, German-Americans had the
opportunity to support a candidate who had been one of their most fervent
supporters during the war and the post-war years, Senator Robert La Follette
of Wisconsin. La Follette's Progressive movement received immediate support

from the German-American Citizens League in Chicago. At long last,
League president Louis Link proclaimed, German-Americans would have a candidate whom "they could call their own."[46] The Steuben Society joined in the
support of LaFollette as it urged all German-Americans to fight the parties
"of Wilson and Harding." In a manifesto titled "Why We Are For La Follette,"
the Society pictured Calvin Coolidge as "out of sympathy with citizens of
German origin." The Republican had defended "the black horror on the Rhine"
and had supported a policy whereby "races of inferior civilization" were
allowed free association "with the pure Aryan stock of the German nation."
In contrast, John W. Davis, the Democratic candidate, came "directly from
the ranks of the international bankers who made the war the means of
colossal profits . . . ." Both parties had disgraced themselves in the
post-war years by turning deaf ears "to the appeal of charity for the relief
of thousands of starving children and their mothers." LaFollette was the
only candidate who deserved the support of German voters.[47]

Some Republican Party leaders feared that La Follette would draw
enough votes away from Calvin Coolidge to throw the election into the House
of Representatives.[48] These leaders feared that a major desertion by
German voters, who had given Harding 80% of their ballots in 1920, would
increase the possibility of a deadlock in the electoral college. Therefore,
party strategists decided that the Middle West, with its large numbers of
German voters, would be the major battle ground of the election.[49] "The
'revolt' in the West," a survey indicated, "may have deeper inspiration
than Washington now believes," and it warned the Republican leaders that
La Follette was very popular in Iowa and Kansas.[50] In order to retain
the German vote the party sent vice-presidential candidate Charles Dawes

on three speaking tours through the Middle West.   The Republican strategy was to attack La Follette and ignore John Davis.   Dawes's message stressed three issues of major appeal to German-American voters: aid to Germany, opposition to radicalism, and support for the United States Supreme Court.

Dawes had gained an international reputation as "the man who had saved Europe."[51]   Late in 1923 the Chicago banker had been appointed by Calvin Coolidge to represent the United States at an international meeting of experts called to investigate financial conditions in Germany and report on the German ability to continue paying reparations.   These experts produced what came to be known as the Dawes Plan, a proposal whereby Germany would receive a $200,000,000 loan from the Allies.   The Committee also recommended that all French troops be withdrawn from the Ruhr.[52]   Dawes announced on his return to the United States, and after having accepted the vice-presidential nomination, that he would not discuss the reparations question or his plan because "he had no desire to make political capital out of what was undertaken and carried through in Europe as a non-political task."   Yet, reputation preceded him, and in most places he was introduced as "the Savior of Europe."[53]

To retain their votes, Republicans called on Ambassador to Germany Alanson S. Houghton, to address German-Americans in Chicago, St. Louis, Milwaukee, and in smaller cities in North Dakota and Minnesota.   He maintained that unless Calvin Coolidge was elected the Dawes Plan would not go into effect, and without that plan, he warned, Germany would devolve into total chaos.   The Dawes Plan alone would give Germans the opportunity to get back to work again, and only then "would the threat of Communism vanish."[54]

Republicans had high hopes that the Dawes Plan would be a winning issue among German voters. An advisor to Dawes predicted that "the carrying out of the Dawes Plan, will, in the opinion of well-informed politicians, make a favorable impression on Americans of German descent, and they will show their appreciation by supporting the Republican standard bearers . . . ."[55] Such was also the opinion of Frederick Britten who headed Republican campaign efforts among Germans in Chicago. "La Follette has no claim to you," he told Germans in his district. Simply because the Wisconsin senator had voted against the war was not a valid reason for German-Americans to vote for him for president of the United States. "America is about to play its first real part in the resurrection of Germany," he maintained, therefore, it was imperative that German-Americans do nothing "that will impair the success of the Dawes plan"[56] The Dawes Plan, Britten said on another occasion, offered "the only real opportunity to begin making-up for the mistakes of 1917 and 1918."[57]

Germans testified to the worth of the Dawes Plan. The former president of the state of Oldenburg spoke in Chicago during the campaign, explaining that the loan would give Germany the "only possibility of creating a solid economic foundation for Germany's future."[58] A prominent German banker said that the Dawes Plan completely satisfied "the German business world" and would restore a badly needed sense of security to the German people.[59] A former Chicago judge, Theodore Brentano, who had been appointed American Minister to Hungary in 1921, returned home to defend the Dawes Plan, and testified that the Plan was "looked upon very favorably in Germany," and represented the first step toward self-sufficiency for that country.[59]

That German-Americans had ambivalent feelings toward the Old Country and La Follette was demonstrated during a speech by Representative Britten. After praising the Coolidge administration for its "generous and tireless" efforts to restore order in Germany, the Congressman launched into an attack on "Battlin' Bob," but at the mention of the Senator's name the audience arose and burst into several minutes of applause. Britten then concluded with a warning to German-Americans that they had better vote with their heads rather than with their hearts, and that would mean a vote for the Dawes Plan and the Republican party.[60] From the Republican point of view, the plan fit in well with their foreign policy approach; the loans were privately financed and entailed no support of the League of Nations. Politically the Plan had great appeal for a large block of voters whose sympathy was with another candidate. The Dawes Plan demonstrated that the Republican party was, as Ambassador Houghton explained, interested in preventing "the total collapse of Germany."[61]

The second issue with special appeal to German-Americans was that of La Follette's alleged radicalism and disloyalty. The "Bolshevik menace" had special meaning for German-Americans who had been reading about events in the Old Homeland. Ever since the conclusion of the war, reports of the imminent collapse of German democracy had appeared in the press with some regularity, and riots, purges, and revolutions had given a sense of reality to the idea that communism was a real menace.

Charles Dawes left no doubt in the voters' minds as to who was chiefly responsible for the trouble: Robert La Follette, he told a Milwaukee audience, was "the master demagogue," who was undermining the "foundations of our country" by attempting "to amalgamate" those who are "justly dis-contented . . . with the Socialists, flying the red flag."[67] La Follette's running mate, Burton K. Wheeler, dubbed "Bolshevik Burt" by Republican speakers, responded to Dawes' charge by reminding voters of the Teapot Dome and other scandals; these people were really undermining the Constitution and "destroying American traditions," he charged, and these were the "men in the Cabinet of the United States grafting at wholesale."[68] Dawes continued to assail the La Follette movement as the gravest danger to American traditions, however. In Sioux Falls, South Dakota, Dubuque, Iowa, and Galena, Illinois, he raised the issue of "Coolidge or Chaos!" In St. Cloud, Minnesota, he expanded on this theme: "The international demagogues have brought Europe to the verge of an abyss . . . . We have had an orgy of demagogues in the United States in the last few years . . ." and the only appropriate response was to reaffirm the Constitution.[69] La Follett was "a menace to American institutions and American government," Dawes told rallies in Davenport, Iowa and Omaha, Nebraska, while in Duluth, Minnesota, he called on all Americans to help defeat the "dangerous mobilization of extreme radicalism" led by Robert La Follette. "We may stand for jazz music," he concluded, "but we will never stand for jazz politics in America."[70]

La Follette's attack on the Supreme Court best symbolized his "radicalism," and was of vital importance to German-Americans. According to La Follette's plan, the Court would be deprived of its exclusive power to declare laws unconstitutional. Instead, Congress could re-enact any measure declared unconstitutional by passing it with a two-thirds majority.[71] "What kind of government would this be if Congress had the right to pass a law telling you where to go to church?" Dawes asked crowds in the Middle West.[72] "It so happens that during the war," a German language newspaper pointed out, "laws were passed in numerous states prohibiting use of the

German language. . . . Attempts to withdraw such laws at the end of the war brought no results. . . . . One had to appeal to the courts." The lesson was obvious; if left to Congress, "the laws prohibiting the use of German would stand."[73]

The Supreme Court, in Meyer v. Nebraska, had defended German-American rights. Tampering with the Court might endanger such protection. Also pending before the Court was a case involving an Oregon law which abolished all private elementary schools. The "La Follette Idea" thus constituted "a deadly menace to Christian Day schools and Religious liberty," a group of Lutheran ministers in Chicago warned.[74] The success of the plan would "take the United States back to pre-reformation days, leaving the Church and individual defenseless against any attack of fanaticism and intolerance." The Supreme Court was the last defender of religious and constitutional liberty; a vote for La Follette, the ministers argued, would be a dangerous threat to those liberties. The Republican National Committee sent out thousands of German language pamphlets which denounced La Follette's "assault on religious liberty" and warned that Congress, under La Follette's plan could "take away religious rights that the Supreme Court has always protected. So, Vote For Coolidge, regardless of your religion."[75]

La Follette supporters in Chicago answered all the charges against their candidate at the German Day celebration of 1924, which had been turned into a giant "Support La Follette Day." Fifteen thousand supporters of the German-American Citizens League and the Steuben Society gathered in Riverview Park to hear Philip La Follette defend his father and explain his program. Pastor Alfred Meyer opened the festivities by recounting the Wisconsin Senator's wartime record; La Follette had been and was "the only leader we have had in the battle for our people's freedom. His name is, for us, a release from bondage." Leopold Saltiel, first speaker of the Illinois Turners, praised the Wisconsin Senator for being one of the few men in America with "the courage of his convictions." With his election "the prohibition fraud would be concluded," and America would be restored to "the ideals of personal freedom so beloved by the Founding Fathers of this Republic." "God has given us a man," he concluded, "like Washington, and Lincoln, whose soul is touched with greatness, and who will consume himself in fulfilling his promises." Philip La Follette addressed the issues most concerning German-American voters. He refuted the Republican charge that the Progressive's Supreme Court plan would "undermine the constitutional foundations of the country" by arguing that it would instead return power to the people. The Progessive movement retained a belief "in the sacredness and sovereignty of the people and we want to give Congress, the true representative of the people, a veto over the Supreme Court." Next, the younger La Follette asked for a national referendum before any declaration of war. German-Americans should be more sensitive to the need for such a referendum than other ethnic groups in the country. As for charges of radicalism and disloyalty, he continued, it was good to remember that Jefferson and Abe Lincoln had once been considered radical. The Progressive movement was dangerous "for certain people," mainly the rich and powerful, because its aim was to remove these people from power "and restore sovereignty to the people." La Follette closed his speech with a defense of his father's war record: "He has no need to apologize for anything he said," and neither did German-Americans; "Americanism has nothing to do with coming over on the Mayflower," he pointed out, because "much more

important was what an individual or group accomplished after its arrival."
In those terms, German-Americans had contributed much and could be proud
of their loyalty and Americanism.[76]

The Wisconsin Senator responded to Republican attacks by defending
his record and that of German-Americans during the course of the war.
Questions of loyalty had a special meaning for American Germans, he told a
crowd of 30,000 of them gathered in Yankee Stadium. The true proof of
Americanism, he explained, was not ancestry but the determination to bring
the government of the United States to its true purposes. The war-time
experience of German-Americans, who had survived the reign of terror with
courage and honor, proved beyond a doubt "their dedication to the fundamental principles" of our government.[77]

La Follette became more strident as his campaign drew to a close.
After a particularly vociferous attack on the Versailles Treaty before a
large German-American audience in St. Louis, his campaign manager, Ernest
Gruening, advised him to tone down his rhetoric for fear of alienating
Polish, Czech, and other East European nationalities. Only "the international
bankers, oil companies, and other exploiting interests" had profited from
the policies of Wilson and his successors, La Follette had maintained.[78]

In order to counter La Follette's attacks on Republican foreign
policy party leaders persuaded Charles Nagel to support Coolidge. Nagel
said he would vote for Coolidge because of the administration's plans for
Germany. "All other nations," Nagel said, "including France and Germany
look to the Dawes plan for a way out of chaos. Under these circumstances
the defeat of Coolidge would be disastrous." Nagel was considered one of
the most important spokesman for German-America in the country, and his
support was considered crucial among Republican strategists. The former

Secretary of Commerce had a divided conscience, however. German-Americans
could not forget La Follette's war record, he explained; "in the days of
blind intolerance . . . and vindictive persecution" La Follette had
exhibited great courage. But, Nagel concluded, that was no longer the issue
because a vote for La Follette would only endanger the Dawes Plan.[79]

On election day only the Wisconsin Senator's home state supported
him. The Coolidge-Dawes ticket carried states with large German populations
such as Minnesota, Missouri, Nebraska, North Dakota, and Iowa. In German
areas of Chicago the Republicans got 53 per cent of the German vote, with
La Follette getting 33 per cent and Davis 14 per cent. Social class made
little difference as 31 per cent of the German middle class and 34 per cent
of the working class supported the Progressive movement candidate.[80]

La Follette had given German-American voters an opportunity to
express their ethnic consciousness, but only one-third of them still felt
German enough to make that choice. William Lemke, Republican state chairman
of North Dakota, argued that his party's emphasis on the Dawes Plan saved
many voters in his state from casting their ballots for Robert La Follette.
Such may also have been the case in Chicago, but it was also true that a
candidate with a very pro-German record made a very poor showing among
German-American voters. Thus it seems that despite the rhetoric German
issues, e.g. the Dawes Plan, the foreign language question (Meyer v. Nebraska
or Bolshevism in Germany, were not salient. As in the 1923 mayoral election
the German candidate did not get a majority of the German votes.

IV

Events in Germany, such as "the black outrage," the Ruhr invasion,
and the debate over the Dawes Plan failed to arouse an ethnic consciousness
among German-Americans. In the first five years after the war, chaotic

conditions in the Old Homeland had little effect on the mass of German-
Americans. Only a few leaders seemed intent on preserving a ethnic identity
in the United States. German-Americans were even reluctant to contribute
to relief programs in the Old Country as several efforts had shown. Apathy
seemed the dominant theme; not even Robert La Follette could arouse a
spirit of revenge. German-Americans were divided by class, religion, and
politics. Nothing seemed to remain around which to build ethnic identity.

As prosperity returned to Germany even the issue of a violated
homeland disappeared from the rhetoric of German-American leaders. Yet,
they attempted to keep the idea of a unique identity alive through speeches
and festivals, sermons and editorials. Politicians, too, kept the idea
alive by appeals to ethnic blocs, like the German-Americans, and used foreign
policy issues, even in local elections, to win votes from people bored
with traction reform, sewer bonds, gas company scandals, and zoning laws.
The major issues for German ethnic leaders would be German cultural
superiority and English barbarity; for politicians interested in "the German
vote," the major appeal would be an anti-English isolationism. William Hale
Thompson would make that issue a major theme in the remainder of his
political career. Thus, leaders and politicians would unite in a campaign to
de-Anglicize American life and recapture the glories of the German heritage
in the United States.

Examples of rhetoric concerning German greatness filled the pages of
the Abendpost. "The 10th is greater than the 11th," Alfred Meyer told a
Schiller's Birthday Celebration. He explained that Schiller, born on
November 10th, had been the greatest "apostle of liberty in human history."
Therefore, his birthday, not the 11th, "the day of disgrace for Germany,"
should be the day of celebration for German-Americans. Fritz Gissibl, a

young Austrian wounded in the war, expressed a similar point of view in
a speech to the Teutonic Americans. Gissibl, who had arrived in the United
States in 1923, discussed the "Kriegschuldfrage," the "war-guilt question,"
and denounced the betrayal and deception of the German people at Versailles.
Germany had been enslaved by Britain and France, Gissibl argued, "because
she had been forced to accept sole guilt for starting the war."[81]

The war-guilt question became part of the campaign to restore German-
American consciousness. The campaign developed several themes, e.g. that
English propaganda had been largely responsible for the "anti-German" feeling
in the United States before the war and that the German army had not been
responsible for as many atrocities as charged. One speech illustrating this
view was given by reporter Oswald Schuette. He had talked to "Belgian
and British soldiers," he reported, but had never found anyone who was an
eyewitness to numerous atrocities described in the British and American
press. How any American could have believed stories of German soldiers
chopping off the hands of children and prisoners-of-war, or reports that
Germans were using the bodies of dead British soldiers to produce soap and
cooking-oil, Schuette could not comprehend. Such "outrageous lies" resulted
from a deliberate mis-translation of the German word for "cadaver."
"Cadaver utilization" in German referred only to animal bodies, not human.
Yet, most people were willing to believe that Germans had become complete
barbarians. German-Americans, Schuette concluded, had an obligation to
make the truth known and help restore the reputation of the German nation.
Efforts to excuse Germany from its confession of sole guilt for starting
the war would make up part of the argument for a distinct German-American
identity.[82]

Doubts as to the sole guilt of Germany appeared as early as September, 1919, with the publication of 352 documents captured by the Soviet government. These documents showed that Austria had dragged Germany into the war against the better judgment of German statesmen. Sidney Fay used some of this evidence in his article "New Light on the Origins of the World War," which appeared in the American Historical Review of July, 1920. Fay concluded that Germany was not alone responsible for the war. The first book-length treatment of the subject in the United States appeared in 1922. Written by Frederick Bausman, a second generation German-American serving on the Supreme Court of the State of Washington, the book, Let France Explain, argued that Americans "were innocent and naive" about European politics. Therefore, they were easy prey for Allied propagandists. Chief responsibility for the war lay with the Allies who had goaded Germany and Austria into declaring war. The United States had been tricked into the war and Germany had been forced into signing an unjust peace.[83]

The Central Commission for Neutral Investigation of the Causes of the World War, established in the Hague in 1921, pressed for "a purely objective" study of the facts. New York lawyer William Bayard Hale headed the American branch; in Chicago, Dr. Otto Schmidt attempted to organize a local group of supporters. Convinced that the "present story of the war is a monstrous falsification of the facts the Commission hoped its studies would vindicate the wisdom and patriotism of those, in any countries, who refused to be carried away by frenzied propaganda." The Versailles Peace was "a crime. . . . The legislators, the accusers, and the judges in the case, were the same, and moreover they were, again one party to the quarrel." The false pretension "was set up that the Entente Powers were fighting for all the high ideals of humanity against the evil principles represented by the Huns."[84] The Commission, through books, pamphlets, and discussion, hoped to show the world that Germany alone had not started the war.

There would be a major catastrophe in the future, the Norwegian and Swedish organizers of the Commission predicted, if Germany continued to be blamed for the war. "The consciousness of suffering injustice is the consciousness of being a slave. But humanity will not acquiesce in being slaves; Germans will--never! The ghosts of those who have been sacrificed by the passions of recent years will haunt Europe for many a generation, many a century, and will claim their dire revenge in wars and sorrows inconceivable--unless they are laid at rest by some sentence approximating justice." A similar message was presented to the Steuben Society of Chicago by a former member of the German Parliament. The myth of German war guilt built into "the scandalous treaty of Versailles" had forced Germans to admit that they were "huns and barbarians." German-Americans had to push for a revision of the Versailles Treaty, the Society was told, so that Germans could once again be restored to a place of honor in the world.[85]

Lack of support for fund-raising efforts disappointed the Commission's chief organizer in the Middle West. Many German-Americans, he reported, responded like Charles Nagel, who regretted that he could be of no service to the organization because "conditions in our country have been such that if a citizen bearing a German name has regarded anything in the German people as commendable, or has entertained doubts about the real causes of the war, his suggestion will be received with hesitation, if not suspicion." Because of the negative attitude toward things German, Nagel responded, "I have concluded that this avenue of service is closed to me."[86] After a year in the Middle West, the organizer admitted defeat and suggested that fear of "losing social standing" prevented many wealthy

German-Americans from contributing to the Commission. German-Americans

appeared no more interested in the war-guilt issue than they did in other

ethnic questions.[87]

German-American leaders appeared unconcerned by these failures,

however. They continued to speak as if being German made a difference and

was an important matter. For Professor George Scherger, the German sense

of order and purpose and discipline stood as a bulwark against English and

American decadence. Other ages had produced gangsters and grandiose evils,

Scherger said, thinking particularly of the Italian Renaissance and the

Medici, but they had also produced much that was praiseworthy. The gangster

era in Chicago had, as yet, produced nothing noble of worth saving.[88]

Missouri Synod Lutherans used their German heritage as a defense

against life in the modern world. The Northern Illinois District convention

condemned "modernism, liberal theology, unionism, lodgism, nonattendance

at church, lack of Christian education of the children, of love and zeal

for the Kingdom of God, family altar, mammon worship, the dance, the

theater, birth control, entertainment, gambling devices; increasing

opposition against the holy Christian church, also against the preaching

of God's Word."[89] The Synod protected its members with stern warnings

against participation in the world, thus, theology was the bulwark.

For others, opposition to permissiveness remained more difficult;

no threats of Hell hung over the heads of Turners or vereine members.

Yet, the feeling of being different remained. "The German oak still remains

although many storms have raged over the tree in the last eleven years,"

Ernest Kruetgen told a crowd of 3,000 gathered to dedicate a statue of

Fritz Reuter, a minor German poet. "The root remains firmly entrenched," and the branches would blossom again, Kruetgen, a second-generation student of German culture predicted, "if German-Americans stood together." One point was certain, "a German who denies his German descent is like Judas, the betrayer, and deserves to be despised by all respectable people."[90]

What differentiated German-Americans from other Americans, except accident of birth, was the subject of debate in the American Turnerbund, or American Gymnastic Union. At the annual meeting in Elkhart Lake, Wisconsin, Turners heard national president George Seibel of Pittsburgh talk of the damage done by the war, and of the immediate problems facing Turner groups. Attributing most of the problems encountered in membership losses to "the conflicts between the original German membership and the new generation that can be only relatively called German," Seibel looked forward to a "new dawn and a new era of fruitfulness." By appealing to the latter group through the publication of an English language paper, Seibel and his supporters hoped to re-invigorate Turner ideals. Thus, the language issue was finally settled in favor of English, though bi-lingual programs were also authorized.[91]

That position was rebuked by defenders of the German language in Illinois who argued that it was "the bond which holds us together. We cannot separate ourselves from it" without losing hold of our ideals. Supporters of the use of English argued that holding on to German would only prove German thickheadedness. "If we have learned nothing from the sufferings of recent years," Alfred Meyer argued, "then we are even more ignorant than our enemies think we are." Use of English was very important if Turners ever hoped to "help clear the Augean stables" of American society.

In 1921 Turners had voted to leave the language question up to local groups. The language use, national president Theodore Stempel argued, made little difference "because real Americanization is more a matter of the spirit than of language."[93] In 1925, the language argument was alive. Opponents argued that a change to English would corrupt the original Turner ideals, but delegates finally gave their approval to the proposition, "finances permitting." An English language newspaper was published until 1928 when it merged with George Sylvester Viereck's American Monthly to which Seibel contributed a column devoted to Turner activities.[94]

Leaders of the German Day Association sought to retain the "German ideal" in the United States through a yearly celebration of German culture and German contributions to American history. The 1924 celebration had turned into a rally for Robert La Follette however, and newly elected leaders of the Association were determined to celebrate German Day, 1925 "in a manner which is not offensive to other Americans." Therefore, politics and religion would be excluded. Instead, the Day would be devoted to renewed efforts to show Americans that German-Americans "have always been good citizens." "What is it we want?" Professor Phillip Allen of the University of Chicago asked. "We want the German language permitted in public schools . . . a German theater and museum . . . and recognition, which because of our history and our numbers, we have a right to claim." Ernest J. Kruetgen added to the list of German-American desires; speaking in English he demanded an end to "the gigantic lie of the sole guilt of Germany in the war." Soon it would become clear, he predicted, that the efforts of the Germans, "that heroic people which fought for over four years against a world of enemies in the name of freedom," had not been in vain. "The spirit of Moloch still rules in the Rhineland and German people cry out from their deep oppression," but the day of vindication will come "because mighty is the truth and ultimately she will win." The German-American cause was clear, Leopold Saltiel proclaimed in the concludin speech. "In the future development of our land we must see that German ideals become more and more the common property of America." Thus, a purpose for German-Americans became clear: to assimilate German ideals into American society, and to help restore the honor of the Old Homeland. Few German-Americans seemed to hear that message, however.[95]

In the eight years since the war, German-Americans had not achieved the unity leaders of the German-American Citizens League and of the Steuben Society hoped for. The only response they received from American Germans was disinterest. For those Germans seeking unity, or at least recognition, through stressing German cultural and historical contributions to American society, the future appeared bleak. One of the major problems was in defining differences between German-Americans and Anglo-Americans. A few leaders like Professor Scherger and ministers from the Missouri Synod found moral objections to American society, and German Turners and liberals objected to the "fanaticism" of the prohibitionists. But these were religious and moral issues, not ethnic ones. The two things most necessary for an ethnic consciousness--language and loyalty to the Old Country--had disappeared from the lives of American Germans. Few students were learning the German language and still fewer studied German-American history. The issue of an abused and violated homeland no longer remained. Germany was becoming prosperous again. Still, however, leaders of the German community in Chicago continued to press for a renewal of ethnic pride among their people.

Chapter 4

1. <u>Abendpost</u>, February 8, 12, 19, 23, 1923; <u>Tribune</u>, February 23, 1923.

2. <u>Abendpost</u>, July 22, 1923.

3. <u>Abendpost</u>, February 23, July 30, 1923.

4. <u>Abendpost</u>, August 20, 1923.

5. <u>Abendpost</u>, August 22, 1923.

6. <u>Abendpost</u>, September 4, 1923.

7. <u>Abendpost</u>, October 1, 1923.

8. <u>Abendpost</u>, October 8, 1923.

9. Charles Strickland, "American Aid to Germany, 1919 to 1921," <u>Wisconsin Magazine of History</u> XLV (Summer 1962): pp. 256-270.

0. <u>Abendpost</u>, November 10, 1922.

1. "Report of Committee Appointed at Chicago, November 1922," Otto Schmidt Papers, Box 1, Folder 11, Chicago Historical Society.

2. Voluntary Conference called to Detroit . . . Friday, January 19, 1923, Minutes, Box 1, Folder 12, Schmidt Papers, Chicago Historical Society.

3. Richard Barthhold to Otto Schmidt, January 24, 1923, Schmidt Papers, Box 1, Folder 12, CHS.

4. <u>New York Times</u>, February 3, 7, 1924; <u>Abendpost</u>, February 7, 1924.

5. Cleveland A. Newton to H. W. Geller, February 29, 1924, Schmidt Papers, Box 1, Folder 12, CHS.

6. U.S. Congress, House, 68th Cong., 2nd sess., June 5, 1924, <u>Congressional Record</u> 65: 10963-10964; 10991.

7. Jacob Babler and George Seibel to Calvin Coolidge, October 18, 1923; May 18, 1924; Calvin Coolidge Papers, Library of Congress, Microfilm Edition.

8. C. Bascom Slemp to Henry C. Block, September 13, 1923, Coolidge Papers.

9. C. Bascom Slemp to Henry C. Block, September 21, 1923, Coolidge Papers.

20. German-American Citizens League to Calvin Coolidge, January 28, 1924, Coolidge Papers; U.S., Department of State, Foreign Relations of the United States, 1923 Vol. 2 (Washington, D.C.: Government Printing Office 1938), p. 204.

21. Steuben Society Bulletin, Vol. 2, No. 8, January 16, 1924.

22. Chicago Daily News, November 30, 1923; Abendpost, December 23, 24, 1923.

23. Abendpost, Jan. 26, 1923; Feb. 28, 1923.

24. Abendpost, March 5, 1923.

25. Abendpost, April 2, 1923.

26. Christian Science Monitor, March 24, 1923.

27. Abendpost, March 27, 1923.

28. Abendpost, March 23, 30, 31, 1923.

29. New York Times, April 3, 1923.

30. Chicago Tribune, April 1, 1923.

31. New York Times, April 3, 1923.

32. Our Sunday Visitor, October 29, 1922.

33. Chicago Tribune, April 3, 1923.

34. Chicago Tribune, March 31, 1923.

35. Chicago Tribune, March 14, 1923.

36. Allswang, A House for All Peoples, p. 42, 192.

37. Charles Merriam and Harold Gosnell, Non-Voting: Causes and Methods of Control (Chicago; University of Chicago Press, 1924), p. 205.

38. Merriam and Gosnell, Non-Voting, pp. 219-220.

39. Ibid., pp. 26-27, p. 113.

40. Abendpost, July 6, 1923.

41. Abendpost, July 24, 1923.

42. Abendpost, October 8, 1923.

43. Minutes, Germania Club of Chicago, October 24, 1923, Germania Clubhouse.

44. Minutes, Germania Club of Chicago, November 15, 1923.

45. Abendpost, July 6, 1923: in Meyer v. Nebraska, 262 U.S. 390 (1923) the Court ruled that a Nebraska statute prohibiting the teaching of foreign languages in elementary schools was unconstitutional. Justice McReynolds, for the majority, argued that the Fourteenth Amendment guaranteed liberty which included the right to bring up one's children according to the dictates of individual conscience. See: Alfred H. Kelly and Winfred A. Harbison, The American Constitution: Its Origins and Development, 5th ed. (New York: W. W. Norton & Co., Inc. 1976), p. 663.

46. Abendpost, August 9, 1924.

47. New York Times, August 31, 1924.

48. C. Bascom Slemp to Casper S. Yost, October 6, 1924, Coolidge Papers.

49. "La Follette and the German Vote," Literary Digest 83 (October 11, 1924), pp. 10-11; O. G. Villard, "Summing Up the Campaign," The Nation (October, 29, 1924), pp. 67-68; "La Follette and the German-American," New Republic XL (October 1, 1924), pp. 108-110; New York Times, October 1, 5, 10, 13, 20, 25, 26, 1924.

50. O. G. Welles to Calvin Coolidge, August 2, 1924, Coolidge Papers.

51. Chicago Tribune, October 13, 1924.

52. Betty Glad, Charles Evans Hughes and the Illusion of Innocence: A Study in American Diplomacy (Urbana, Ill.: University of Illinois Press, 1966), pp. 227-228; Bascom Timmons, Portrait of an American: Charles G. Dawes (New York: Henry Holt & Co., 1953), pp. 215-225.

53. Chicago Tribune, August 28, October 13, 1924.

54. Abendpost, October 5, 14, 19, 1924; New York Times, October 20, 23, 25, 26, 1924.

55. Unsigned, undated memorandum, Charles Dawes Manuscripts, Department of Special Collections, Northwestern University.

56. Chicago Tribune, October 12, 1924.

57. Abendpost, September 4, 1924.

58. Abendpost, October 29, 1924.

59. Chicago Tribune, October 13, 1924.

60. Abendpost, June 23, October 29, 1924.

61. Chicago Daily News, April 28, 1923.

62. Charles Dawes Diary, June 8, 12, 1923, Dawes Manuscripts.

63. <u>Literary Digest</u>, May 26, 1923, p. 15.

64. <u>Abendpost</u>, June 19, 1924.

65. <u>Abendpost</u>, September 12, 1924; <u>New York Times</u>, September 12, 1924.

66. <u>NYT</u>, Sept. 16, 1924.

67. <u>NYT</u>, Sept. 20, 21, 1924.

68. <u>NYT</u>, Sept. 27, 1924.

69. <u>NYT</u>, Oct., 3, 7, 1924.

70. <u>NYT</u>, Sept. 22, 1924; <u>Abendpost</u>, Sept. 22, 1924.

71. <u>Literary Digest</u>, Sept. 20, 1924, p. 81.

72. <u>NYT</u>, September 21, 1924.

73. <u>Omaha Daily Tribune</u>, Aug. 30, 1924, Clipping in Dawes Papers.

74. <u>CT</u>, Oct. 11, 28, 1924.

75. Edward S. Van Zile, "La Follettes Angriff und die Religiose Freiheit," Republican National Committee, 1924, Coolidge Papers; Kenneth MacKay, <u>The Progressive Movement of 1924</u> (New York: Columbia University Press, 1947), pp. 162-63.

76. <u>Abendpost</u>, October 6, 1924.

77. <u>CT</u>, Nov. 2, 1924.

78. <u>NYT</u>, Oct. 15, 1924.

79. <u>NYT</u>, Oct. 16, 1924.

80. John Allswang, <u>A House For All Peoples</u>, p. 42, 192.

81. <u>Abendpost</u>, November 11, 13, 1924.

82. <u>Abendpost</u>, January 11, 1925.

83. <u>Let France Explain</u> (London: George Allen and Unwin, 1922); On revisioni see especially: Warren I. Cohen, <u>The American Revisionists: The Lessons of Intervention in World War I</u> (Chicago: University of Chicago Press, 1967); Selig Adler, "The War-Guilt Question and American Disillusionmen 1918-1928," <u>Journal of Modern History</u> XXIII (March 1951), pp. 1-28; Ralph Haswell Lutz, "Studies of World War Propaganda, 1914-1933," <u>Journal of Modern History</u> V (December 1933), pp. 496-516.

84. Memorandum, Central Commission for Neutral Investigation of the Causes of the World War, Schmidt Papers, CHS.

85. _Ibid._, Schmidt Papers, CHS.

86. Charles Nagel to George Fasting, June 12, 1923, Schmidt Papers, CHS.

87. George Fasting to Rudolph Pagenstecher, January 21, 1924, Schmidt Papers, CHS.

88. _Abendpost_, July 11, 1924.

89. _Lutheran Witness_, XLIV (June, 1925), p. 341.

90. _Abendpost_, July 13, 1925.

91. _Abendpost_, June 26, 28, 1925.

92. _Abendpost_, Nov. 14, 1918; April 28, June 17, 1919; May 2, 1921.

93. _Abendpost_, July 1, 1921.

94. _Abendpost_, June 28, 1925.

95. _Abendpost_, August 16, September 21, 1925.

CHAPTER V

RESPECTABILITY AND POWER, 1927-1930

The search for a respectable past preoccupied German-American leaders in Chicago in the immediate postwar decade. By 1927, the Dawes Plan had led to a rebirth of the economy in the old homeland and a renewed respect for Germany in the eyes of American citizens; the crisis seemed to be over. In Chicago, the 1927 mayoral election, leaders predicted, would give German-Americans another opportunity to show their power and unity. That old friend of German-Americans, William Hale Thompson, was running again and he raised an issue particularly sensitive to German-Americans, the Anglicization of their children's history textbooks. Thompson promised to restore true Americanism to the texts and fired the school superintendent responsible for introducing "pro-British propaganda" into Chicago's schools. The trial of that superintendent would provide a forum for pro-German spokesmen to excoriate Anglo-Americans, defend "true Americanism," and present their views as to who was really responsible for starting the Great War.

The 1928 presidential election provided German-American leaders further opportunity to proclaim the power of their people. Both candidates had their appeal to various elements in the German community. Al Smith supported repeal of the Eighteenth Amendment and was Catholic, while Herbert Hoover (or Huber, as some Germanists would proclaim) appealed to those German-Americans unwilling to see prohibition as the only issue

132

affecting their lives. Hoover's conduct after the war, when he was in charge of feeding the nations of war-torn Europe, became an issue for some leaders in the German-American community, but the major support for the Republican candidate came from leaders of the Missouri Synod who could not abide the idea of a Catholic in the White House. Results of the election indicated that religious differences still split German-American voters, at least in elections where a Catholic directly opposed a non-Catholic.

By 1930, some leaders of German-Americans in Chicago felt that the damage done by the wartime experience had been largely repaired. The long sought goal of political unity had not been achieved, but some leaders still saw unity as a future possibility. On the positive side, the German language was being taught again in Chicago schools, a German theater had been opened in the city, and German Day celebrations were drawing larger and larger crowds. Germany had apparently been restored to economic health, though the blot of war guilt still hung over her head; the image of the Hun seemed to be disappearing. A few radicals from the Teutonia Society complained that the leadership of German-American societies was timid and cowardly, but such criticism was quickly dismissed as nonsense. Few German-Americans would listen to the ravings of hot-headed young Fascists, it was predicted, and Germanists could go on building respect for German-American culture among all Americans.

I

The "German-Amrican" candidate in 1923, Arthur Lueder, had lost the mayoral election by a substantial majority with German voters displaying little unity. In 1927, these voters would receive yet another opportunity to coalesce.

William Hale Thompson campaigned vigorously for the "German vote" in the primary and general election. When he announced his decision to seek the mayorality again in 1927, he emphasized three themes of special importance to German-American voters: opposition to the League of Nations and the World Court, opposition to prohibition, and opposition to the educational policies of School Superintendent William McAndrew. McAndrew was a lackey of the King of England and a pro-British propagandist, according to Thompson, who promised that "when I am elected McAndrew will be out the window." The superintendent was specifically charged with having chosen textbooks for Chicago schools which neglected the contributions to American history of Germans as well as of other ethnic groups. On the question of prohibition enforcement, Thompson proclaimed that if any policeman in Chicago entered the house of a citizen in order to find alcohol, that policeman would be discharged immediately.[1]

Arthur Lueder, feeling he had been betrayed, charged that Thompson's organization had not given him its full support in 1923. He presented the Republican party a petition signed by "75,000 German-Americans" asking that it endorse him once again for mayor. The Chicago postmaster accused "Big Bill" of insulting "local Germans" with appeals to "beer, sausages, and tobacco." These were not the highest ideals valued by Germans, Lueder insisted, as Thompson should have known. "It must be recognized," Lueder insisted, "that during the war Thompson took a position thoroughly in harmony with the principles of the Constitution, but, it must be added that it seems he spoke only with his lips and not with his heart." As evidence of this charge, Lueder pointed out that despite German support in 1915 and 1919 Thompson "had not returned his debt" to the German community "in terms of jobs and programs."[2]

Lueder, however, did not become "the German candidate" in the Republican primary. That job fell to Edward Litsinger, owner of an automobile dealership and a prominent Lutheran layman. Litsinger received the support of the reform wing of the Republican party led by Senator Charles Deneen. At first, Litsinger stressed that though he was "an American of German origin," he was not an "ethnic candidate," but the candidate of all "citizens of good sense." Voters who wanted to support "the German candidate," he told members of the Burgerbunder Mannerchor, should work for William Hale Thomspon.[3] Despite his protestations, however, Litsinger could not avoid being "the German candidate." For, much to the delight of the editors of the Abendpost, he showed in several speeches that he could even speak German. Litsinger had been a leader in the post-war campaign to feed the hungry in Germany, the editors pointed out.[4] And the candidate himself acknowledged that he had been "an active participant in the strivings of Chicago's Germans, before, during, and after the War."[5] German organizations thus had a difficult decision to make whether to support "Kaiser Bill," and to continue repaying him for his wartime conduct, or whether to support a member of their own ethnic group. The German Club opted for one of their own, but few other groups followed suit. As leaders of the German-American William Hale Thompson for Mayor Booster's Club explained, "in the aftermath of the war a German-American could never be elected mayor of Chicago; so vote for Thompson who can be!"[6]

Litsinger stressed his business credentials and attacked Thompson's "looting of the public treasure" in his past terms as mayor. Thompson stressed fears of foreign, and especially pro-British, interference in American society, and said he would open the 10,000 saloons Mayor Dever had closed during his term. Litsinger expressed amazement at Thompson's campaign tactics. "For one hour straight we hear him talk and not say one thing about Chicago," he told an audience at the Social Turner Hall. "He talks of the world court, England, international affairs, and yet some people believe that this man can work out their salvation. . . . How does Big Bill settle the traction question?" Litsinger wanted to know; "by waving the flag and yelling 'America First'!" he answered.

A third candidate in the primary, Dr. John Dill Robertson, ran with the support of Thompson's former political mentor Fred Lundin. Robertson campaigned against Thompson's past failure to enforce the Eighteenth Amendment, and promised that he would not allow the law to be violated in such a flagrant manner. Robertson attracted little attention in the German-American press, and little support from German-American voters, who gave William Hale Thompson 68% of their votes in the Republican primary.[7] Litsinger's appeal to business sense and honesty in government apparently had little chance of success against Thompson's appeal to ethnic unity and pride.

In the general election Thompson faced William Dever. The major issues were ethnic pride, schoolbooks, and corruption. The German-American Dever Club set the tone of the campaign with its announcement that Thompson lied when he gave the impression that "he is a great friend of the Germans." In truth, Thompson had "given his most tender attention, not to the Germans, but to the Negro population of Chicago."[8] Several prominent German Republicans attacked Thompson's ties with Al Capone. "Shall we let ourselves be deceived again?" Dr. Otto Schmidt asked. The lawless and corrupt elements support Thompson. Is it necessary to get in the same boat with criminals to demonstrate German pride?" "German-Americans! We call upon the spirit of Pastorius Muhlenburg, Zenger, von Steuben, Leisler, and Schurz, and the thousands of others who gave their all for America and for us. Shall we disappoint them? Shall we support Thompson and thus let ourselves be branded by our enemies as a worthless race without pride, principles, or intelligence?" If German-Americans supported Thompson again, the German-American Republicans for Dever Club concluded in its appeal, "it would only give our enemies further cause for slanderous attacks."[9] The <u>Abendpost</u>, too, doubted the wisdom of supporting Thompson. He had stabbed Arthur Lueder in the back in 1923, the editors charged, and therefore no longer deserved the support of German-American voters.[10]

Thompson received the support of the German-American Citizens League and the German Day Committee, the two groups most militant in their defense of German pride. Thompson promised German-Americans that after his election he would build a giant concert hall in which "twenty-five thousand German singers could assemble, if necessary," and recalled his war-time efforts to protect freedom of speech. "During the war they called me 'Kaiser Bill,'" he told a League gathering, "simply because I defended the Constitution and protected all the inhabitants of Chicago, including German-Americans." For that, he concluded, he was now being attacked, but, he promised, he would never regret his war-time performance.

The teaching of history in Chicago schools became a major issue in the campaign through the efforts of the German-American Citizens League. As early as 1923, after a successful effort to remove some "pro-British" textbooks in New York City, the League began demanding the removal of such material from Chicago elementary and secondary schools. Thompson raised the issue in several speeches and frequently repeated his promise to remove Superintendent McAndrew. In February 1927 the School Board received numerous complaints from German-American groups about the presence of two anti-German stories in a fourth grade reader. The stories, "A Little Soldier of France," and "A Brave Little Frenchman," were "a direct affront to all German-Americans," a spokesman for the Citizens League declared. The Steuben Society also protested the depiction of the German characters in the stories. In the first story, the Society argued, Germans were pictured as barbarians, and in the second they were referred to as "beasts."[1] In response to petitions from the German community, Mayor Dever appointed Dr. Otto Schmidt to the School Board, and then made him head of the Citizen's Committee on History Books in Public Schools which was specifi-cally to investigate charges of "anti-Germanism."[12] The Committee issued its report on March 12 and found no evidence of anti-Germanism in history textbooks, though it did regret that General von Steuben was not mentioned. "The textbooks in use in Chicago are used by progressive school systems throughout the country," Schmidt announced, and should be retained. In regard to the stories in the reader, the publisher expressed his regrets for the book's "lapse of good taste" and promised to issue a new edition without the references to Germans.[13]

The Steuben Society rejected the Schmidt report. "The insidious way in which history was being taught" in Chicago schools damaged forever a German-American student's love for his homeland and his American heritage. The textbooks used "purposely colored and distorted statements much more favorable to a pro-British unhistorical conception of our American history than is justified." The Society not only regretted the failure to mention von Steuben, it was outraged that the general's "great deeds . . . are ignored" and that "no credit is given the very large percentage of Germans and Irish soldiers who battled for American liberty."[14] The Society, in cooperation with the Irish American Historical Society, took out advertisements in several Chicago newspapers denouncing Dever and Schmidt for having "ignored" the importance of the schoolbook issue during the campaign and urged voters to support Thompson. Schmidt's efforts to fill the moderate's role earned him only enmity.[15]

The Democratic Party attempted to make anti-black fears the major issue in the campaign, going so far as to send calliopes through white neighborhoods on election day playing "Bye, Bye Blackbird,"[16] Trains loaded with thousands of blacks were reportedly ready to leave the South for Chicago the day after a Thompson victory. That racial appeal found little success among German voters who gave "Big Bill" 63 per cent of their votes, the highest percentage they had ever given a Republican mayoral candidate. The vote was an 8 per cent increase over that received by Arthur Lueder in 1923. Both middle and lower-middle class German-Americans increased their support for the Republican candidate. Thompson received 46 per cent of the lower-class vote, up from 40 per cent in 1923; among middle class voters he received 80 per cent of the vote, up 9 points. Thompson's supposed allegiance with Chicago's criminal element had little effect on his popularity among German-American voters. Thompson received 52 per cent of the vote in the city as a whole, with Dever getting 43 per cent. (John Dill Robertson got 5 per cent of the vote). German-American leaders took much of the credit for electing Thompson and therefore expected him to act quickly in making good on his campaign promises, especially that of getting rid of the "pro-British" superintendent of schools.[17]

II

One of the major problems troubling German-American leaders was the image portrayed of Germans in public school history texts. There had been an unsuccessful attempt to ban some "anti-German" textbooks from New York City schools in 1923, but the Steuben Society, now joined by members of the German-American Citizens League, and the Concord Society, had not given up their fight to present a more positive image of Germans in history textbooks. Mayor Thompson had made a pledge to review the texts used in Chicago and Germanists saw this as an opportunity to make their case. The hearing deteriorated into bufoonery on the part of the mayor and some of his cohorts, but for the Germanists it represented a victory since at least they had an opportunity to be heard.

Upon taking office Thompson called for a review of the history texts used in Chicago schools, and of those used in teacher education classes at the University of Chicago and other places. He maintained that books used in teacher training, such as Arthur Schlesinger's New Viewpoints in American History (1922), developed "an unsympathetic picture of American colonists" and pictured George Washington and others as rebels and radicals. "If teachers have read this book and believed its content," the mayor opined, "then they must be inhuman if they do not impress these opinions on their students." Schlesinger not only denigrated the Founding Fathers he also omitted names like Von Steuben, Schurz, and other German heroes.[18]

Thompson kept his campaign promise and suspended Superintendent of Schools William McAndrew pending an investigation of his conduct. The School Board voted to approve the suspension with Otto Schmidt casting the

only vote in oppositon. The Superintendent was charged with "insubordination"
for, among other reasons, recommending in 1925 the adoption of history
textbooks "which contained pro-British propaganda and which omitted the
names and exploits of many foreign and native born heroes of the American
Revolutionary War." These books were "not true histories," the statement
of charges continued, but were written "for the purpose of promoting
propaganda of the English Speaking Union." The latter group, organized,
according to a spokesman, for the purpose "of establishing world peace"
through the teaching of a common language, became the principal of the
prosecution during the trial. McAndrew's purpose in recommending the
"flagrantly unpatriotic" texts was clear; he and his fellow conspirators
were intent on "undermining and distorting the ideal of American nationality." Among the conspirators listed were Charles E. Merriam and Charles
H. Judd; these men had entered into "an unlawful confederacy" at the
University of Chicago "to destroy the love of America and loyalty" among
students by encouraging future teachers to read "pro-British, un-American,
and unpatriotic textbook's. . .replete with false and disloyal statements,"
like Arthur Schlesinger's volume. The Board brought a total of sixteen
charges against McAndrew, including his failure to call teacher councils
together for advice, but most important in the eyes of interested German-
American and other ethnic leaders were charges that school superintendent
was instilling "anti-American" ideals among teachers and students.[19]

The proceeding against the superintendent, dubbed the "Chicago Scopes
Trial" by the New Republic, began early in October, 1927. Thompson appointed
former Congressman John J. Gorman as "special investigator" of the textbook
question. In his opening statement to the Board of Education, Gorman

charged McAndrew with being the "tool of the English-Speaking Union. . .," which he described as "a sinister organization" headquartered in New York City. The texts introduced by McAndrew showed "a clearly defined tendency to endeavor to unite Great Britain and the United States," and they also "showed definitely seeds of the Rhodes scholarship, and the Carnegie Foundation," as well as the English Speaking Union. These comments indicated that the trial would, as Mayor Thompson insisted, not only investigate the conduct of a suspended superintendent, but would involve the whole issue of "pro-British propaganda" and its disseminators. He was not "just playing politics," the mayor insisted; he had serious questions about the influence of British thought in American foreign and domestic policy. "Big Bill" mentioned that an article he had read in The American Mercury of October, 1927, "Under Which Flag?," by Frederich Bausmann, the man who had written the first American book on the "war guilt" question, raised serious questions in his mind as to the extent of British influence. Because of that article he instructed Gorman to call Judge Bausmann as a witness in the case against McAndrew.[20]

Thompson also wanted the most prominent German-American journalist of the time, H. L. Mencken, to testify, but "the Sage of Baltimore" declined. "That is certainly a good show Mayor Thompson is running there in Chicago," Mencken commented, "I would very much like to go over and see it, but I cannot possibly spare the time now." Mencken did agree with the intent of the trial, however, and told Thompson that he was correct in his suspicion that "the Anglomania which was official during the war has found its way into the schoolbooks." The major problem from Mencken's point of view was that "every American thinks an Englishmen is better than he is, . . ."

Any efforts to change that conviction, Mencken felt, should be encouraged.[21]
McAndrew demonstrated his feelings toward his opponents by talking to the
Chicago Literary Club about "Life Among the Boneheads."[22]

Judge Bausmann led off the parade of witnesses who appeared to
speak against McAndrew. The trial, in his view, involved the security
and integrity of the United States. The British sought to conquer America,
not with shells but by "the rain of propaganda." Such seemingly innocent
institutions as the American Library Association, Columbia and Princeton
Universities, and "Mr. George Peabody," were in reality agents for the
distribution of propaganda. The president of the A.L.A. was a Canadian by
birth, Bausmann charged, who during the war had directed the distribution
of British propaganda in North America. The aims of the textbook writers
and pro-British historians, "aided by the finances of England," were two-
fold: "first, the full cancellation of England's war debt to the United
States, and second, the placing of the Union Jack wherever now flies the
Stars and Stripes." Bausmann denied he was pro-German, insisting instead
that he was "truly neutral"; after all, he pointed out, he had been born in
Pittsburgh and his mother was English. A conspiracy existed among American
publishers and British bankers, he insisted, to keep the truth of the origins
of the World War hidden. "England fears that if American gets to know
England was a guilty party in the causes of the war, America will no longer
fawn at her feet."[23]

Otto Schmidt emerged as the chief defender of the superintendent
during the inquiry. But his role as mediator earned him only scorn from
other German-American leaders and led Mayor Thompson to accuse the doctor of
being neither a good American, nor a good German. "I have lived in Chicago

longer than" the mayor, Schmidt responded, "I have attended the public
schools here and I have read American history earnestly . . . I feel I am
as capable as" the mayor "of forming an individual opinion." The Steuben
Club of Chicago found little to disagree with in the mayor's conduct:
"There are 600,000 Americans of German descent living in Chicago who are
almost daily held up to ridicule because of efforts they are making to get
recognition for the illustrious achievements of their ancestors in the
founding, preserving, and development of this country," a Club spokesman
asserted, and he urged the press to take these efforts seriously.
Representatives of almost every German society in Chicago joined with the
Steuben Club to denounce the attempt to treat Thompson's "defiance of the
British crown facetiously."[24] Such attempts to return dignity to the
proceedings suffered from statements such as that of Gail S. Carter of
Springfield, grand dragon of the Illinois chapter of the Ku Klux Klan,
who found "a spiritual bond between Thompson" and himself. "We both
believe unquestionably that McAndrew should be chased out of town." German
leaders from the Steuben Club tried to emphasize the seriousness of the
hearings but had little success in that endeavor. With statements like that
of the Grand Dragon, the hearing was easily portrayed as a farce in the
English language press.[25]

Frederich F. Schrader, 71-year-old former editor of George Sylvester
Viereck's pro-German American Monthly, testified next and charged that
the "agents of King George" controlled American education and sought to
destroy loyalty. "We meet determined propaganda to denationalize America,"
Schrader discovered in his reading of American history texts. "We find
this propaganda is tainting the source of our unification, polluting the
very books of history with which our boys and girls are supplied in our

public schools." Schrader recommended that entirely new texts be written which reflected a truly American point of view, by which he meant a view not completely Anglo-Saxonized.[26]

Witnesses from German-American groups predominated at the hearings, but other ethnic groups, including the Poles and Italians, sent representatives to testify against McAndrew. A delegation of American Indians visited the mayor and complained to him of the detrimental view of Indians in the history texts. The mayor told the Grand Council Fire of American Indians that they, indeed, were the real "100 percent Americans." "Mayor Thompson's scheme of rewriting and revising the history of America is one of the greatest things that has ever occurred in late years," the President of the group exulted. Thompson, in another meeting with Council members, put on a headress, did a war dance, and promised to do all he could to see to it that Indians would no longer be depicted as "savages" in the history books.[27]

At the hearings, Oscar Durante, a Thompson supporter on the School Board, raised a touchy issue with Italian-Americans when he promised "to remove the Viking blot" from the pages of any text which credited Leif Erickson with founding America.[28] Board members also heard the views of Charles Grant Miller, a New York journalist, who attacked "the treason spirit" at Columbia University, and Charles Edward Russell, a Socialist writer, who charged that Great Britain wanted the "amalgamation of English speaking countries" everywhere. "You must understand," Russell explained, "that the British Empire is a religion with the English. To them it represents the chosen instrument of the almighty to civilize and Christianize the world. But England is going to lose India . . ." and therefore would turn its attention to North Africa. In "fertile Africa," Russell believed, the British would come into conflict with the French, and for that reason the British were propagandizing in the United States, because they would need American help in their fight with "the Latins" for Africa. Such testimony only added to the comedic image of the hearings.[29]

Involved and confusing testimony such as Russell's finally drove McAndrew out of the hearing room. Late in November he simply walked out on the Board and refused to have anything further to do with "what is almost universally regarded as a burlesque." The Board decided to go on with the hearings without the presence of the accused.[30] Charles Grant Miller, leaders of the newly organized Patriotic League for the Preservation of American History returned for additional testimony and continued his attacks on "treason histories." Historians knew the British history of America, he contended, and were good "scandal-mongers and mud-slingers," but offered little positive information for children to admire. A new biography of George Washington by Ruppert Hughes symbolized the attitude of historians, Miller said, they were "busy woodpeckers picking out maggots." That comment elicited a response from the American Historical Association which termed the entire proceedings "absurd and harmful."[31]

Hearings continued until March 22, during which time McAndrew announced his retirement, a step he had been required to take no matter what the results of the trial. Nevertheless, the Board voted 8-2 to condemn the Superintendent, and along with a plea that the hearings be taken seriously, charged that "evidence that there is an organized pro-British anti-American propaganda effort of stupendous proportions" existed in abundant supply.[32] Several months later the final step in the proceedings was taken when the Board announced that all the books discussed at the trial, including Thomas B. Hart's School History of the United States, Everett Barnes, Short American History, and David Muzzey's American

History, would not be used again in Chicago schools. The one text approved, Wilbur Fiske Gordy's History of the United States (1922), would have to undergo a few changes, specifically a picture of George Washington would have to be added, and a picture entitled "The Resplendent Redcoats" would have to be removed.[33]

Thus, what had been seen by some German-Americans as an opportunity to improve the image of their group ended in failure. German-American history would not yet become part of American history. "Big Bill" Thompson had saved George Washington from the de-bunkers and was satisfied with that victory, feeling that he had protected the integrity of a great hero. "American patriotism upon the nobility of George Washington," the mayor observed, "father and founder of the nation, and the righteousness of the cause of freedom and independence that he led. Take that away and the patriotic structure falls, leaving but the shell of commercialism." People needed heroes. "Drop the heroes from the country's histories," he concluded, "and you take the stars out of the firmament of patriotism."[34]

The pleas by Board members that their case be taken seriously indicated a desire that the case for a multi-ethnic approach to American history be taken seriously. But the quality of some of the witnesses who seemed more intent on fulminating against Great Britain than anything else, and the reputation of "Big Bill" Thompson whose every move was interpreted as that of "a power hungry fool," made implementing such a plea difficult. Offensive school books were gone but the various ethnic groups involved in the events had not gained in recognition or prestige. If anything, Thompson's antics and the testimony of the pro-German witnesses only added to the caricature of German-Americans as a group unwilling to assimilate into the

American mainstream. If a group gets its image from its leadership, as
John Higham suggests, then the image received from the testimony of German-
Americans such as Frederick Bausmann and Frederich Schrader during the
McAndrew hearings, as well as the public statements of Chicago's Steuben
Society and other German groups, was one of an embittered group of men who
saw pro-British-conspirators almost everywhere.[35] .Evidence that this is
precisely the image adopted by the English language press is shown by the
refusal of papers like the Tribune and the Daily News to take the hearings
seriously. Schrader, especially, speaking with a heavy German accent,
appeared as the caricature of a stubborn minded "Teuton." Mayor Thompson's
antics, and his close association with the "Kaiser Bill" image only
sharpened the negative image of Chicago's "Teuton population."

During the course of the trial William Hale Thompson became a
national celebrity and began laying plans for a bid for the presidency. The
mayor organized a nationwide campaign "for better citizenship based on
loyalty and patriotism," under the banner of "America First." He asked for
donations of $10 from all Americans interested in the work of the America
First Foundation. Mayors of St. Paul, Toledo, New Orleans, and Davenport
were among the first to join.[36] Thompson's plans included an appeal to
members of the American Legion, the Spanish War Veterans, and the Daughters
of the American Revolution. These groups, he hoped, would join together
in an effort to show "the anti-Americans" that they "are not going to
teach . . . that the Constitution was drawn up by a lot of drunken bums."
Thompson's presidential aspirations never got off the ground, however,
because the trial of Superintendent McAndrew appeared ridiculous to many
American leaders, as did the mayor. Even the Abendpost questioned the
wisdom of the proceedings and urged German-Americans to follow the example

of Dr. Schmidt, who, according to the paper, conducted himself with more
dignity than most of the witnesses.[37]

III

German-Americans leader felt their group would play a decisive part
in this election. Early in the campaign, the Chairman of the Republican
National Committee Hubert Work received assurances that German-Americans
would deliver "95%" of their votes to the Hoover-Curtis ticket. Organizers
from the Steuben Club made this estimate based on the Republican Party's
position on the revision of the National Origins Act and Herbert Hoover's
conduct in feeding Germans after the war. Originally the Society had
determined to vote for Smith because Hoover had been "too pro-British," but
after a meeting with the Republican nominee, leaders apologized for the
injustice of their initial stance.[38]

The Steuben Club of Chicago was organized early in 1928 by dissident
members of the Steuben Society of America who felt the latter was too
moderate. The Club published a monthly magazine, The Progressive, and
joined forces with the National Historical Society, a group dedicated to
German-American history. The Historical Society published books such as
Frederich Schrader's filiopietistic Germans in America, and several studies
of the "war guilt" question. In June, The Progressive had come out for
Al Smith, but in its August issue the editors admitted they had been
victimized by an "atrocious lie." Democrats had charged that Hoover "was
bitterly antagonistic to the people of Germany after the armistice," but an
investigation of those charges made by the magazine had proven those charges
to be totally without foundation. A second reason for supporting Hoover
was his position regarding the immigration question. The National Origins

Clause, which limited immigration in any year to two percent of the total
number of immigrants in the country according to the Census of 1890, (chosen
in order to reduce quotas from Southern and Eastern Europe), was to have
changed in 1927. New quotas would be determined by a special board appointed
by the President, which, The Progressive felt, endangered "the Scandinavians,
the Irish Free State, and Germany." Secretary Hoover opposed that change,
however, and to him "belongs the credit for having prevented this iniquitous
National Origins Clause from going into effect."[39] In its October issue,
the magazine gave another reason for supporting the Republican cause, "the
election of Alfred Emmanuel Smith," it predicted, would mean "the revival of
Wilsonism." Copies of The Progressive articles were mailed to "every
Lutheran Minister in the United States."[40]

German-American National Republican Campaign Committee headquarters
were established in Chicago, with August Siebel, president of the German
Club of Chicago, serving as chief spokesmen and director. The Committee
urged German voters to remember that "the questions with which the election
is concerned are of greater importance economically and politically than the
'beer question.'" It cited the immigration question and the question of
church-state relations, as the two predominant issues of the campaign.[41]

The Lutheran Church-Missouri Synod had similar concerns over voter
priorities. Spokesmen hoped that no member would sell out the Church "for
a glass of beer." Prohibition was far better than "a papist in the White
House," Walter Maier suggested. Herbert Hoover assured a worried Lutheran
clergyman that he was "opposed to the encroachment of the Federal Government
on local self-government in any direction," including encroachment on
parochial education.[42] Lutherans were also concerned about the change in

immigration quotas. The manager of the Missouri-Synod-owned Concordia Publishing House wrote a pamphlet which aroused fears that 1920 census figures would cut the German quota in half and let in more immigrants from the predominantly Catholic countries of Southern and Eastern Europe. The Lutheran case against a Catholic in the White House was summarized by the editors of the Lutheran Witness: "All who know the history of popery know that its path is trailed by tyranny, bloody persecutions, deceit, and tricky dealings." Al Smith was a devout member of the Church of Rome, and therefore subject to the declarations of the Pope, "who himself insists that he dare not be subject to any government." What if a Catholic president reached a conflict between what was good for the United States, and what was good for the Church of Rome? The example of Mexico offered a possible answer to that question. "The rebellious insurrection of the Roman clergy against the government in Mexico shows what the Roman Church and devout Roman Catholics will do when there is a conflict between their Church and the government."[43] The answer for Synod members was clear, devout Catholics would follow the Church. To prohibit the "mingling . . . of politics and religion" it was necessary to keep a Catholic out of the White House. A vote against Smith would be the best protection for "the political and religious freedom and liberty which God has granted us."[44]

Lutherans feared statements such as that found in The Catholic Union and Times, published in New York: "Were a Catholic elected tomorrow, the drowning man in the person of the Protestant Church would quickly shrink from view," the editors wrote. "The straw at which he has grasped as an anchor would disappear with him. The remnants of Calvinism, Lutheranism, Wesleyan teachings, and Episcopalianism would die, as their sects are disintigrating from division, discord, and dissension." A statement in

The Missionary, the official organ of the Catholic Missionary Union, also
caught the eye of the editors of the Lutheran Witness: the presidential
campaign was "so plainly a part of our divine Lord's own age-long and world-
wide campaign" that "all Catholic lovers of Christ" were "feverishly praying"
for the success of the Democratic ticket.[45] The Lutheran case against Al
Smith was explained most precisely by Dr. Charles L. Fry of New York City whe
he asked, "Shall we have a man in the White House who acknowledges allegiance
to the Autocrat on the Tiber, who hates democracy, public schools,
Protestant parsonages, individual right, and everything that is essential
to independence?" Church-going Germans had seriously to consider these
issues before casting their ballots; the Battle of the Reformation had not
yet been won by either side.[46]

The American Turnerbund remained neutral during the campaign, but
its national president, George Seibel of Pittsburgh, put forth a set of
"Fundamental Principles" to guide members in making their decision. First
among these was opposition to prohibition; "the reason for our opposition
to such legislation is because it deprives human beings of a natural right;
. . . because it breeds hypocrisy, espionage, graft and crime; . . . and
because it creates a dangerous precedent, upon which a hundred other in-
vasions of liberty, other agencies of coercion and confiscation, can be
erected." Other principles beyond the "beer question" had to be kept in
mind too. "We hold that every war, except defense against invasion,"
Seibel wrote, "is a crime against the law of nations, and should be out-
lawed by every nation. . . ." Since the Kellogg-Briand Pact outlawing war
had recently been signed, Turner voters would have to keep Secretary
Hoover's support of that treaty in mind. But Seibel also opposed "Protection
and supported "Free Trade" because "protective tariff policy . . . is one

of the most potent factors in our present economic distress." "Inhuman
Immigration Laws" also needed to be changed, but in the end Turners would
have to remember, "No man of German descent should become the slave of any
party. . . . Government may be a necessary evil, but it does not necessarily
follow that it must be administered by scoundrels and selfish hucksters. We
may not be able to weed them all out, but the Turner Principles will help to
sift some of the chaff from the wheat." Beyond that advice, leaders of the
American Turnerbund would make no recommendations.[47]

The German-American Al Smith Committee, headed by Ernest Kruetgen,
pressed the prohibition issue. "Whoever is against prohibition cannot be for
Hoover," Kruetgen believed. The Committee's advertisements called Hoover
"an outspoken friend of the British," and denounced his post-war efforts in
Europe as "anti-German." Senator Robert Wagner, "the only senator of German
birth," the Abendpost observed, talked about "his old friend Al Smith" at a
Chicago rally. Smith, at least, was forthright and honest, the Senator
claimed, while Republican campaign tactics were "underhanded and bigoted."
Prohibition was the major issue in the campaign, according to Wagner, and
Smith had openly called for repeal. Albert Ritchie, German-American governor
of Maryland, spoke in Chicago on two occasions, stressing the religious
issue both times. "When politics is preached from the pulpit," he told
German-American audiences, "regardless of how clear the motives may be, it
is more harmful to the church than it is helpful to politics." He called
for an end to anti-Catholicism and a return to the issues, neglecting to
realize that from a Lutheran perspective, as well as that of other Protestant
churches, anti-Catholicism represented real theological differences and was
a real issue.[48]

A slogan in The Progressive illustrated the feelings of some German-Americans toward Al Smith on other issues; "Herbert Hoover: Prosperity, Ability, and Americanism. Al Smith: Hard Times, Tammany, and Wilsonianism." Republicans in Illinois hit hard at Smith's Tammany connections; "Smith is a good person at a picnic or at a fish fry, or at a night-time get-together after which everyone has a hangover," Senator Ottis Glenn remarked, "but as for being president, he is hardly significant enough."[49] Republicans were aware of their own image problems with William Hale Thompson, but as Colonel Theodore Roosevelt Jr., remarked, "The great difference between the national Republican Party and the national Democratic party . . . is that we did not nominate W. H. Thompson of Chicago for President. They did nominate the leader of Tammany Hall."[50] Judge Frederic Bausmann, who said he normally voted Democratic, changed his mind in 1928. Bausmann noted a flaw in the Democrats anti-prohibition argument; despite Al Smith's claims a president by himself could not change the 18th Amendment, for that he would need the help of Congress. Congress, of course, would not act because of the opposition from the very dry, very Democratic, Solid South. Smith's proposal to add another amendment to the Constitution allowing each state to determine whether it would be "wet" or "dry" was also rejected by Bausmann because the amendment would do little to help "wets in dry states." So, forget the prohibition propaganda, the Judge argued, and vote on matters of substance like world affairs.

In the area of foreign policy the choice was simple: Smith simply did not have one. Hoover was "soundly American" in his views; he was not a victim of the "foolish sentimentality" popularized by Democratic spokesmen who argued that the United States had not "done its duty to Europe" and should, therefore, continue to interfere in purely European affairs.[51]

Colonel Edwin Emerson, a New Yorker who had lived in Germany during the war, told German Republicans that, Herbert Hoover was really Herbert "Huber" and that, Democratic charges to the contrary, "against the heavy odds of French and British hostility to the German people Hoover had to fight at Versailles before he could break down the inhuman barriers of the blockade." He had succeeded in that mission and "millions of German civilians, women and children" had been saved from starvation.[52] Cleveland Newton, Missouri congressman active in the campaign to aid Germany after the war, and Senator Robert Owen of Oklahoma, who had made the first speech in the Senate questioning Germany's sole responsibility for the outbreak of war, also defended Hoover's record in Germany. "Hoover, like a quiet huge electric dynamo," Owen wrote, "organized the work to free the women and children."[53]

The German-American Citizens League opposed prohibition but refused to support Al Smith because in its view the immigration question loomed as importantly as did the "beer question." The League finally decided to support Hoover because in his acceptance speech the Republican candidate had announced opposition to the concept of national origins as a basis for immigration quotas. It was impossible to determine quotas "accurately and without hardships," Hoover announced, and quotas should be rejected for that reason. Smith did not express his views on this issue. The Citizens League supported Hoover because maintenance of the quota system would lead to the rapid "Anglicization of the United States." Britain would receive almost 50% of the total number of immigrants under the plan which used the 1890 census, whereas it had less than 25% under the 1920 census, the League claimed.[54]

In the closing days of the campaign, the Republican drive for German-American votes reached new heights as the questions of religion, loyalty to

Germany, opposition to prohibition, and the personal integrity of the candidates were raised again and again. The Foreign Language Division of the Hoover-Curtis Campaign Committee presented endorsement after endorsement of Dr. Francis M. Schirp, a prominent Catholic layman from New York City. The "beer question" was demeaning to German-Americans, Dr. Schirp insisted; Herbert Hoover exemplified higher ideals. He had saved the German people from Bolshevism after the war, and for that alone deserved the votes of all German-Americans.[55] Hoover picked up more endorsements from Germans when he greeted members of Germany's most famous Zeppelin crew. The captain of the airship visited Hoover in the Commerce Department and announced that Hoover had been "the savior of Germany during the post-war period." Had it not been for Hoover "thousands of our people would have starved."[56]

The Republican party sent former Ambassador to Germany Alanson B. Houghton, engaged in a campaign for the U. S. Senate in New York, on a tour of the Midwest as had been done in 1924. He spoke in Chicago, St. Louis, Milwaukee, and other heavily German cities. He reminded listeners of the success of the Dawes Plan and defended Hoover's post-war record in Germany. "The only person responsible for the fact Germans did receive foodstuffs was Herbert Hoover. . . . You cannot imagine the bitter feeling that comes over me when I hear that Hoover was unfriendly to German children that is a hateful lie."[57]

German-American Democrats took out an advertisement in the Abendpost to respond to Houghton's charges. The Republicans had also distributed leaflets urging voters to "Remember 1916: Prohibition was the work of Democrats," it was pointed out, "and they also gave us a war." The Democrat responded that "it would be better not to stir up all the hatred of the war again." After all, it had been Theodore Roosevelt who had begun the slanderous attacks on German-Americans; he had been the first to call them "hyphens." And Herbert Hoover in his preface to a book on the First World War, had called Germany "a nation of dishonor" and Germans "a decaying and contaminated people."[58] Former Democratic congressman Richard Barthhold, of St. Louis, entered the debate at this time and quoted Hoover as saying in 1918 that "we are not concerned about Germany." Barthhold charged that of $33 million raised by Hoover's Relief Commission only $1 million had been used to feed German children.[59] Such charges and counter-charges continued to election day, leaving voters to wonder, as the Lutheran Witness charged, if the real issue of the campaign was whether they wanted "a baby-killer or a soak?"[60]

The "German vote" split on religious lines on election day. As Douglas Stange has shown in a study of the Lutheran vote, Hoover won handily in counties over 60% Lutheran. Smith did somewhat better in German Lutheran counties than in Scandinavian Lutheran counties, possibly owing to his stand on prohibition. Smith carried only 2 of 29 Lutheran counties averaging 40% of the vote in those counties he lost. In Chicago, Smith received 58% of the German vote according to Allswang, the largest majority a Democrat had received from German voters since 1892.[61] Smith did far better among working-class Germans, getting 71% than he did among middle-class Germans where he got 45%. In heavily German Lutheran suburban towns, Hoover received as much as 74% of the vote.[62] A report on the election prepared by Hoover's transition staff pointed out that "at the beginning of the campaign it was considered impossible to receive but a small percentage," yet Hoover had received a "magnificent vote" in German-American areas. Surveys conducted by staff members indicated that "35 percent of Democratic German-American women voted the Republican ticket; and it is estimated that 18 percent of our usual support for the presidential ticket was lost, on account of Democratic propaganda was pro-British." It was also

estimated "that our loss due to the wet and dry issue was about 10 percent."
Whatever the causes, the German Republican vote in the city had slipped from
82% in 1920 to 54% in 1924 to 42% in 1928. German Lutherans remained within
the Republican column, though some apparently did prefer a glass of beer to
a papist in the White House and voted for Smith. Far fewer German Catholics,
apparently, voted for Hoover. War-time memories had been aroused by some of
the campaign rhetoric but religion was the decisive issue in the election.
Thus, in the presidential elections of 1924 and 1928 the German vote was
split, in the first instance because of the appeal of the anti-war candidate
Robert La Follette, and in the latter election by theological conflicts.

The war-guilt issue continued to interest some of German-American
leaders. Only a few weeks after the election, the Concord Society began
a nationwide campaign for a re-investigation of the causes of the war and of
the evidence which reportedly pointed to Germany as the instigator of the
war. The focus of the campaign was a resolution introduced in Congress by
Senator Henrik Shipstead of Minnesota which instructed Congress to renew its
inquiry into the causes of the war.[64]

Shipstead, a Farmer-Laborite, said that the "war-guilt clause" had
been "forged in the fires of war" and the time had come for a unbiased
investigation. Congress had already sponsored one investigation in 1925.
Senator Robert Owen sponsored the resolution which led to the accumulation
of "an impartial index of all authentic important evidence, heretofore made
available in printed form or otherwise readily accessible, bearing on the
origin and causes of the World War . . . ." Charles C. Tansill, professor
of American History at American University, was placed in charge of the
project which lasted one year.[65] The Government Printing Office refused to
publish the results of Tansill's investigations, however, contending that

the completed volume was too favorable to the Germans. Other senators accused Tansill of being in continuous contact with the German embassy during the course of his research, thereby biasing his results. Shipstead, with the help of the Concord Society, demanded that the Senate Foreign Reltions Committee reopen the discussion, but his motion was tabled. In 1931, he asked the Senate to declare the "war guilt clause" a falsification of history, but it was not until the Nye Committee hearings investigating the munitions industry in 1934 that the Senate gave serious consideration to the question of war guilt.[66]

Other issues to which German-Americans responded in some numbers were immigration restriction and the restoration of German language to Chicago schools. In March, 1929, over 2,000 people gathered in Orchestra Hall to demonstrate against quotas; many felt that Britain would gain the most from a new system and were angry at the "favoritism showed one nation." Irish-Americans joined in the protest sponsored by the National Historical Society, and argued that the new quotas would stamp all non-British immigrants as inferior. "We stand with Herbert Hoover in his assertion that this law is unworkable," the group resolved. On the language question, delegates to the German Day Committee petitioned the school board to reintroduce the teaching of German, but the board declined at this time saying it had not received sufficient support from German parents to make the language available again.[67]

The major cultural event of the year for German-Americans was the Carl Schurz Centennial. Late in 1928 the Carl Schurz Memorial Foundation had been established by Albert Faust of Cornell University, Franz Boas of Columbia, and other leading German-American scholars. The Foundation, it was urged, should remain non-political and attempt to "accomplish something never before done in the history of the German element in the United States, to found an institution of which the on-coming generations may be proud." As an example of the goals in mind, members were urged to look at "the Scandinavian element," which had "succeeded in establishing" just such an exemplary foundation to award scholarships for study in the Old Country and brought visiting students and lecturers to the United States. "The Germans in the United States are far more numerous and they are more wealthy. Will they fail? . . . Only if they are not united, if a countrywide effort is lacking."[68]

The times were not the best for a nationwide effort to raise funds the group soon found out. Dr. Otto Schmidt, chief fund-raiser for Illinois, blamed the bad economic situation in 1931 along with the general "apathy" of German-Americans toward their own history, for the difficult time he had raising money. With the help of Julius Rosenwald and the Warburg family of New York the Foundation raised $500,000 and began its program of cultural exchange. The central purpose of the Foundation, according to executive director Wilbur K. Thomas, was to replace the war-time image of German "Kultur" with a proper image of Germany.[69]

Leaders of the Steuben Club disagreed with the cultural approach to achieving recognition in American society. Club president Leopold Saltiel, who was also First Speaker of the Illinois Turner District, saw political action as the best means to achieve status for German-Americans. After all, he argued, few members of the Steuben Club could even speak German anymore and most did not care to learn how; political power, not cultural under-standing and exchange, would lead to recognition and respect.[70] The German-American Citizens League also continued to urge political solidarity.

Germans had a future in the United States, a spokesman for the group announced, if they but remembered their differences from Anglo-Americans. The central difference lay in the attitude towards government; the "narrow-minded puritans" who now governed the land were attempting to "make saints of everybody through their laws." The "German idea," on the other hand, which was also the ideal of true Americans such as Washington and Jefferson, was that of "personal freedom and liberty" in domestic life. In the field of foreign relations the "German idea" also corresponded with that of the Founding Fathers: "independence from all foreign obligations" was the rule to follow. Thus, as Professor George Scherger pointed out to a League meeting, German-Americans were the true descendants of the Founding Fathers because they rejected prohibition and internationalism. America would become America again only by returning to the traditions exemplified "by the German character.[71]

An opportunity to put the themes of the "German Idea" into practice came in the 1930 senatorial election in Illinois. James Hamilton Lewis faced Ruth Hanna McCormick in a contest in which prohibition and internationalism became the chief issues. The German-American Liberty League, headed by Ernest Kruetgen, backed Lewis and the repeal of the Eighteenth Amendment. Legalizing liquor would not only restore personal liberty, but it would also restore prosperity by increasing employment and tax revenues. McCormick, serving as Congressman-at-Large from Illinois, said that she supported prohibition, but would bow to the wishes of the electorate if they voted for repeal in a referendum being held at the same time as the election. Defender's of Mrs. McCormick in the German community argued that Lewis was using "a beer stein" to tempt voters from an intelligent consideration of the issues. Lewis had been a follower of Woodrow Wilson, they argued, and had supported the League of Nations. "No German-American should sell his soul for a glass of beer," advertisements in the Abendpost read. Frederick Britten, unopposed for his 9th District congressional seat, even argued that the Republican Party offered the best hope for repeal. "The light of Revolution" against the Eighteenth Amendment was "beginning to burn in the Republican camp." The Democratic party held within it the chief supporters of dry laws, southern Democrats; he urged, therefore, "to support repeal by voting Republican."[72]

McCormick had received the support of Mayor Thompson in the primary because he was eager to defeat Senator Deneen. During the campaign against Lewis, however, Thompson repudiated Mrs. McCormick and came out for Lewis; she after all was the sister-in-law of his arch enemy Robert McCormick, publisher of the Chicago Tribune. She also took the wrong position on the issue of the World Court, though she ultimately pledged to oppose a Senate resolution that would ratify American membership. In the closing days of the campaign Lewis charged the congresswoman with trying to buy the campaign with McCormick money and attacked the idea of a woman running for the Senate. "You cannot buy a landslide nor win an Illinois senatorship by sex appeal," he claimed. The election proved no contest as Lewis received over 80% of the votes in the state, and 85% of the German vote. Perhaps, the Abendpost remarked, "the Senator would be friendlier to Germans now than he had been in 1917." The fact that Lewis had been a disciple of Woodrow Wilson did not make that hope too bright. The combinatio of McCormick's personal approval of prohibition, plus her reluctant opposition to the World Court had brought the greatest unity to the German vote sine 1920. Dreamers of a united "German bloc," such as leaders of

the Steuben Club or the Citizens League, could not be faulted if they saw
the results as proof of the truth of their position, but the dream of unity
was not to last for long.[73]

A new divisive element was entering German-American politics and
cultural life. Delegates to the planning session for the 1931 German Day
were greeted with leaflets urging them to fight "the un-German German Day in
Chicago." Signed by "The German Emergency Association," composed of members
of the Stahlhelm (Union of German Soldiers of the World War), the National
Socialist Party (Teutonia), and the Organization of King Louis, Chicago
Group, the leaflet accused Chicago's German leaders of never having accomplished anything for German-Americans. Leopold Saltiel, president of the
German Day Association, was charged with having had "pro-French" sympathies
during the war. Saltiel called the charges "the ravings of a rabid dog"
and urged delegates to throw "the crazies and fools" out of the room.
Fritz Gissibl, leader of the Emergency Committee, was led to the door after
a nearly unanimous vote asking for his ouster but promised to be back. As
he left he called upon people to attend the next meeting of Teutonia, which
would discuss "Who Is Hitler?"[74]

Local elections, the school book controversy, presidential elections
and cultural pursuits all involved the leadership of the German-American
community in Chicago in a search for respectability, because respectability
and a new image for German-Americans would have to come before the attainment
of power. Reason for hope existed by 1930. The old homeland appeared to
be on the road back to its pre-war position in Europe, and in Illinois and
Chicago interest in German Day was on the increase. Bad economic times hurt
the effort to raise funds for the Carl Schurz Society, but it was hoped
those circumstances would change in the future. The German Aid Society and

the newly organized German-American Liberty League, formed to help free
Americans from the enslavement of the Eighteenth Amendment, both had held
well-attended rallies to raise funds to assist unemployed Germans in the
city. The United Male Chorus held a concert that raised $12,000 for those
in need. The problem, though, as Michael Girten, president of the German
Aid Society explained, was that the contributions were never enough. The
problem of widespread unemployment added another dimension to the difficultie
encountered by German-American leaders in Chicago. Between 1927 and 1930,
they had made several attempts to save their group from disppearing from
American life. Politically some success had been achieved. William Hale
Thompson had been elected mayor of Chicago with the help of German voters,
and these same voters had shown a remarkable unity in the 1930 election
for United States Senator. Unity, of course, had not been achieved in 1928
because of religious differences, but those differences, it was felt, could
be overcome. The crusade to drive British propaganda from school textbooks had ended in ridicule and farce, but there would be further attempts
and the goal seemed worth pursuing. Giving the total picture, however, it
appeared, as several German business and political leaders told the
Chicago Evening Times, that the German Community in Chicago was regaining
its old vitality.[75]

NOTES

Chapter 5.

1. <u>Abendpost</u>, December 7, 1926.

2. <u>Abendpost</u>, Dec. 19, 1926.

3. <u>Abendpost</u>, Jan. 7, 1927.

4. <u>Abendpost</u>, February 12, 1927.

5. <u>Abendpost</u>, February 13, 1927.

6. <u>Abendpost</u>, Feb. 19, 1927.

7. <u>Chicago Daily News</u>, February 16, 17, 1927.

8. <u>Abendpost</u>, March 16, 1927.

9. <u>Abendpost</u>, March 29, 1927.

10. <u>Abendpost</u>, April 3, 1927.

11. Statement of Steuben Society of Chicago to Board of Education, April 18, 1927, Schmidt Papers, CHS.

12. William Dever to Otto Schmidt, March 1, 1927, Schmidt Papers, CHS.

13. <u>Abendpost</u>, March 12, April 18, 1927.

14. <u>Chicago Tribune</u>, April 4, 1927.

15. <u>Abendpost</u>, April 9, 1927.

16. Harold Gosnell, <u>Negro Politicians: The Rise of Negro Politics in Chicago</u> (Chicago: University of Chicago Press, 1935), pp. 39-41.

17. John Allswang, <u>A House for All Peoples</u>, p. 42, 161.

18. <u>Abendpost</u>, April 18, 1927.

19. Specifications and Bill of Particulars . . . Against William McAndrew, 29th Day of August, 1927, Schmidt Papers, CHS.

20. <u>New York Times</u>, October 13, 1927; <u>Chicago Tribune</u>, October 14, 15, 16, 1927.

21. <u>NYT</u>, October 19, 1927; <u>CT</u>, October 19, 1927.

22. <u>NYT</u>, October 19, 1927.

23. <u>NYT</u>, Oct. 20, 1927; Bessie L. Pierce, <u>Public Opinion and the Teaching</u> of History in the United States (New York: Alfred A. Knopf, 1926), pp. 204-244, discusses earlier attempts to censor books in Chicago; Lawrence Martin, "Higher Education in Chicago," <u>The Nation</u> 125 (Nov. 16, 1927), pp. 538-540; George S. Counts, <u>School and Society in Chicago</u> (New York: Columbia University Press, 1928), pp. 267-281.

24. <u>Abendpost,</u> October 23, 1927; <u>NYT</u>, Oct. 23, 1927.

25. <u>CT</u>, Oct. 22, 1927.

26. <u>NYT</u>, Nov. 3, 1927.

27. <u>NYT</u>, Nov. 2, Dec. 2, 1927.

28. <u>NYT</u>, Nov. 17, 1927.

29. <u>NYT</u>, Nov. 24, 25, 1927.

30. <u>NYT</u>, Dec. 1, 1927.

31. <u>NYT</u>, Dec. 5, 1927.

32. <u>NYT</u>, Mar. 22, 1928.

33. <u>NYT</u>, Au. 25, 1928.

34. <u>Current History</u>, XXVII (February 1928), pp. 619-625.

35. <u>Abendpost</u>, May 9, 1927; John Higham, "Introduction: The Forms of Ethnic Leadership," in <u>Ethnic Leadership in America</u>, ed. by Higham (Baltimore: John Hopkins University Press, 1979), pp. 1-19.

36. <u>NYT</u>, Oct. 29, 1927.

37. <u>Abendpost</u>, Dec. 21, 1927.

38. George W. Angerstein to Herbert Hoover, July 17, 1928, Pre-Presidential Papers, General Correspondence Series, Box 5, Herbert Hoover Papers, Hoover Library.

39. <u>The Progressive</u>, 1, 2, 3 (August, September, October, 1928). Copies in Pre-Presidential Series, Newspapers-Foreign Language, Box 216, Hoover Papers, Hoover Library.

40. George Angerstein to Herbert Hoover, August 21, 1928, Pre-Presidential Papers, General Correspondence Series, Box 5, Herbert Hoover Papers, Hoover Library.

41. <u>Abendpost</u>, Sept. 19, 1928.

42. *Walther League Messenger*, VII (Aug-Sept. 1928), pp. 119-121.

43. Herbert Hoover to J. R. Bausmann, September 8, 1928, Pre-Presidential Series, Box 8, Herbert Hoover Papers, Hoover Library.

44. *Lutheran Witness*, 47 (March 6, 1928), pp. 95-96.

45. *Lutheran Witness*, 47 (March 20, 1928), p. 111.

46. *Catholic Union & Times*, Oct. 4, 1928; Also see: "Catholics and the Presidency," *Fortnightly Review* 35 (January 1, 1928), pp. 3-9.

47. *American Monthly* 13 (October 1928), p. 26.

48. *Abendpost*, Oct. 11, 12, 1928.

49. Robert Moats Miller, "A Footnote to the Role of the Protestant Churches in the Election of 1928," *Church History* XXV (June 1956), pp. 145-58; Paul A. Carter, "The Campaign of 1928 Re-Examined: A Study in Political Folklore," *Wisconsin Magazine of History* XLVI (Summer 1963), pp. 263-272.

50. *Abendpost*, Oct. 4, 1928.

51. Theodore Roosevelt, Jr., "Comments on the Candidates," September 27, 1928, Campaign and Transition Series, Box 12, Herbert Hoover Papers, Hoover Library.

52. *American Monthly*, 13 (October 1928), pp. 22-24.

53. Edwin Emerson, "Statement on the Campaign Issued by the Republican National Committee," October 11, 1928, Campaign and Transition Series, Box 168, Herbert Hoover Papers, Hoover Library; Cleveland A. Newton, "Germany and Central Europe Fed Through Efforts of Hoover," Campaign and Transition Series, Box 168, Herbert Hoover Papers, Hoover Library.

54. *Abendpost*, Oct. 15, 1928; Robert Divine, *American Immigration Policy, 1924-1952* (New Haven: Yale University Press, 1957), pp. 31-41. The animosity towards the immigration quota reflected the anti-British feelings of many German-American leaders. German-Americans were not usually thought of as an aggrieved group, so opposition to the quota system by various leaders was surprising. That the British part of the quota would be the largest galled these leaders, hence their opposition.

55. Frances M. Schirp, "Why German Catholics Should Vote for Hoover," Campaign and Transition Series, Box 182, Herbert Hoover Papers, Hoover Library.

56. *NYT*, Oct. 19, 1928.

57. Alanson B. Houghton, "Why Germans Should Support Hoover," October 17, 1928, Campaign and Transition Series, Box 168, Herbert Hoover Papers, Hoover Library.

58. Abendpost, Oct. 27, 1928; NYT, Oct. 23, 1928.

59. Abendpost, Oct. 26, 1928.

60. Lutheran Witness 47 (November 13, 1928), p. 382.

61. Douglass Stange, "Al Smith and the Republican Party at Prayer: The Lutheran Vote in 1928," Review of Politics 32 (July 1970), pp. 347-64; John Allswang, A House for All Peoples, p. 42, 192.

62. John Allswang, A House for All Peoples, p. 192.

63. Republican National Committee, "Election Figures: Chicago, Illinois," Presidential Campaign Series, Box 273A, Hoover Papers, Hoover Library.

64. Abendpost, Nov. 23, 1928.

65. U.S. Congress, Senate, 68th Cong., 2d sess., Congressional Record 66: p. 3789.

66. NYT, June 22, 1931.

67. Abendpost, March 28, May 18, 1929.

68. "A Draft of the Plans and Purposes of the Carl Schurz Memorial Foundati• undated mimeographed copy, Schmidt Papers, Box 13, CHS.

69. Otto Schmidt to William K. Thomas, June 26, 1931, Schmidt Papers, Box 1: CHS.

70. William K. Thomas, "The Carl Schurz Memorial Foundation," American Monthly 15 (July 1930), p. 131; NYT, July 12, 1930.

71. Abendpost, Sept. 6, 1930; June 30, 1930.

72. Republican National Committee, "General Political Survey, March 4, 1931• The Election of 1930--The Middle States, Illinois," Presidential Campaign Series, Box 273A, Hoover Papers, Hoover Library.

73. Abendpost, Nov. 2, 6, 1930; John Allswang, A House for All Peoples, p. 51.

74. Abendpost, Oct. 25, Nov. 1, 4, Dec. 16, 1930.

75. Abendpost, Dec. 8, 1930; Chicago Daily News, July 1, 1929; Chicago Evening Post, Feb. 22, 1930.

CHAPTER VI

THE FIGHT FOR RECOGNITION, 1931-1934

German-American leaders continued to feel that their group was not receiving proper recognition from American politicians and cultural leaders. The image of their group, and of their old homeland, seemed to be improving as memories of the Great War dimmed. Germans in Chicago seemed to be re-asserting their political power, as indicated by the 1930 senatorial election, and by the deomonstration of support for William Hale Thomspon in 1927. Culturally, the German language theater had been revived, the organization of a German Literary Society was being contemplated, and both the German Club and Germania Society had gained members despite the declining economic situation in the city. Leaders remained confident that with the return of prosperity German culture in the city would flourish.

Between 1931 and 1934 efforts were made to achieve even greater political unity among German-Americans. Reform-minded German Republicans challenged William Hale Thompson in the 1931 primary in the same manner and with the same results achieved in 1927; they lost. The fight against Thompson, however, was also an attempt to rebuild the image of German-Americans. The mayor's antics and close association with "the German vote," heightened by Democratic propaganda which continued to designate Thompson as "Kaiser Bill." Any restoration of a positive image for German-Americans would have to include disassociation from political leaders like Thompson.

German-American leaders, especially Republicans, felt they had a strong supporter in the White House in Herbert Hoover. They admired him and urged all German-Americans, depsite the depression, to support him in 1932 chiefly because of his foreign policy and his general friendliness toward Germany. His moratorium on German reparations payments indicated his wisdom and, German-Americans were assured, would help restore the economic health of the world. Franklin Roosevelt was attacked for his anti-German statements in his 1920 campaign for the vice presidency by German-American Republican leaders. In his bid for the German vote in 1932, Roosevelt publicly proclaimed his friendship for German culture. German Democratic leaders attacked Hoover's attitude toward Germany in his relief mission after the war, as they had done in 1928, and implied that Roosevelt's election would lead to a quick end to Prohibition. Ethnic and foreign policy issues thus continued to play a role in the political life of German-Americans.

The search for a national voice and organization speaking for German-American cultural values also continued between 1931 and 1934. An organizing meeting for a German American Federation of America was held in New York City, and a short time later another national group, the Friends of the New Germany, was organized in Chicago, New York, and other cities. The Friends were more successful than the Federation in terms of numbers and finance, though neither group really achieved its purpose of building a united front of German-Americans. The coming to power of Adolph Hitler led to renewed interest in Germany, and to a hope expressed by some German-American leaders that he would restore Germany to world power status. Criticism of German internal matters was deemed to be unnecessary and unfair. Both Nazi racial policy and the subsequent call for a boycott of German goods by Americans were considered unwise. Just at the time when German prestige was being restored, an event which could only help restore the prestige of German-Americans, some fanatics were moving to destroy that prestige. A Congressional inquiry into Nazi activities in the United States, held at the urging of Samuel Dickstein, could also be viewed as an attempt to revive the "Hun" image at a time when that image was beginning to disappear. German-Americans had proven their loyalty once, but it appeared that their patriotism was being called into question again.

The Mayoral Election of 1931.

In the midst of the Depression the Democratic party of Chicago turned to a candidate with wide ethnic appeal, Anthony J. "Tony" Cermak, to defeat William Hale Thompson. As in 1927, Thompson also faced opposition in the Republican primary. Judge Thomas Lyle led one faction of reformers while Alderman Arthur Albert, a German-American and long-time critic of "Big Bill's" leadership, led another. Lyle opposed prohibition and charged that Thompson had made the city a laughingstock to the rest of the nation; during Thompson's reign the city had been turned over to gangsters and racketeers, Lyle said, and he promised to clean them out.[1] Another group of Republican reformers, many of whom had been associated with the Litsinger challenge in 1927, sought a German-American candidate to oppose Mayor Thompson in the primary. Frederick Britten, who had been returned to Congress without opposition in the elections of 1928 and 1930, declined an invitation to run. Alderman Albert, a city councilman for ten years, accepted the opportunity to run against the man he had frequently called inept and corrupt.[2]

At a mass-meeting called in support of Albert, German-American leaders again expressed the feeling that if only Germans could unite they

could control the office of mayor. The recent election of James Hamilton
Lewis to the Senate was pointed to as an example of the ability of German-
Americans to unite. Forgotten were the unique characteristics of that race.
Lewis had received 80% of the German vote, but his opponent was a woman,
supported prohibition, and reluctantly opposed the World Court. Edward
Litsinger, who had lost to Thompson in 1927, led the German-American support
for Albert, though he expressed doubts about the ability of German voters to
stick together. "Other nationalities made their numbers felt, but the
Germans only rarely"; their effect on Chicago and American political life had
been "zero." But here in 1931 was another chance to show solidarity and
gain some respect from other nationality groups. A vote for Arthur Albert
was a vote for German-American pride and prestige, according to Litsinger.

Albert promised the leaders of 138 German societies that when he
became mayor German-American would receive the "recognition due them in the
city." Thompson had sought German-American votes but had done little to provide jobs or respect. He was a "political clown" whose major contribution
to the city was the construction not of new buildings but of "the crime
syndicate." What the city needed, Albert concluded, was a return of "the
German tradition of honesty to the city government."[4]

During the primary Thompson ignored the charges of corruption brought
against his administration and concentrated on arousing feelings against the
King of England and celebrating his wartime defense of civil liberties.
Albert hoped that "the German people" were no longer "afraid of the King,"
and that their war-time experience was long behind them. Thompson, he said,
had been repaid enough for his protection. The issues were now honesty and
good government. Thompson ridiculed Albert's concern for honesty, "You know

little Arthur," he said, "he wears a little halo around his little head, but his halo has a little dent from his little head in it." Instead of worrying about the King, Albert insisted, Chicagoans should be more interested in getting people back to work; so he suggested constructing a subway.[5] Thompson said little about unemployment but produced a plan for a lottery in which persons could buy tickets for 25¢ and win as much as $100,000.[6]

A number of German-American political figures again supported Thompson. The mayor's building commissioner, Christian Paschen, headed the German-American Thompson for Mayor Committee. Leopold Saltiel, leader of the Illinois Turners, active in the German Day Association, and Thompson's appointee to the Library Board, issued several strong statements defending the mayor. Saltiel's brother William, who had recently been appointed attorney for the School Board, praised Thompson's record in keeping taxes down and also recounted Thompson's efforts at getting British propaganda out of Chicago schools and libraries.[7]

Thompson addressed a crowd at the Lincoln Turnhalle in his own version of the German language, and the crowd responded wildly. "Us Germans mussen zusammensticken . . ." he began. He attacked prohibition. "Who profits from Prohibition? The King of England. How? By supporting a rum fleet" off the coast of the United States. "There are no Italian, German, or French rum fleets," he pointed out. "Why? Because those countries are not controlled by King George!" Presidential politics, the mayor said, demanded that he be renominated and re-elected; "if I lead the Illinois delegation, . . . I would vote for Calvin Coolidge. I have never voted for Herbert Hoover and never will; nor would I vote for King George." Thompson concluded by denouncing prohibition and promising to "stand for you in the future as I have in the past. I have always been the German-American's best friend."[8]

Albert stressed his city council record of honesty and opposition to Thompson. Advertisements for Thompson recalled that in 1917 "British propaganda" had led to a crusade against everything German in the United States. "Hang the Hun! Close German Newspapers! Close German Theaters! Down with the Germans," the propagandists shouted, and it happened every-where "except in Chicago," thanks to Mayor Thomspon. "Don't dare insult those Americans of German origin," the mayor was quoted as saying in 1918, "they are the real patriots. I will call out the police to insure their rights under the Constitution."[9] Thompson also paraded through the city leading a donkey and an elephant, who he said represented his opponents, and refused to meet with his opposition in public debate; instead, on occasion, he debated the donkey and the elephant.[10]

On election day, Albert failed to carry even his own ward, though he did much better in his home territory (35%) than he did in the city as a whole (15.6%). Judge Lyle, popular among Scandinavian and white middle class voters, ran behind Thompson and Albert in German areas, but received 35.9% of the city vote to the mayor's 46.6%. The split in the forces opposed to Thompson may have prevented Lyle from winning the primary, though it seems just as likely that Albert's vote among German-Americans could have gone to "Kaiser Bill." Lyle made little attempt to win the German vote; Albert, on the other hand had attracted little attention out-side the German community and appealed only to members of his own ethnic group.[11]

In the general election, Tony Cermak refused to concede the German vote to his Republican rival. He responded vigorously to a charge, raised

by the German-American Thompson Committee, that he had run an "anti-Hun"
campaign in his 1918 race for sheriff. In a speech to thousands of German-
Americans at the Lincoln Turnhall, Cermak recalled that he had led a
campaign to support the German Red Cross in 1919, and that in 1918 he had
travelled to Washington to testify against the suppression of foreign
langugage newspapers. He had also, he said, worked to get many German-
Americans released from jail during the war and was a great admirer of
German music and culture.[12] Cermak's long-time leadership of the United
Societies for Local Self Goverhment, which took the lead in opposing
prohibition in Chicago, had brought him in contact with many German- American
leaders and established his credentials as a sincere friend of ethnic voters.
The Democrats also showed their interest in the "German vote" by naming
Edward Kaindl, a second generation German-American, as candidate for city
treasurer. That fact alone was enough to win the support of the Abendpost
which even forgave Cermak his anti-Hun comments of 1918.[13]

     Cermak crusaded against "Thompsonism" in his campaign and appeared
at rallies with a "broom brigade" of women supporters who were ready to
"sweep the city clean." Thompson was "un-American," Cermak charged; Big
Bill had "injured the sacred principles of American society" by openly
consorting with gangsters, and by openly "sowing" the seeds of ethnic and
racial hatred in order to get votes." Thompson answered the first charge
by declaring that "there are more untruths printed against Capone than
against Thompson. Any time a newspaper don't know where to lay a crime
they try to hang it on Capone."[14] As to charges of un-Americanism, Thompson
felt than on this issue he was beyond reproach. "Remember the times when
it was a crime to be a German?" he asked. "Remember when waves of British
propaganda threatened to destroy the city, and when Germans were thrown in

jail? Surely you recall the painful experiences of those days! And who was your one true friend? Vote for him--William Hale Thompson."[15]

Thompson wanted to be mayor during the up-coming 1933 World's Fair in Chicago. So, he asked voters. "Tony, Tony, where's your pushcart at? Can you imagine a World's Fair mayor with a name like that?" Cermak responded, "He don't like my name. Its true I didn't come over on the Mayflower. But I came over as soon as I could."[16] A straw poll conducted by the Tribune indicated that Thompson was in trouble in all areas of the city, and among all religious groups. Only the Italians stood firmly behind the mayor, 61% to 39%. German Lutherans gave Cermak 59% of their straw ballots. German Catholics gave "Pushcart Tony" 65% of their votes.[17]

On election day, German-Americans gave the Democratic candidate 58% of their votes, up from 37% in 1927. Cermak received the same percentage in the city as a whole, his 58% being the highest percentage any Democrat had received in the city's history.[18] With unemployment reaching 25% in some industries in the city, it appeared that economic issues took precedence over ethnic issues, but it should be pointed out that Cermak talked little about economic issues during his campaign. Voters, it seems, had replaced one style of ethnic politician with another. Thompson's image of "100% Americanism" had been tarnished by his association with Capone-style gangsters, except among Italian voters who gave Thompson 53% of their votes, and by the economic crisis he seemed unable to deal with. Perhaps the stolid conservatism of Tony Cermak reassured voters more than the wild antics of "Big Bill" Thompson. Both candidates had appealed to the voters on the basis of ethnic issues; the times seemed to dictate a less colorful and flamboyant leader for a city on the verge of bankruptcy.

II

The radical nationalists who had been escorted out of the German Day Committee meeting in 1930 returned in larger numbers in 1931. The executive committee voted 25 to 21 to keep German Day celebrations "non-political" but the closeness of the vote indicates the growing strength of the insurgents. A proposal to invite Senator Shipstead to talk about his "war-guilt" resolution at the next German Day was also defeated. After a lengthy debate members decided to exclude representatives of National Socialism from the celebration of German culture. If the "Young Fascists," refused to abide by that decision, one delegate threatened to report them to immigration officials. Others argued, however, that the threat posed by Fritz Gissibl and his followers was minimal because if they were true friends of Adolph Hitler, as they claimed to be, the radicals would soon be returning to Germany to build the Third Reich. Until that time, moderates argued, the "young Fascists should be kept in the German Day Committee so that they can be brought to their senses." On this occasion, however, the exclusionists won out.[19]

Exclusion did not last long. At the next monthly meeting the insurgents returned again and were given permission to participate in German Day activities. They could do so only if they appeared as representatives of groups other than the Teutonia Society, and if they promised to conduct themselves peacefully. They would not be able to wear their uniforms, however, and they would not be allowed to march in the German Day parade. On another matter, members were urged to boycott the showing of "All Quiet on the Western Front." The movie, Dr. Otto Schmidt observed, depicted "the atrociousness in the actions of the Germans," but not of any other group.

Another movie, "Hell's Angels," added to the unfavorable reputation of
Germans, and delegates voted to boycott it too. In "Hell's Angels," the
commander of a German airship "ordered his men to jump overboard, for the
glory of the Fatherland, rather than to surrender," and they jumped,
willingly. Such fanatic obedience to orders, Committee members objected,
was not part of the German character.[20]

The Young Fascists accepted the restrictions placed on them by the
German Day Committee. One of their proposals, that English language speeche
be prohibited at future celebrations, was approved. The Teutonia Club
demonstrated its true militancy at the "Hitler's Birthday" party on April 27
Several hundred people attended with many in full National Socialist uni-
form, which many members admitted had been made from their Illinois National
Guard equipment. The birthday celebrants pledged loyalty to Hitler, and
heard a poem exulting the leadership qualities of "der Fuhrer" recited by a
woman member. The Principal speaker of the evening was Walter Kappe, who
had immigrated from Germany in the 1920s. Kappe wanted to acquaint
Chicagoans with Hitler and his goals, chief among them "to keep Germany pure
and tightly welded together, and to restore hope, love, loyalty, and honor"
to the German people. Hitler wanted to show Germans that "the casualties
of the war" had not suffered and given their lives in vain. German-American
were also asked not to forget that a mighty Germany would help them recaptur
some of their lost glory and gain the recognition always denied them.[21]

The Chicago National Socialists demonstrated their fervent commitmen
to the cause on a rainy Sunday afternoon in June set for the German Day
celebration. It rained so hard that only two groups, the Teutonia Society
and the Stahlhelm, showed up for the parade. The others did not parade unti
a week later when 30,000 people gathered under more favorable skies to

celebrate German culture. Mayor Cermak led the list of speakers and described
his program for ending the great unemployment problem in the city. Prohibition was the major cause, according to Cermak. The decrease in revenue
experienced by the city through the loss of brewery jobs and liquor taxes had
led to a financial disaster symbolized by the unbalanced budget he had
inherited. The principal German language speaker of the afternoon,
Professor Erich von Schroetter of Philadelphia, did not speak of the "beer
question" or unemployment. Instead, he talked about the "plague of
Versailles and the insuperable burdens it placed on the leaders of Germany. . .
Do not let the sacrifice of eight million Germans be in vain," he pleaded.
"Support the Shipstead Resolution" which would "brand as a lie the cruel
idea of sole war-guilt" for Germany. Only if that lie was stricken from
the historical record could "Germany be freed from the chains of Versailles."
During the professor's speech a small airplane circled Soldier Field
dropping leaflets printed by the Chicago Teutonia Society calling on
German-Americans to "Awake" and support the true interests of their homeland by supporting Adolph Hitler. German Day officials severely critized
Fritz Gissibl for his group's actions; the "non-political" nature of the
activities had been violated and he was asked to promise again not to
inject politics into the proceedings.[22] He refused to make such a promise.

The moratorium and reparations question would become issues in the
1932 election as would problems closer to home like unemployment. That the
situation was going from bad to worse in the city was indicated by the
report of the German Aid Society. Over 100 people a day visited its offices
in search of employment, but the Society had been able to find only 56
jobs for people in one month. Several thousand dollars a month would be

needed to keep the Society open, President Girten reported, otherwise it could only declare bankruptcy.[24] The Germania Club and the German Club found themselves in similar financial straits. The Depression did not harm the Teutonia Society, however, as it announced plans to build a new clubhouse on the north side in the heart of the German community.[25]

III

The German-American Citizens League, under the new leadership of Julius Klein, a radio personality and newspaper columnist, planned to use the moratorium issue to re-kindle interest in its activities. The League also hoped to rebuild the power of the German-American bloc in the Republican Party. The Grand Old Party could win the German vote, Klein wrote President Hoover, by stressing friendship for Germany and downplaying Prohibition. Klein included an editorial from the Abendpost which termed the Republican plank on the liquor question "bombastic foolishness." The platform called repeal a "step backward for America," but in reality, the editors argued, repeal represented the only chance for ending the Depression. Abolition of the 18th Amendment would mean more jobs and more tax revenue--points which Republicans would have to stress if they hoped to win.[26]

Klein, running for congressman-at-large, surprised party professionals by winning the primary on a program that called for repeal of the Eighteenth Amendment, and an end to "Government extravagance and foreign entanglements." He received support from the Steuben Society, the Germania Club, and other important German-American organizations. The former reporter for the Chicago Herald and Examiner attributed his victory to strong support from German groups. His objective was to bring "well-deserved recognition" to the Germans of Illinois. "The records of history, the gravestones in national cemetaries, the monuments to heroes, and the German names in our social, political, and business life, are constant reminders to us all . . . of the irreparable and unforgetable parts the German blood and tradition have infused into the very life of our national existence. Twenty-seven percent of the blood that flows through our veins is German," he concluded.

Former minister to Hungary Theodore Brentano, though 78 years old, came out of retirement to lead Klein's campaign staff. Emil Wetten, an associate of William Hale Thompson, served as chairman of the Klein Campaign Committee.[27] On economic issues, Klein argued that the Depression resulted from the "unjust peace and the cruel terms" reached at Versailles. If the Democrats captured the White House and Congress they would reinstate "the same elements who supported Woodrow Wilson" which would only increase the problems for Germany and the United States.[28]

Paul Mueller, owner and editor of the Abendpost, warned Franklin Roosevelt of the charges being spread about Democratic attitudes toward Germany. Roosevelt replied that German-Americans had nothing to fear from him, "I learned to speak German when I was eight years old, having had a German governess for a year." He reported how the Roosevelts' had visited Germany on many occasions, and that he had been in Germany "every summer" until his fourteenth birthday. Therefore, Roosevelt concluded, he was thoroughly acquainted with the country and its people . . . . I am still able to speak after a fashion and even to read the German part of your paper," Mueller was assured. As to charges that he had made anti-German "utterances" while serving as Assistant Secretary of the Navy, Roosevelt replied that though he may have made anti-German statements, they were directed at the government and not the "German people."[29]

The Republicans continued to attack the Democratic party and its Wilsonian heritage. "The whole Wilson gang wants to get back in power," he told a downstate audience, "they fooled us once in 1916 and then in 1919 Wilson wrote the Versailles Treaty, which dismembered and bankrupted Germany." A vote for the Democrats would be a sign of support for those past violations of German and German-American rights.[30]

Chicago postmaster and former mayoral candidate Arthur Lueder headed the nationwide organization of "Americans of German Descent for Herbert Hoover." Lueder's group extolled the virtues of Hoover's German background and praised the war-debt moratorium as an act that prevented "the dramatic economic collapse of Germany and all it implied." Roosevelt, Lueder continued, had denounced German-Americans in his 1920 campaign for the vice-presidency and had sought "American votes only." As to prohibition, the Republican program appeared the only feasible solution. Hoover, in his acceptance speech, favored a change in the Eighteenth Amendment which would give each state the right to deal with the problem as it determined. Political reality dictated this approach, Lueder believed, because Southern Democrats, who controlled Congress, might support Hoover's program as long as state's rights were protected. The thing that had to be avoided, Lueder, the son of a Lutheran clergyman, concluded, was the return of "the saloon system" and all its evils. Concerning the depressed economic conditions of the country, Lueder warned his fellow Germans that the system had to be protected from radical change, not in order to protect millionaire or Robber Barons, but so that "this generation will be able to hand on to the next a heritage of freedom unimpaired." Lueder turned to Lutheran theology rather than economic explanations to find the source of the nation'

difficulties; it was a "time of penance and suffering" for unnamed sins of
the past, a punishment that God in his wisdom, had ordained.[31]

German Day, 1932, turned into a Republican political rally.
Julius Klein spoke and assailed Woodrow Wilson while crediting Herbert
Hoover with "saving Germany." Roosevelt, in 1920, had sought only "to
profit politically by the unfortunate disaster" that had beset Germany.
The crowd of 15,000 passed a resolution praising the Hoover moratorium, and
another which asked that Germany be restored its "Polish corridor." (The
latter resolution led to a clash with the Polish National Alliance and the
Polish Roman Catholic Union. Both groups asked for "an unequivocal
condemnation of this deplorable and dishonest" action by a "German nation-
alistic group." The president of the German Day Association refused to
condemn the resolution.[32])

As in the presidential elections of 1924 and 1928, the Republican
party sent the Ambassador to Germany, now Frederick Sackett, on a tour of the
Midwest to solidify German votes. The Moratorium, Sackett told a meeting of
German-American political leaders in Chicago, had done "more good for
Germany than the Dawes plan." Germany was still in a critical economic
situation, having suffered a fifteen year long depression, but release from
reparations payments had helped the situation considerably. Another speaker,
Franklin Fort, chairman of the board of the Federal Home Loan Bank, recalled
his experiences while working in Europe in 1919 under Herbert Hoover. Had
all the recommendations made by Hoover been written into the treaty of
Versailles, Fort explained, most of the ills which had befallen the world
would have been avoided.[33]

The president of the German Club of Chicago, Captain A. C. Weideling,
pleaded with his fellow German-Americans that they not allow themselves to

be purchased by "Democratic promises of beer and pretzels." Charges such
as those made by Mayor Cermak that "prohibition caused the Depression"
would founder under any "clearheaded and sober analysis." It was "the
peace treaty of Versailles" that was the principal factor "which had brought
Germany to the brink of destruction," and it had been "the loss of this
major customer which had led to the depression in the United States."
German-Americans should bear that in mind when casting their ballots and
vote for Herbert Hoover who had a truer understanding of the causes of the
economic disaster.[34]

The Steuben Society made no recommendation for president; but it
urged German-Americans to cast ballots for "liberal candidates." A
"liberal candidate" opposed prohibition and supported an old age pension,
a five-day work week, and unemployment insurance. Domestic concerns took
precedence over foreign policy questions the Society determined.[35]

Roosevelt generally ignored foreign policy during the campaign since
he had no quarrel with Hoover on his policies.[36] The German-American
Democratic Organization of Cook County had a quarrel with Hoover's policies,
however, and expressed its attitudes in several pamphlets and advertisements. Republicans had charged Roosevelt with being anti-German, so the
Democrats raised the charge heard in 1928 that Hoover had "designated the
Germans as the most worthless nation in Euorpe," and that he had told his
relief administration staff that German children could "go to hell." As
for domestic policy, the German-American Democratic Society urged a vote
for Roosevelt because of his concern for "Work, Bread, and Repeal."[37]

In the final week of the campaign, Hoover addressed a largely
German-American audience, in St. Louis. He declared the moratorium as

one of his major efforts to meet and beat the depression. "I know that the proposal of the Moratorium diverted the entire current of thought and changed the history of what otherwise would have been a tragedy to the whole of civilization. It brought to a new understanding the realization of the burdens under which Germany has been laboring. . . .there came out of this agreement a great measure of redemption to the German people." The Moratorium, he claimed, "served greatly in the healing of the wounds of the great war."

In one of his last campaign speeches, Hoover raised the specter of Communism when he charged that Roosevelt's philosophy would destroy the American system of government. The Democratic party, he claimed, had drawn its flavor from the "witches's cauldron" boiling in Red Russia. He also refuted the Democratic assertion that he was not an American citizen, a charge based on the fact that his name appeared on a London voter's list, indicating that he was an English citizen. The President admitted he had once rented a house in London but assured everyone concerned, that he no longer did. [39]

Despite the vigorous campaign conducted by local German Republicans and the support Hoover received from the German Club, the German Day Association, and the German-American Citizens League, Franklin Roosevelt received 69% of the German vote in Chicago. That figure represented an 11% increase over Al Smith's total in 1928. [40] Prohibition may have been the decisive factor, but as the American Monthly, which backed Hoover, pointed out, "release from the reign of terror produced by the Volstead Act is practically assured whichever candidate occupies the White House after March 4th next." [41] Hoover had promised to work towards allowing states to make their own choice in the matter. The Democratic party, of course, had long symbolized "Repeal," and added inducements of work and bread seemed more important to voters than inducements to "Hang on to Hoover," however friendly he had been to Germany.

Julius Klein was unsuccessful in his bid for congressman-at-large. During the last week of the campaign he had stormed-off the stage of a Chicago theater rather than listen to anti-Semitic remarks being addressed at Henry Horner, Democratic candidate for governor, by an aide to William Hale Thompson. Thompson supported the old party warhorse Len Small. Klein attacked the Thompson "machine" for introducing racial hatred into the campaign. Klein pointed to this incident as decisive in his loss, since he believed Thompson forces "knifed" him in the back for defending Horner. Judge Horner had little trouble defeating Small and received 67% of the German vote, evidence that little anti-Semitism existed among German voters in 1932.[42]

In October 1931, German-American organizations from 18 mid-western and eastern states agreed to attempt a revival of the old German-American National Alliance. The new group would be called the German-American Federation of America and would present a united front that would speak for German-Americans everywhere.[43] At the first national meeting of the proposed Federation, held in New York City in October, 1932, delegates heard speeches by Charles Nagel; Alanson B. Houghton, not of German extraction but a friend of German culture and former ambassador to Germany and England; Victor Ridder, publisher of the New Yorker Staats-Zeitung, and Harry Elmer Barnes who addressed the question of German war-guilt and received an award for his historical revisionism concerning the origins of the World War.

More than five hundred delegates attended the conference and heard resolutions calling for the establishment of a national university in the

United States "through the agency of which there shall be perpetually assured a full and adequate opportunity for the proper study of Germanic culture" and for the creation of a German Art Academy and German drama guild. Creation of these institutions, proponents argued, would help overcome the number one problem of German-Americans, lack of recognition. Ambassador Houghton claimed that "as long as the united German element in the United States does not fight for recognition and is not proud of its great German heritage, it will remain without influence."

The Congress decided it would be best to refrain from political activity and adapt programs of cultural exchange much like those favored by the Carl Schurz Society. Renewed study of German-American contributions to American history was suggested as the best means of restoring respect for members of the group. Professor Barnes assured those present that "we know now that the Allies were the aggressors in 1914, and that there was not the slightest probability that Germany would have attacked the United States had she been victorious." Therefore, he concluded, "the only moral argument" in favor of France and Britain had been totally destroyed. Historical scholarship had removed that blot from the German self-image. The Congress ended with a call for German-Americans to take part in conferences and meetings which sought to abolish all of the anti-German sections of the Versailles treaty.[44]

Eight months later another group of Germans in America met in Chicago to discuss the revision of the Versailles Treaty and other matters. The group, calling itself the Friends of the New Germany, was formed by members of the old Teutonia Society in Chicago and by other supporters of Hitler's Germany from throughout the country. Fritz Gissibl, who had lived in Chicago since December, 1923, was chosen national president. Gissibl worked as a printer for the Daily News and had led the "Young Facists" who had attempted to exert their influence in the German Day Association. He remained a German citizen though he said he had intentions of one day becoming an American. Gissibl was a dynamic speaker addicted to the Fuhrenprinzip who soon left Chicago for New York City at the command of his superiors.[45]

Germans in Chicago heard conflicting views about the meaning of Hitler's rise to power. On the one hand, a visiting member of the German parliament told a gathering at the Germania Club that Hitler was interested only in his "personal ends" and was attempting to become a "dictator more powerful than Mussolini." Hitler attracted the attention of the German people because he promised "redemption," and for "redemption Germans were ready to follow blindly almost anybody, including a demogogue like Adolph Hitler." The Abendpost, which ten years earlier had found much to admire in the Nazi program, reacted more cautiously as it warned of the dangers of radicalism and, as in 1923, criticized the dangerous anti-Semitism displayed by Hitler's followers, though it claimed treatment of Jews in Germany was an internal matter.[46] Professor George Scherger, speaking to the German Club, took a more positive view of the situation in Germany likening Hitler's leadership abilities to the skills of great German statesmen in the past like Bismarck; both men were "imbued with the traditional German sense of duty and those old-fashioned ideas of exact rectitude."[47]

Hitler became German chancellor on January 30, 1933. Almost immediately allegations of mistreatment of Jews appeared in the press. The German Ambassador to the United States denied any mistreatment and declared that law and order would be maintained in his country. Hitler assured the world that "undisciplined acts" of individuals against Jews would be prevented.[48] A major anti-Jewish riot took place early in March, however, and the American Jewish Congress called for a nationwide protest against German treatment of Jews. German Jews in Chicago and New York called for a period of calm. Leaders of German-Jewish congregations issued a statement which expressed confidence in a report issued by the Central Union of German Citizens of the Jewish Faith, a group founded in 1893 to unite all Jews in Germany. The Central Union claimed there had been "no attrocities" in Germany and urged the A.J.C. not to hold its proposed protest demonstrations. Such rallies, the German Jews argued, would only provoke a more violent anti-Semitic campaign by the Nazis. The American German-Jews expressed the view that reports of violent attacks on Jews were exaggerated and "based on unproven information."[49] The American Jewish Committee refused to cancel its planned rallies. On the following day the Nazi party announced that if American Jews did not stop spreading "Atrocity propaganda" the party would call for a boycott of Jewish owned stores throughout Germany.[50]

Frederick Sackett, serving as Ambassador to Germany until the appointment of a successor, denied seeing evidence of any atrocities against Jews in his trips through Germany and asked for understanding on the part of Americans, since in his view the violent phase of the "Nazi revolution" had almost run its course. Other groups in Germany, such as P.E.N., an international association of writers, sent special messages to German-Americans asking them to make an effort to get the truth out that "reports of attrocities were lies," what was needed was a renewed spirit of co-operation.

On March 28, an Anti-Nazi Rally, addressed by Rabbi Stephen A. Wise, Bernard Deutsch, president of the A.J.C., and Senator Robert Wagner of

New York. was held in New York City. The Nazi boycott of Jewish owned
stores in Germany began on April 1. A few German-American organizations,
such as the German Society of Maryland and the American Turners, issued
statements denouncing Hitler's treatment of Jews. The Maryland Germans sen
a personal appeal to the German chancellor asking him to exercise a spirit
of justice and humanity in dealing with the minorities question, while the
Turners, at their annual convention condemned the "oppression of free
speech, press, and conscience" in Germany. The dissolution of the Turner-
schaft and the forceful suppression of "the peaceful activities of a
minority" also were denounced.[51]

On the other hand, the Steuben Society refused to condemn Hitler.
Its National Council issued a statement challenging the right of Americans
to protest Hitler's treatment of an internal problem. Americans would
respond with outrage if other nations took it upon themselves to hold mass
meetings, declare boycotts, and have parades "in protest of our treatment o
the colored races," so why should anything different be expected from the
Germans? Hitler's removal of Jews and Socialists from public offices, the
Society claimed, "was no more than the spoils system in operation, and to
the "victor belong the spoils." Besides, Hitler was not really acting agai
Jews, he was really acting against Communists and Bolsheviks. Only disloya
elements in the United States, the statement concluded, would protest again
events in Germany.[52]

Leaders of the Lutheran Church-Missouri Synod also saw Hitler in
a more favorable light. Walter A. "WAM" Meyer, editor of the youth-oriente
Walther League Messenger, and soon to become the leading spokesman for the
Synod as "Voice of the Lutheran Hour," saw Hitler as the saviour of German
Christendom. Hitler's "repudiation of communistic ideas and his unqualifie

insistence upon a return of the German nation to the God of its fathers" held out great hope for "the reconstruction of Germany." Germany would be saved from "pornographic literature, Hollywood films, nudist colonies, and the rampant social evils of a demoralized nation . . . . Communists, international Jews, foreign capitalists, of course, regard this with undisguised animosity," but the task would be done. Germany would be saved.[53]

A German Catholic journal was quite impressed with the new government in Berlin. "Germany at present is truly the scene of portents and miracles," it quoted from a letter from a "well-informed Catholic observer in Berlin. Marxists were being "hard hit," the author continued, and "the Jewish problem, too, is being handled with consistency. The reports of Jewish atrocities that have been printed in foreign newspapers are hysterical fables." Chancellor Hitler, the letter concluded, was not anti-religious as some newspapers reported; instead, German-American Catholics were reassured, he had "repeatedly given public expression to his respect for religion . . . ." A prominent Jesuit pointed out in another journal that Fascism was a great bulwark against Communism, which was the greatest danger "that threatens our liberties and our peace."[54] Thus, both Lutheran and Catholic leaders of German-Americans, in the early days of Hitler's rule, found little reason to criticize him.

The Chicago Abendpost attributed Hitler's rise to power to the cruel inhumanity of the Versailles treaty. Hitler had come to power because of the "failure of democracy. The German people naturally staked their hopes on a man who had promised to reconstruct the Reich from its very foundation." Only time would tell whether "Hitler was the Moses who would give the German people good laws and lead them into the promised land," but Germany and Hitler deserved that time.[55]

The most vociferous defenders of Germany were members of the
Friends of the New Germany. At opening ceremonies of the Friends' new
clubhouse, Fritz Gissibl praised the new spirit of National Socialism he
found growing both in Germany and in Chicago. the Nazis "were the true
representatives of the German race" and he pledged to increase their influence in American politics. A few weeks later at opening ceremonies for
the German House at the Chicago World's Fair, Gissibl demonstrated how he
proposed to increase that influence. At meetings of the German Day
Association attempts had been made to get approval to fly the swastika as
the official German flag, but the requests had always been refused. German
Day officials wanted the traditional black, white, and red flag to be
hoisted; the swastika they insisted was the flag of a party, not of the
German nation. Dr. Otto Schmidt also pointed out the swastika was "a
symbol of anti-Semitism" and therefore had no business at an American
fair. On the day of the ceremonies only the traditional flag was visible,
but during a speech, Gissibl and some of his associates stormed the flag-
pole, hauled down the German flag and raised the swastika. After heated
words with Dr. Schmidt and Bernard DeVry, president of the German Day
Association, Gissibl was ordered to remove the flag or be held for the
police. The swastika was removed and Gissibl left quietly. The incident
illustrated the view of some leaders of Chicago Germans that all was not
well in the New Germany and that the swastika represented only a political
party in Germany and not the entire German nation. The anti-Nazis in
America generally were associated with the Turner movement, or like Doctor
Schmidt were identified with liberal causes. To members of the Friends of
the New Germany, on the other hand, these opponents were "non-Germans," men
who had forgotten or rejected their racial heritage.[57]

Soon after the flag incident Fritz Gissibl and his associates
decided to give up their tactic of infiltrating traditional German societies
from within. "Germans must be separated from non-Germans," Gissibl declared,
since "anti-German propaganda" was again being spread throughout the United
States "and a united effort had to be made to oppose it." The Friends refused to participate in further German Day activities "because of the
continued insults to the German flag and the Government of the German people
made by German Day Association members."[58]

German Day at the World's Fair was attended by 25,000 German-
Americans who took part in the choral singing and cultural displays. At a
rally in Soldier Field, the participants heard denunciations of German war-
guilt and a call to "remove the war-guilt lie from history books." It was
also time to get the pigeonholed Shipstead Resolution out of committee, a
speaker declared.[59] The Hitler government was not praised or commended, a
circumstance which led a prominent rabbi, Dr. Gerson B. Levi of Temple
Israel in Hyde Park, to commend "the speeches, the wording of them, and
more particularly the spirit." The Rabbi commended German-American leaders
for keeping the "hot-heads" away.[60]

Dr. Schmidt, however, took a different view of the proceedings and
warned that German-Americans should not become indifferent to the situation
in Germany. Unfortunately, he lamented, most of the opinions on Germany
he heard expressed were "based largely on ignorance or on statements that
are so frequently set forth both in newspapers and private conversations . . .
that only a relatively few people of the Jewish faith are affected" by the
racial policies of the Hitler government. The truth simply was not being
heard, Schmidt believed, and the truth from his knowledge of German affairs

was that "the sum total of the barbarism is practised now with a greater finesse and with greater harm" than ever before.[61]

One small German-American anti-Nazi group existed in the city in 193 the Action Committee of the German Progressive Societies of Chicago. The Committee published pamphlets exposing the "true activities" of the Nazi party such as Nazis Among Themselves, a description of the activities of the Friends of the New Germany. The Friends had replaced the National Socialist Labor Party, a group made up of German nationals living in the United States which had about 50 members in Chicago. The National Socialists had been disbanded by order of Rudolph Hess in reaction to criticism of alleged German government control of the party. In the summer of 1933, Hess ordered all German nationals out of the party in an attempt to mollify publi opinion in the United States; most of these nationals had simply moved into the Friends of New Germany, though that group officially was open only to American citizens or to those who had taken out first papers for American citizenship. The Action Committee kept a close eye on the activities of the Friends in the city, at times picketing Nazi meetings and holding counter-rallies. The Action Committee conveyed the message that "Germany is ruled by maniacs and "Hitlerism leads to ruin."[62] The group apparently had about as many members as did the Friends of the New Germany in 1933 but did not grow as rapidly as the Nazi group did after that year.[62]

The Friends, which by now had become the most visible German-American group, organized separate sections for women and children. Fritz Gissibl told the "German Womanhood" that they were not to serve a political function within the community but they were expected to help create a "German school" and "help to raise funds to support the unemployed" in the area. All German-Americans were also urged to help fight the growing

boycott of German-made products organized by several Jewish groups across
the United States.[63]

The Chicago branch of the Anti-German Boycott Committee held its
first meeting in September 1933. Delegates elected as president Max
Korschak, Cook County Assessor, and resolved to "boycott all German merchandise and trade as long as the present German government continues in its
policy of suppression." Committee members were urged to agitate to stop
all Americans from buying German merchandise, or from using German ships,
and from travelling to Germany or from reading German publications and
propaganda. Opposition to these resolutions came from Judge Harry Fisher,
who claimed to represent the German Jews in Chicago. Judge Fisher denounced
the boycott; never before had Judaism deviated from a policy of patient
endurance in times of trouble, and by following that policy "Jews had always
achieved great victories." He saw no need to deviate from that policy despite
what Hitler might be saying; the boycott would only worsen the conditions of
German Jews since it would only make economic conditions in Germany much
more difficult.[64]

The Steuben Society denounced the boycott in much the same terms as
Judge Fisher. President Theodore Hoffmann said it was economically
disastrous for both the United States and Germany. After all, he argued,
Germany owed American investors "more than $2 billion" and these debts could
not be repaid by cutting off trade. "If the German economy suffered any more
shocks," Hoffmann warned, "the only alternative is Communism." He denied his
group was anti-Semitic, citing statements of German Jewish leaders who had
urged the outside world to desist from economic sanctions since such action
would tend to "inflame already highly wrought feelings." Hoffmann also
denied his group was "pro-German," maintaining that the Society was "an

American organization, interested in American institutions and American principles."[65] Nevertheless, the American League for the Defense of Jewish Rights, headed by Samuel Untermeyer, the originator of the boycott movement denounced the Society as "completely under the influence of Nazi proposals."

Stories in the Abendpost cast doubt on the need for a boycott to protest treatment of Jews in Germany. The German government through the Ministry of Economics and Labor had recently issued an order which prohibited the boycotting of Jewish establishments, the publication of blacklists, and reprisals against Jewish firms; also intimidation of persons patronizing Jewish shops, pickets on Jewish premises, leaflets and placards calling for a boycott of Jews, and the photographing of customers entering Jewish shops. Jewish firms had to have a chance to exist, the ministry explained, because they provided so much employment.[67] Thus, if the German government or the statements of some German Jewish leaders could be believed, the need for a boycott seemed wildly exaggerated.

While the boycott movement was being debated, Representative Samuel Dickstein of New York, a Russian immigrant who chaired the House Committee on Immigration, announced that his committee would investigate charges that "aliens" sent to the United States "for the purposes not only of forming a branch of Hitler's government . . . but to establish here racial and religious hatred and bigotry" were gaining control of many German-American groups. Dickstein likened the new wave of "German propaganda" flooding this country to the German government's effort prior to World War I. He asked for and was granted a special investigation of Nazi activities in America.[68]

After several weeks of hearings in Washington and New York city which developed little in the way of evidence to show any large pro-German movement in the United States, Chairman John McCormick of Massach. setts brought his Special Committee on Un-American Activities to Chicago. With Dickstein leading the questioning, several leaders of the Midwest Bund testified in closed-door hearings. In the spring city elections an un-named "German leader" had noticed that the "nazi (sic) movement had con-siderable political significance in certain wards where both democrats and republicans are seeking German-American votes." He attributed the growth in the Nazi movement to the fear of reprisals against relatives remaining in Germany. The brother of the president of a "hot-bed of propaganda," the German-American Citizens League, had actually been elected Democratic ward committeemen from the 50th ward. After these charges were made, the president of the Citizens League, Fred Rixmann made the same claim to the Un-American activities committee investigators.[69] Fritz Gissibl was also interrogated, but Dickstein had little success getting him to admit he was an agent of the German government. The Friends of the New Germany had been founded as an "American organization," Gissibl insisted, and had as its goal the promotion of German-American relations. "Can you name any American organization," the congressman asked, "which denies the privilege of membership to the ones you deny the privilege?" Gissibl answered, "The Union League Club in Chicago." Dickstein did not argue with that answer. The leader of the Chicago Nazis concluded his appearance by announcing his decision to take out his first papers to become an American citizen as soon as he left the hearing room, an intention he never fulfilled since he eventually returned to Germany.[70]

The other German-American group investigated by the Un-American Activities Committee was the Stahlhelm (Steel Helmets), a war veterans association. The group's former commander testified that the group had about

250 members in Chicago and that held regular monthly drills. He likened the organization to the American Legion and proudly boasted that most members belonged to the Illinois National Guard. The aims of the group were fraternal: the continuation of wartime comradeship, educating members to accept the full responsibilities of American citizenship, and the furtherance of friendship between veterans of all countries. The group, he assured Dickstein, did not spread propaganda.[71]

On the basis of such evidence McCormick announced that his Committee was ready to "bare a Nazi plot" against America; he also was glad to say that "there has been no evidence of any Americans of German blood born in the United States having taken part in the efforts of the Nazi party in Germany." A Nazi plot would be exposed at the open hearings beginning in July, he promised.[72]

The Committee concluded its investigation in New York City where Dickstein talked with friends and associates of Bruno Hauptmann in an effort to link the alleged Lindbergh kidnapper with the Nazi underground. Hauptmann's landlady remembered that he had received many "German" friends at his apartment, and had given many parties that had lasted until late in the evening. She had never heard Hauptmann utter any pro-Hitler statements, however. Four friends of Hauptmann testified in a similar manner. After failing to link the kidnapping to pro-Nazi activities, the Committee turned its attention to William Pelley's Silver Shirts, a native American Fascist movement and temporarily forgot about German-Americans.[73] The protestations of Representative Dickstein notwithstanding, the Un-American Activities Committee had not discovered a major plot to propagandize America or to encourage the growth of "Hitlerism" among German-Americans.

Charges made by Committee members, however, helped raise doubts about the loyalty of German-Americans. Again, as in 1917, loyalty to the homeland for German-Americans meant loyalty to a government considered unfriendly to the United States.[74]

The New Germany and the rise of Hitlerism gave some German-American leaders the feeling that the time for a rebirth of German culture in the United States had arrived. Among other leaders, however, particularly those associated with Turner societies and other liberal groups, there was an awareness that the National Socialist government did not represent all that was true and noble in the German character. The German image in the American mind had been that of "the Hun" and "the uncivilized barbarian" once before. The racial policies and dreams of world power expressed by Adolf Hitler and his followers in the United States could easily revive that image.

NOTES

Chapter 6.

1. <u>Abendpost</u>, Nov. 21, 1930.

2. <u>Abendpost</u>, Dec. 24, 30, 1930.

3. <u>Abendpost</u>, Jan. 20, 1931.

4. <u>Abendpost</u>, Feb. 17, 1931.

5. <u>Abendpost</u>, Feb. 10, 1931.

6. <u>Abnedpost</u>, Feb. 7, 1931.

7. <u>Abendpost</u>, Feb. 12, 1931.

8. <u>Abendpost</u>, Feb. 12, 1931.

9. <u>Abendpost</u>, Feb. 21, 1931.

10. <u>Chicago Tribune</u>, Feb. 19, 1931.

11. <u>Chicago Tribune</u>, Feb. 25, 1931.

12. <u>Abendpost</u>, March 27, 1931.

13. <u>Abendpost</u>, April 4, 1931.

14. <u>Chicago Tribune</u>, March 31, 1931; <u>Abendpost</u>, April 3, 1931.

15. <u>Abendpost</u>, April 1, 1931.

16. Alex Gottfried, <u>Boss Cermak of Chicago: A Study of Political Leadership</u> (Seattle: University of Washington Press, 1962), p. 242.

17. <u>Chicago Tribune</u>, March 30, 1931.

18. John Allswang, <u>A House for All Peoples</u>, p. 42.

19. <u>Abendpost</u>, Jan. 31, 1931.

20. <u>Abendpost</u>, Feb. 28, 1931.

21. <u>Abendpost</u>, April 27, 1931.

22. <u>Abendpost</u>, June 8, 15, 1931.

23. Abendpost, June 24, July 11, 1931; Louis Lochner, Herbert Hoover and Germany (New York: Macmillan Co., 1960), pp. 82-112.

24. Abendpost, October 18, 1931; Joseph Martini, interview at German Aid Society of Chicago, August 11, 1977.

25. Germania Club of Chicago, Minutes of Meeting of Board of Directors, October 20, 1931, located in Germania Club of Chicago.

26. Abendpost, June 17, 1932.

27. Julius Klein to Herbert Hoover, June 22, 1932, "Address Delivered and Made by Julius Klein . . . at the State Convention, May 27, 1932," Presidential Subject File--Newspapers-Foreign Language Papers, 1929-33, Box 273, Hoover Papers, Hoover Library.

28. Chicago Daily News, June 25, 1932; Abendpost, June 25, 1932.

29. Franklin Roosevelt to Paul Mueller, August 22, 1932, PPF 5539, Box 11, Deomocratic National Committee Papers, Roosevelt Library.

30. New York Times, August 8, 1932.

31. Arthur Lueder, "Wahre Sachurhalt bezurglich der Prasidenten Herbert Hoover fur Amerikaner deutschen Abkunft," Presidential Subject File-- Republican Party, Foreign Language Groups, Box 273, Hoover Papers, Hoover Library.

32. Abendpost, Sept. 26, 1932; CT, Sept. 26, Oct. 18, 1932.

33. Abendpost, Oct. 30, 1932; CT, Oct. 30, 1932.

34. Abendpost, Oct. 26, 1932.

35. Abendpost, Oct. 8, 1932.

36. Frank Freidel, Franklin D. Roosevelt: The Triumph (Boston: Little, Brown and Company, 1956), p. 357.

37. Abendpost, Oct. 30, 1932.

38. CT, Nov. 5, 1932; Lochner, Herbert Hoover and Germany, pp. 110-112.

39. CT, Nov. 6, 1932.

40. Allswang, A House for All Peoples, p. 42.

41. American Monthly 16 (October 1932), p. 11.

42. Chicago Herald & Examiner, Nov. 1, 1932; Abendpost, Nov. 20, 1932.

43. NYT, Oct. 26, 1931.

44. _American Monthly_ 16 (November 1932), pp. 10-11; _NYT_, Oct. 28, 30, 1932.

45. _Abendpost_, Jan. 15, 1933.

46. German Club of Chicago, _20th Anniversary and World's Fair Year Book, 1913-1933 . . ._ (Chicago: n. p., 1933).

47. _Abendpost_, January 19, 31, 1933.

48. _NYT_, Mar. 22, 1933; _Abendpost_, Mar. 23, 1933.

49. _NYT_, March 26, 29, 1933.

50. _Abendpost_, March 30, 1933.

51. _Abendpost_, July 1, 1934; NYT, April 3, 1933.

52. _NYT_, May 4, 1933.

53. _Walther League Messenger_, XLI (April 1933), p. 461.

54. _Fortnightly Review_, XL (June 1933), p. 134; F. K. Wentz, "American Catho Periodicals React to Nazism," _Church History_, 31 (Summer 1962), pp. 400-

55. _Abendpost_, July 16, 1933.

56. _Abendpost_, July 20, 1933.

57. _Abendpost_, July 20, 1933.

58. _Abendpost_, Aug. 12, 1933.

59. _Abendpost_, Aug. 12, 1933.

60. Rabbi Gerson B. Levi to Otto Schmidt, August 15, 1933, Schmidt Papers, Box 11, CHS.

61. Otto Schmidt, Memorandum, August 17, 1933, Schmidt Papers, Box 11, CHS.

62. _Abendpost_, Sept. 15, 1933; Donald S. Strong, "Anti-Revolutionary, Anti-Semitic Organizations in the United States Since 1933," (Ph.D. dissertat University of Chicago, 1939), pp. 35-36.

63. _Abendpost_, Sept. 28, 1933.

64. _Abendpost_, Sept. 29, 1933.

65. _NYT_, Oct. 18, 1933.

66. _NYT_, Oct. 19, 1933.

67. _NYT_, Oct. 18, 1933; _Abendpost_, Oct. 18, 1933.

68. _NYT_, Oct. 10, 1933.

69. <u>NYT</u>, June 7, 1934.

70. <u>Chicago Daily News</u>, April 2, 11, 1934.

71. <u>U.S., Congress, House, Special Committee on Un-American Activities, Investigation of Nazi Propaganda Activities and Investigation of Certain Other Propaganda Activities, Public Hearings</u>, 73rd Cong., 2d sess., 1934, pp. 80-81.

72. <u>NYT</u>, June 8, 19, 1934.

73. <u>NYT</u>, Sept. 28, Oct. 2, 1934.

74. See: Samuel Dickstein to Franklin Roosevelt, Oct. 17, 1933, "Confidential Committee Print: Historical Sketch of the Origin and Extent of Nazi Activities in the United States," File 198A, Presidential Papers, Roosevelt Library. Dickstein explains to the President that his pamphlet shows "how extensive this propaganda has become."

CHAPTER VII

"A TIME OF TESTING": GERMAN-
AMERICANS AND THE "NEW GERMANY", 1935 to 1938

The resurgence of power by Germany led to new efforts towards the
rebirth of militant Germanism in the United States. The Friends of the New
Germany, which became the German-American Bund (League) in 1936, was the
most outspoken and visible of the supporters of militant Germanism in the
United States. Though the German government itself was embarrassed by the
activities of the Friends and the Bund, and preferred to deal with more
traditional German-American societies, the leaders of the Friends and the
Bund acted as if they were the official spokesmen for all German-Americans
in the United States. Publicity given these fanatic groups in newspapers
and congressional hearings implied that thousands of Germans in the United
States were outright supporters of the policies of Adolf Hitler and were
engaged in activities aimed at the overthrow of the American government.
Leaders of traditional German-American groups were caught between a desire to
support Germany--after all Hitler was going about restoring German pride--and
a desire not to be considered un-American once again. This conflict between
loyalty to the old homeland and loyalty to the United States continued to
trouble leaders of German-American political and social organizations.

The dream of political unity continued to haunt German-American
leaders. The Republican party in Chicago in 1935 again turned to a German-
American to lead its ticket, though by this time, at the depths of the

204

Depression, the Republican party had all but disappeared from the city.
Ethnic questions and foreign policy hardly influenced the 1936 presidential
election, though leaders of the Lutheran Church-Missouri Synod launched an
effort to defeat Franklin Roosevelt. Increasingly, throughout the 1930s,
the emphasis among German-American leaders in their efforts to build group
consciousness was on foreign policy. Loyalty to Germany came to be seen as
the most important factor in restoring power and prestige to German-Americans
in the United States. Throughout the 1920s, speakers at German Day celebrations and ethnic society meetings had emphasized the problems of a defeated,
enslaved Germany. The Versailles Treaty had been condemned again and again
as the major cause of Germany's economic and social problems; the "war guilt"
question had been raised on numberless occasions. With the expansion of
German power in Europe, and Hitler's rebuff of the Versailles Treaty, German-
American leaders could forget about the humiliations of World War I.

Hitler's internal policies and racial views presented a more
difficult problem for German-American leaders, but not one that was
insurmountable. His racial policies could be dismissed as an internal matter
much as America's treatment of her Negro population. Criticism of Nazi
programs, in the eyes of German-American spokesmen, could easily be
dismissed as just more British propaganda, comparable to the charge that
Germans during the Great War had used the bodies of prisoners-of-war to
make soap and lard. Just as that latter charge had been proven false, so
all the rumors concerning mistreatment of German Jews could be refuted.
Thus, German-American leaders could defend the German government without
disloyalty to the United States. The reputation of Germany and German-
Americans had been badly abused during the Great War; if such abuse was

allowed to go unchallenged another time it was feared that German
culture would be destroyed.

I

An overflow crowd attended the Midwest District meeting of the
Friends of the New Germany held in Chicago on August 27 and 28 1934.
Hundreds of delegates from Cincinnati, St. Louis, Milwaukee, Cleveland, and
Hammond, Indiana, heard Fritz Gissibl and other leaders discuss plans for
uniting German-Americans into a powerful political bloc. The Dickstein
hearings, according to Gissibl, would not deter the Friends from pursuing
their goal. The Friends had suffered a severe blow earlier in August when
the German government had again ordered all German nationals out of the
group. This was done in response to advice from Richard Sallet, the
representative of the Ministry of Propaganda in the German embassy in
Washington. In Sallet's view, the Friends would be "a burden to us as long
as it engages in political activity." If Germany wanted to build its
prestige among "the mass of patriotic Americans" it would have to refrain
from "playing a part in domestic politics." By the participation of Reich
subjects in the Friends, "the Jews" had been able "to cloak themselves in
a mantle of patriotism" against a group allegedly composed of "un-American
agitators." Germany's best hope lay in convincing German-American organizations, and other Americans, "particularly in the Middle West," of the
righteousness of the German cause.[2] It was essential for Germans in the
United States to avoid the appearance of disloyalty while trying to help
their homeland.

The German American Citizens League attempted to maintain a
balance between being German and being American. At a picnic in Chicago,

the crowd shouted approval of a resolution acknowledging Germany's right
to manage its internal affairs "as it sees fit," and applauded Reverend
George Scherger's call to fight "for the victory of the German spirit," by
which he meant the victory of toleration, liberality, and open-mindedness.[3]
Unfavorable economic circumstances were blamed for the "meager success" of
a state-wide recruitment campaign, but as soon as the "bad times" were over
the membership committee expected many more members. The League called for
an economic program stressing a reduction of the number of working hours;
the abolition of child labor; the introduction of an old age pension system,
and a law which would have allowed only one adult in each family the right
to work. Then the convention delegates, after a long, loud, and acrimonious
debate, voted to support the anti-Jewish boycott organized by the Friends
of the New Germany.[4]

Leaders of the boycott held their convention in Chicago late in
October. Over 100 delegates from throughout the United States met to
discuss plans for the future. C. K. Froehlich, president of the United
German Societies of New York, chaired the meeting and explained the purpose
of the boycott. "As an American of German birth," Froehlich told newspaper
reporters, "I experienced painful impressions when I saw how a small group
of fellow American citizens and non-citizens placed a boycott on German
goods." That boycott had "poisoned" relations between two friendly nations
and had defamed the image of German-Americans. For those reasons "tens of
thousands" of German-Americans were banding together "to bring a halt to
the shameless activities of the opponents of the German people." Other
speakers emphasized that their group was not a "hate" organization; it was
not like the opposition in that respect. The German-American Economic
Association (D.A.W.A.), boycott organizer, would tell people where they

could buy without harming "the economic life of their birthplace, or the birthplace of their ancestors."[5] Eventually, it was hoped, appropriate stickers would be placed in the windows of all stores which did not take part in the boycott of German goods.

Another opportunity to demonstrate loyalty to the old homeland arose for German-Americans in December 1934. According to the Versailles Treaty a plebiscite was to be held in the Saarland early in 1935, and anyone who had resided in the Saar when the treaty had been signed was eligible to vote. At a Saarfest in Chicago, several thousand dollars raised to send 196 former residents back to the Saar for the election. Mayor Kelly attended and gave a $100 contribution to the travel fund. Both the German Day Committee and the Friends of the New Germany sponsored the event.[6] At a celebration in the Steuben Society building after the plebiscite on January 13, 1935, both groups exulted in the victory for Germany. One of the Saarlaenders spoke of his experience in the Old Country and reported in glowing terms of the glories of the New Germany. Social justice was the ultimate aim of the nationalist movement, he maintained, and Hitler had restored pride to the German people. Dr. Rolf Jaeger, the consul general, also spoke and thanked Chicago's Germans for their support for efforts to make German reunification a reality. Walter Kappe, of the Friends, closed the celebration with a call to fight "for the maintenance of German ways and to unite German-Americans into a true people's community which would find new strength in its unity."[7] Dr. Scherger held a special service in St. Paul's in commemoration of "Hitler's repudiation of the Versailles treaty." In his sermon, he praised the German chancellor's "genius" in reforming German morals and religious life. Hitler was on the right track, in Scherger's view, "in urging the simple life over against the mechanical, automatic city life."[8] The

Saarland episode showed that hundreds of Chicago Germans were ready to come to the aid of the old homeland when it needed assistance.

The Friends of the New Germany capitalized on the growing interest in Germany. Early in November it began a weekly series of Sunday afternoon concerts by the Friends of New Germany orchestra. Leaders of the group frequently criticized the older German-American organizations. "We are the revolutionary movement of German-Americans," one leader said. "We are not weaklings content to drink beer and bowl. We have other things to do." Leaders of the Steuben Society resented these attacks, and accused the Friends of being "un-American." Differing goals divided the two groups. The Friends wanted to go beyond protecting German culture. "If some day it becomes necessary to free America from the menace of communism, America can expect more from the Friends of the New Germany than from the Steuben Society," a leader insisted; the Friends were at last preparing for the final battle.[8]

In a meeting with Adolph Hitler, Theodore Hoffman of the Steuben Society complained that the Friends were hurting his groups efforts to organize German-Americans. Too many Americans assumed that the Friends received their orders from Berlin. The American Nazis were giving a bad image to all German-Americans. The German government had already issued an order banning German nationals in the United States from participating in the activities of the Friends of New Germany. It was hoped that this order would alleviate fears that the German government was interfering in American domestic affairs by supporting a political group.[9] The German ambassador in Washington, Heinrich Dieckhoff, suggested that the German government support the traditional leaders of German-American clubs and political organizations because the "excess of zeal" displayed by the Friends was "particulary outlandish and un-American" and had done "not inconsiderable damage" to the German cause in the United States. The best policy to pursue, the Ambassador argued, was to have cultural exchanges with American groups and a program to encourage tourists to travel to the New Germany. Such a course would allow for a much wider acceptance of Germany by Americans than would support for a belligerent, pro-Nazi political group.[10] Dieckhoff found little reason to believe German-Americans would support an openly pro-Nazi appeal to join their ethnic brothers in a world-wide crusade for Fascism.

II

The mayoral election of 1935 gave Germans in Chicago an opportunity to demonstrate the strength of their support for Fascist principles because one of the three candidates involved ran as an open supporter of the ideals personified by Adolf Hitler. Edward Kelly replaced the assassinated Anton Cermak in 1933 and was running for re-election. Also on the Democratic ticket was Gustave A. Brand, who had long been active in Turner affairs and the German Day Association. Brand was running for city treasurer. The Republicans chose Emil Wetten, a German-American who had been William Hale Thompson's campaign manager in 1931. Newton Jenkins headed the People's Party and was dedicated to advancing the philosophy of Adolf Hitler.

Jenkins, who had worked for Robert La Follette in 1924, had attracted little attention during his previous bids for political office. In 1935, however, he wrote a booklet and campaigned on an issue which brought him prominent attention. In several speeches he denounced the "pack of crooked Jews who have disgraced our city" and who had easy access to power. Jenkins had visited William Pelley, head of the Silver Shirts, in North Carolina and

Pelley had returned the visit during the mayoral campaign. The Anti-Defamation League charged that Jenkins sought and received the support of the Friends of the New Germany.[12]

Jenkin's anti-Semitism reached a new shrillness in the closing days of the campaign when he attacked the "ring of Jewish masters in chancery" who were wrecking the city and who preyed "upon Jew and Gentile alike." Those remarks led Paul Douglas, professor of economics at the University of Chicago, to warn his fellow Chicagoans about the extreme danger involved in the People's Party's program. "If Mr. Jenkins should poll a big vote in the municipal election," Douglas declared, "he would use it as a spring-board to carry out his Hitler policies on a state and national scale." This attack was only the first in a series of warnings published in editorials and newspapers stories concerning the dangers of a vote for Newton Jenkins. The Abendpost supported Mayor Kelly and said that Jenkins had no chance of winning implying that a vote for him would be wasted.[13]

Emil Wetten, who was ill for most of the campaign, had reluctantly accepted the Republican nomination after no one else could be found to run. Wetten made only six speeches all on the radio, and paid for the limited advertising the Republicans took out with his own money. Wetten stressed "good government" and an end to "machine politics." Mayor Kelly wanted to impress the Roosevelt administration with his power to produce votes, so he made an all-out effort to get as many votes as possible. He pledged no new taxes, and helped fight a 1¢ sales tax proposed by Governor Henry Horner. Kelly promised jobs for 100,000 Chicagoans and promised it would cost the city little or no money since he would "go after all the money we can get" from the federal government. Kelly swept to victory with his program.

On election day Kelly received 75.3% of the votes to 17.2% for Wetten, and 7.5% for Newton Jenkins. Jenkins defeated Wetten in four wards (the 9th, 35th, 39th, and 41st), as Kelly carried every war (50) in the city. The wards in which Jenkins defeated Wetten, with an average of about 20% of the total vote, were also wards with a high percentage of German residents (approximately 20% compared with an average of 10% German for all of Chicago's 50 wards), indicating a higher degree of dissatisfaction with traditional politicians such as Kelly and Wetten in those wards. German-Americans showed a greater tendency to support an anti-Semetic candidate than did other Chicagoans, but it should also be noted that Germans demonstrated no tendency to vote against Henry Horner, who was Jewish, in his gubernatorial campaigns of 1932 and 1936.[14]

Pro-Hitler rhetoric and anti-Semitism did not disappear after Jenkins's defeat, however. For the themes were addressed again in the 1936 presidential election, this time by the Union Party.

Relations with Germany had little salience in the presidential election of 1936.[15] Republican attacks on the New Deal and federal spending highlighted the campaign rhetoric. The German-American League (Bund) endorsed Alf Landon because, as Fritz Kuhn explained, the most important question of the campaign was "whether the tendency of the present Democratic regime toward the left could not easily lead through a sort of people's front to communism and hence chaos." And Landon, in Kuhn's view, stood as communism's "greatest enemy."[16] Landon had earlier rejected the support of "any elements who are endeavoring to bring racial prejudices and religious bigotries into American life." Kuhn's support gave the Democrats an opportunity to charge Landon with being pro-Nazi and accepting the support of an agent of a foreign government; even that foreign government repudiated

Kuhn, however. Dr. Hans Thomsen of the German Embassy declared that the
Nazi government was not intruding in the campaign in any way.[17]

Landon campaigned vigorously on the issue that the New Deal
represented an attempt to change the American form of government. He asked
Roosevelt to answer "whether he intends to change the form of our government--
whether labor, agriculture, and business are to be directed and managed by
government."[18] In general, he assailed the notion of a planned society.
"If we are to preserve our American form of government, this administration
must be defeated," he said in Los Angeles. Hitler's Germany was a perfect
example of the planned society. "The planned society . . . is spreading
rapidly throughout the world. We know only too well how it has worked out
in actual practice. It has destroyed freedom of speech, freedom of the
press, freedom of religion. . . . I do not believe that a temporary depression
is adequate reason for changing our whole form of government," he concluded.[19]
The great question of the campaign, he told a New York audience, was "the
question of whether our American form of government is to be preserved."[20]

Dr. Theodore Graebner, editor of the Lutheran Witness, campaigned
for Landon. "The bearing of the new deal," he told a group of 200 Chicago
Lutheran teachers and pastors, was "toward state socialism," and was closely
related to Communism. "We have never had, within the memory of living men,
so perfectly godless a government as is now established in our national
Capital," he exclaimed to another group. Alf Landon, in his view, would
restore godliness to Washington.[21] Landon's popularity among German
Lutherans was demonstrated in a straw poll conducted by the Chicago Tribune.
Roosevelt led Landon 59% to 41% among all Chicagoans polled in early June.
Among all Germans polled, Roosevelt had a 55% to 45% lead. German

Lutherans, however, supported Landon by a 61% to 39% margin. German
Catholics, on the other hand, gave 70% of their straw ballots to Roosevelt
and only 30% to Landon. The results of this poll compare favorably to a
national Gallup Poll in which Lutherans favored Landon 54% to 46%, while
Catholics favored Roosevelt 78% to 22%.[22] The results demonstrate the
continuing split in the German "bloc" and indicate that many German
Lutherans were returning to the Republican party after experimenting with
Roosevelt at the height of the depression in 1932.

The Abendpost gave its support to Roosevelt, chiefly because of the
president's foreign policy. "He is an enemy of war," the editors explained,
"and will not become involved in any war as long as the country is not
attacked." Roosevelt also deserved the vote of German-Americans because of
his success in freeing the United States "from the fear and confusion that
reigned three years ago. He has led us to a new condition of well-being,"
the paper concluded.[23]

The German-American Citizens League also supported Roosevelt,
explaining that under a Democratic administration "trade with Germany will
revive because of low tariffs." Roosevelt had helped "the underprivileged
toward a better life," the League believed, and he had halted "the greed
of the capitalists and urged them to respect the rights of each individual."
The German-American Democratic Club of Chicago, under the leadership of
Ernest Kruetgen, Chicago postmaster, urged a vote for Roosevelt on the theor
that "Roosevelt's voice is that of the farmers, the workers, the small
merchants, the employees, and the people; while Landon's voice is the
voice of the Liberty League, the munitions barons, the oil billionares,
the dollar-princes, and the 'Extra Class.'" (Membership in the last

mentioned class was not defined.) Voters were reminded that "Sun Flowers Dry Up in November."[25]

In the race for governor both the Abendpost and the Citizens League agreed that Henry Horner, the incumbent, and C. Wayland Brooks, the Republican challenger, were both unacceptable. Only William Hale Thompson, the Union Party candidate, deserved the support of German-Americans.[26] Thompson promised "to find out whether this country is a tail to England's kite," and announced a plan to outlaw taxation on homes whose owners had less than $3,000 income. He also denounced the "Reds and Jewish bankers" who were running the country.[27]

Illinois was one of the few states in which the Union Party presented a full slate of candidates. Newton Jenkins was running for the Senate, and William Lemke, a German Lutheran from North Dakota, was the presidential candidate. Father Charles Coughlin appeared on behalf of the party early in September and attracted a crowd of over 100,000. Lemke spoke the next day, Labor Day, at the same place and attracted less than 8,000 listeners. Lemke, a congressman from North Dakota, told his crowd that if elected he would "tell Congress to go home and make an honest living instead of riding on the backs of taxpayers." He also attacked "the gold dust twins," Landon and Roosevelt, and explained that the Union Party offered the only true alternative to the suffering caused by the Depression. Lemke said nothing about foreign policy in his Chicago speech.[28] Throughout his campaign he attacked "concentrated wealth that had impoverished the masses."[29] In 1936, all the major candidates could claim to be spokesmen for American isolationism, so that factor would have little effect on a voter's choice.

The Republican party pressed hard on the issue of Americanism. In Illinois, Ottis Glenn, running for the Senate, declared that Americans

had to "turn out the new deal because strange voices, and strange theories
now occupy the national capital. Never before in our history have
communists dared to parade the streets of our cities carrying the red flag
of anarchy . . . . Yet none of these communists have been deported,
probably because the ships were too full of New Dealers on their way to
Moscow."[30] Former Illinois governor Frank Lowden addressed a similar theme
in a nationwide radio speech. He predicted that Franklin Roosevelt would
attempt to pack the Supreme Court and then have "declared constitutional
that which was previously unconstitutional." He warned that such an increase
in power had ominous consequences for Americans because "the communist and
Fascist type of government have this in common--that they both depend upon
unlimited power in the head of state." A Republican victory would prevent
such a possibility from arising, Lowden asserted.[31]

On election day, German-Americans rejected the strident pro-Hitler
rhetoric and fringe anti-Semtism of some of their leaders. Republican
scare tactics also failed to drive them out of the national consensus.
Franklin Roosevelt received 65.4 per cent of the German-American votes in
the city with Alf Landon getting 31.1 per cent and the Union Party 3.5 per ce
German-Americans differed little from the rest of the city in these results.
In Chicago as a whole, Roosevelt defeated his Republican opponent 65.0
per cent to 32.4 per cent, and 2.5 per cent for William Lemke.[32] For the
third election in a row German-Americans had cast a majority of their ballots
for the Democratic party. The bitterness toward the party of Woodrow Wilson
apparently had been forgotten. German-Americans in Chicago were now part
of the Democratic coalition but, ironically, many political observers
continued to believe that the "German vote" was always Republican. Perhaps
the confusion could be explained by the difference between urban and rural

Germans. As studies by Alan Lichtman, Gavin Wright, and Michael Rogin have demonstrated, rural Germans continued to vote Republican throughout the 1930s. That Chicago Germans did not follow a similar pattern indicates the important influence of urban living on ethnic voting patterns, at least for German-Americans.[33]

The lack of an ethnic consciousness among German-Americans troubled their leaders as well as officials in the German government. In an attempt to change the situation, the German government sent speakers, encouraged German-Americans to visit the homeland, and distributed movies, books, and German-American societies, desperate for membership, were in no position to reject the gifts of the German government and saw the growing power of the German nation as a boon to their sagging financial position. Much as the coming to power of Mussolini had led to a rebirth of interest in Italian-American achievements would do the same for German-American clubs. The activities of Hitler were extolled in speeches which carried the following themes: whereas Germany had over six million jobless in 1933, "today it is down to one million." National income in Germany rose 25 per cent in the same period, and there had been a great resurgence of culture, music, and art. Ideas of class warfare, on the other hand, which had "done so much damage" in earlier years, had been overcome, and for the first time in history a united German people had arisen. All this success was owed to one man, Adolph Hitler.[34]

Dr. Scherger repeated that message in a speech delivered to representatives of several German societies. Germans everywhere, and at last, could take pride in the power and might of their homeland. German-Americans had only to remember that in order for Germany to continue to flourish the United States would have to remain true to its diplomatic heritage best expressed in the view "that each nation be allowed to develop itself, whatever way it chose." Dr. Hugo Simon of the German consulate in Chicago, soon to become a Northwestern University professor, claimed that many Chicago Germans were becoming "su porters of the Hitler government." He hoped that this new sense of pride in Germany would slow down the process of assimilation and draw German-Americans together. Traditionally, he explained, "localism" had left German-Americans in communities as close as Milwaukee and Chicago isolated; however, with the powerful symbol of a resurgent Germany to lead them on, this provincialism could be overcome.[35]

Hitler's Germany troubled only a few prominent leaders of the German community in Chicago. George Cardinal Mundelein did not consider himself a German-American, though his grandparents had come from Germany, but the Abendpost always spoke of him as a leader of the German community. Because of his name he was considered a German- American leader. So, when he attack the Hitler government in 1937 the paper gave his statement detailed coverage and special editorial attention. In a speech to a group of Chicago priests, the Cardinal expressed surprise that the German people had permitted "a foreigner, an Austrian paperhanger," to bring paganism to their country. The German government's "propaganda against . . the church," he maintained, "made wartime propaganda about German cruelties sound like bedtime stories." Significantly, no prominent leader in the German community in Chicago supported the Cardinal in his remarks. The Abendpost continued its policy of refusing to attack Germany's internal policies.[36]

German-American leaders were reluctant to support an open attack on Hitler. They were also, however, unwilling to show support for Fritz Kuhn and his followers. Several thousand German-Americans attended a Bund picnic in September, 1937 and heard Kuhn discuss his conversation with

Adolph Hitler during the Berlin Olympics. No prominent Chicago German
appeared at the picnic, however. Kuhn explained that his group was an
American organization, dedicated to American principals but few leaders
of Germans in Chicago found it necessary or proper to openly associate
with the antics of the Bund.[37] The German-American Citizens League indicated
its view of Kuhn's organization by barring all "active Nazi sympathizers"
from membership. German-Americans, the League argued, could not be considered agents of a foreign government if they wanted to continue their
fight for non-entangling alliances and non-interference in European affairs.[38]

The patriotism of German-Americans was already being challenged by
Congressman Samuel Dickstein and by newspaper stories reportedly revealing
the inside details of an alleged German plot to take over the United States.
Dickstein received wide coverage for his allegations concerning the thousands
of German-American "storm-troopers" waiting for the day when they would
install a Nazi regime in the White House. Dickstein's charges received some
confirmation from a series of stories in the Chicago Daily Times written by
three reporters who had joined the Bund and had participated in secret
ceremonies and rituals. John Metcalfe, the principal reporter, presented
evidence of preparations under way by Bund members in New York and Chicago
for "Der Tag," the day when Fritz Kuhn and his followers would take over
the White House. (Metcalfe soon became chief investigator for the House
Un-American Activities Committee where he continued to evolve his story of
Nazi plots.) Metcalfe said that the German government was behind Kuhn's
activities, a statement quickly challenged by the German Consul General in
Chicago. Here, the Consul General was reiterating the policy of the
German Embassy in Washington which found the Bund obnoxious and detrimental
to its best interests in the United States. Support for Fritz Kuhn,

Ambassador Hans Dieckhoff had written his government, would only result in bad publicity for the Third Reich.[39] Thus, both the German ambassador and German-American leaders agreed that the best policy to pursue towards the German-American Bund was to avoid it.

"The Bund has failed miserably in its efforts to attract large sectors of the German element," the German Consul in Chicago informed Dieckhoff, and "stands in complete isolation . . . with no possibility of constructive influence." Another analysis of the Bund's strength appeared in a series of articles on "Our Imported Americans" appearing in American Magazine. After interviewing German-American leaders in Chicago, St. Louis, Cleveland, and other cities, author William Seabrook estimated that at least 70 per cent of all German-Americans were "indifferent" to Bund affairs, while 20 per cent were staunchly anti-Nazi, and 9 per cent appeared "pro-Nazi in a sense consistent with loyalty to the United States." Only 1 per cent, Seabrook felt, were "militantly Nazi" and actively loyal to the Hitler government. Seabrook also related that German-Americans were the most difficult ethnic group he had interviewed. Most refused to discuss their views of Hitler and they were generally "suspicious and resentful" that anyone was going to write about German-Americans as a group. They seemed to fear that the anti-German hysteria of 1917-18 was being revived and they wanted to contribute nothing to such a revival. Seabrook found no pictures of Hitler in any of the German-American clubs and saloons he visited, unlike his experience in Italian neighborhoods where he had seen hundreds of pictures of Mussolini.[40]

Another commentator, Frank Hanighen, who authored an essay on "Foreign Political Movements in the United States" for Foreign Affairs, estimated Nazi party membership in the United States at 20,000.

German-Americans, however, seemed more immune to Fascist propaganda than did Italian-Americans. "The solidarity of the Italian groups in large American cities and their resistance to the melting-pot process undoubtedly provide a favorable field for Fascist propaganda," Hanighen concluded.[41] Hanighen did not explain why there was such a lack of solidarity among German-Americans. The World War I experience appeared as a major factor. To avoid a repeat of the anti-Hun hysteria of that period seemed the major motivating force among older German-Americans. Whereas the war had seemingly cut the young off from their roots. Such, at least, was the conclusion of Ambassador Dieckhoff. He estimated that only four to five million German-Americans had "a real consciousness of being German." The others, "perhaps 15 million" were "so completely submerged in the American element that an appeal to their German heritage can no longer arouse any response in them." In 1917, they recalled, "the German element stood miserably aloof, and its sons, without batting an eyelash, went into the battle against the homeland of their forefathers." Dieckhoff's recollections of 1917 were mistaken; German-Americans were definitely not "miserably aloof," instead they took an active role in the anti-war movement, but his conclusions seemed true. By 1938, the great mass of German-Americans had little remaining of an ethnic consciousness.[42]

A small group of German-American leaders continued their crusade for a united German-American community despite the indifference of the great mass. Events in Europe, though, sparked the next attempt by these leaders to awaken their followers. On the night of November 7, 1938, the Third Secretary of the German Embassy in Paris was assassinated by a young Jew whose parents had been taken away to a concentration camp. The ensuing anti-Jewish riots in Germany were condemned by most German-American newspapers, including the Abendpost. That paper concluded that "there is no more future in Germany" for the Jews and hoped that most would be able to leave as quickly as possible. "Germany wants to cut loose from the Jews but it is not willing, perhaps not able, to give them the means which are necessary in order to get outside the forbidden country," the editors concluded. What could be done to help the Jews? That question the Abendpost was unable to answer.[43]

Repercussions from "the Night of Broken Glass," the name given to that phase when Nazi mobs destroyed Jewish property in Germany, were felt in Chicago. Over 1,000 demonstrators broke-up a meeting of the German-American Bund with clubs and sticks and bricks. Police had to be called to protect the 350 Bund members trapped by the anti-Nazi protestors inside the meeting hall. The crowd outside chanted "Down with Hitler" and "Kill the dirty Nazis" during the siege. Twenty of the protestors were arrested and the Bund protested to Mayor Kelly about the lack of police protection.[44]

The attack of an "organized mob of hoodlums" on a lawful and peaceful meeting was also condemned by leaders of the newly organized German-American National Alliance. Organizers of this new group said they were responding to the "un-American hate propaganda" being incited once again against German-Americans. The Alliance would act as a defense group for German-Americans and would dedicate itself to keeping the United States out of another war. Also prominent among the group's principles was opposition to "any program which permits aliens to come into this country in any numbers." This provision argued directly against the claim that the Alliance was not anti-Semitic since Jews were the only group which needed to come to this country in great numbers.[45]

The Alliance received the support of the German Day Committee and its president, Captain George Weideling, a Chicago police officer. The new group, German Day leaders announced, would help German-Americans retain their proud past by uniting them into a political organization that would prevent anti-Germanism from haunting the United States again.[46] George Scherger, newly elected president of the Germania Club also had favorable words of the Alliance as well as for Adolf Hitler. Hitler, in his view, was a bulwark against Communism and a bulwark for peace who "was responsible for saving Europe from a new war" at Munich.[47] The Alliance, Scherger hoped, would be a new voice for Germanism in America.

The period between 1935 and 1938 saw the issue of loyalty to the Old Homeland come before German-Americans once again. For the second time in a generation, loyalty to Germany could be considered disloyalty to the United States. Hitler had returned Germany to the ranks of a world power. His racial doctrine and expansive foreign policy forced many German-Americans to think again about their loyalty to the home of their ancestors. The growing threat of another war, though modified by the Munich Pact, made assimilation into the mainstream even more attractive to German-Americans. For only a small group, leaders of German-Americans clubs and societies and recent immigrants from Germany for the most part, was a defense of ethnic consciousness an important matter. The immigrants, most of whom had come to the United States in the 1920s, had not shared the German-American experience during the Great War and still had close ties to Germany. Thus, many of them were willing to fight for the German cause in the United States. The leaders backed a militant defense of Hitler because they still had the idea of uniting German-Americans in the United States. A strong Germany

with a dynamic _Fuhrer_ would give German-Americans a rallying point.
Respect for Germany in the world would lead to respect for German-Americans.
Hitler, for these leaders, was a cause for hope. His anti-Jewish policies
were an internal matter, the same as was America's treatment of Negroes or
Japanese. The important factor was renewed respect for German power.
Around that respect German-American leaders hoped to build new power for
their societies and political organizations. For these leaders the
opportunity to show other Americans the true meaning of Germanism still
existed.

NOTES

Chapter VII.

1. _Abendpost_, August 27, 1934. See the discussion of the Bund in the
   following: Sander Diamond, _The Nazi Movement in the United States_,
   _1924-1941_ (Ithica, New York: Cornell University Press, 1976); Diamond
   finds two factors important to the development of the movement--the
   immigration from Germany in the 1920s contributed over 90 per cent of
   the Bund's membership, and the Bund preferred to remain aloof from
   traditional German-American societies. Diamond sees the failure of
   the Bund as a sign that the German-American community had disappeared,
   but it could just as well be that many German-Americans rejected the
   Bund because it was too noisy and embarrassing. Even the German
   government preferred to work with more traditional German-Americans
   organizations like the Steuben Society. Cf., Leland Bell, _In Hitler's_
   Shadow: The Anatomy of American Nazism (Port Washington, N.Y.: Kennikat
   Press, 1974), which reaches conclusions similar to Diamond, i.e.,
   that there was little left of the German-American community by the
   1930s, so therefore the Nazis failed. Donald M. McKale, _The Swastika_
   Outside Germany (Kent, Ohio: Kent State University Press, 1977),
   concludes that Berlin quickly realized that the Bund in America was
   detrimental to German ambitions in the United States and "sent only
   insiginficant amounts of cash . . . to the Bund and other German-
   American groups." McKale reiterates the view that the Bund failed
   in the United States because German-Americans were completely
   assimilated into the American "way of life."

2. _Documents of German Foreign Policy_, II, August 3, 1934, pp. 1110-1115.

3. _Abendpost_, Sept. 10, 1934.

4. _Abendpost_, Oct. 1, 1934.

5. _Abendpost_, Oct. 22, 1934.

6. _Abendpost_, Oct. 29, Dec. 10, 1934.

7. _Abendpost_, March 7, 1935.

8. _Abendpost_, March 9, 1935.

9. _Documents of German Foreign Policy_, II, Nov. 6, 1934, pp. 1115-1121.

10. _Ibid._, II, p. 1117.

11. _Abendpost_, Dec. 29, 1934, Mar. 30, 1935; _NYT_, Mar. 31, 1935.

12. _Abendpost_, March 30, 1935; _NYT_, Mar. 31, 1935; Newton Jenkins, _The Third_
    Party (Chicago: Progressive Publishing Co., 1934), p. 3-4.

13. Chicago Daily News, April 2, 3, 1935.

14. CT, Mar. 30, 31; April 1, 2, 3, 4, 1935; ward percentages calculated from Chicago Daily News Almanac for 1924 (Chicago: Almanac Publishing Co., 1925), pp. 721-725. Ward boundaries remained relatively the same between 1924 and 1935.

15. CT, June 10, 15, 1936; on the campaign of 1936 see: Donald McCoy, Landon of Kansas (Lincoln: University of Nebraska Press, 1967), pp. 291-312; James MacGregor Burns, Roosevelt: The Lion and the Fox, 1882-1940 (New York: Harcourt Brace Jovanovich, Inc., 1956), pp. 264-29 Ralph D. Casey, "Republican Propaganda in the 1936 Campaign," Public Opinion Quarterly, I (April, 1937), pp. 34-45.

16. NYT, Oct. 16, 1936.

17. NYT, Oct. 17, 1936.

18. NYT, Oct. 18, 1936.

19. NYT, Oct. 30, 1936.

20. CT, Oct. 30, 1936.

21. CT, Oct. 30, 1936; also see, Dean Kohlhoff, "The Missouri Synod and the Image of Germany, 1914-1941," (Ph.D. dissertation, University of Chicago, 1974), p. 236.

22. CT, June 28, 1936. The poll was conducted outside Chicago churches.

23. Abendpost, Oct. 14, 1936.

24. Abendpost, Oct. 23, 25, 1936.

25. Abendpost, Oct. 28, 1936.

26. Abendpost, Oct. 5, 1936.

27. David H. Bennett, Demagogues in the Depression: American Radicals and the Union Party, 1932-1936 (New Brunswick, N. J.; Rutgers University Press, 1969), pp. 236-37.

28. CT, Sept. 8, 9, 1936.

29. Edward C. Blackorby, Prairie Rebel: The Public Life of William Lemke (Lincoln: University of Nebraska Press, 1963), pp. 217-233.

30. CT, Oct. 18, 1936.

31. CT, Oct. 22, 1936.

32. CT, Oct. 25, 1936, Edward J. Kelly to Franklin Roosevelt, Sept. 14, 1940, "Chicago Poll of Selected Neighborhood Theaters, October, 1936," Roosevelt Library, PPF 3166 "Ed Kelly."

33. The Republican tradition of rural Germans is discussed in: Alan Lichtman, Prejudice and the Old Politics: The Presidential Election of 1928 (Chapel Hill: University of North Carolina Press, 1979), pp. 98-99; Michael Rogin, Mcarthy and the Intellectuals: The Radical Specter (Cambridge: The M.I.T. Press. 1967); Gavin Wright, "The Political Economy of New Deal Spending: An Econometric Analysis," The Review of Economics and Statistics 56 (February 1974), p. 37.

34. Abendpost, Nov. 9, 1936.

35. Interview, Hugo Simon with Dr. Harvey Wish, December 10, 1936, in the "Chicago Foreign Language Press Survey," Works Progress Administration, Chicago Public Library, 1936-1940, Microfilm Edition, University of Illinois at Chicago Circle Library, Reel 58. Wish conducted the interview with Consul General Simon at the conclusion of the Press Survey project of translating German language newspapers in the city.

36. CT, May 18, 20, 21, 1937; Abendpost, Aug. 27, 1937; Documents of German Foreign Policy II, May 20, 21, 1937, pp. 968-69.

37. Abendpost, Aug. 30, Sept. 7, 1937.

38. Abendpost, Sept. 30, 1937.

39. NYT, Dec. 10, 1937; Chicago Daily Times, Dec. 5, 6, 7, 1937; Documents of German Foreign Policy, Dec. 7, 1937, pp. 654-55.

40. Documents of German Foreign Policy, May 30, 1938, pp. 711-12; William Seabrook, "America; ueber alles," American Magazine (October 1937), pp. 48-50 ff.

41. Frank C. Hanighen, "Foreign Political Movements in the United States," Foreign Affairs 16 (October 1937), pp. 1-20.

42. Documents of German Foreign Policy, January 7, 1938, pp. 664-667.

43. Ibid. VI, Nov. 14, 1938, pp. 639-40.

44. Abendpost, Nov. 26, 1938.

45. Abendpost, Dec. 4, 10, 1938.

46. Abendpost, Nov. 27, 1938.

47. Abendpost, Oct. 5, 1938.

CHAPTER VIII

GERMAN-AMERICANS AND THE COMING OF WORLD WAR II

Between 1939 and 1941, German-Americans in Chicago were confronted
with a series of incidents which caused most of them to reject their ethnic
past. Much as during World War I, outside pressures leading to charges of
disloyalty against noisy leaders of staunchly pro-German political groups,
and the association of things German with the name of enemies of the United
States led German-Americans to reject their past and to become more fully
Americanized. The best evidence for this rejection came during the 1940
presidential election, when the Republicans offered a candidate with a
German name who made direct appeals to German-American voters, attainted the
support of most of the traditional German-American groups, yet received
less than 30 per cent of the German-American vote in the city. After the
election, the failure of the campaign to keep the United States out of
the European war led to the disappearance of even the most militant German-
American organizations under a cloud of charges of disloyalty. Most of
these groups never appeared again.

In local politics, for the first time since 1903 no German-American
played a major role in either the mayoral primary or general election. The
Thompson machine was gradually replaced by a machine headed by Dwight Green.
German-Americans had had their chances in 1923 and 1935 and had done badly
each time, so party organizers turned to others to lead the attack on the
Kelly-Nash patronage army.[1]

The rejection of an ethnic identity by many German-Americans in the immediate pre-war years came about chiefly because it became dangerous to be identified with anything German while Adolf Hitler dominated events in Europe. Identification with the old homeland, the one thing remaining to unite American Germans since the First World War had now become impossible unless one wanted to be considered a Nazi storm-trooper. Thus, an important factor in retaining an ethnic identity also disappeared. Why call yourself a German-American when that identification associated a person with the nation considered by many Americans to be the "most dangerous" on earth?[2] Since the elements necessary for the expression of an ethnic identity-- language, most importantly--had already disappeared from the lives of most German-Americans the loss of any attachment to the old country meant that nothing remained to make ethnicity a factor in their lives.[3]

Late in 1939, Democratic congressman Martin Dies came to Chicago to investigate what he called "one of the worst spots in America" as far as the activity of foreign agents was concerned. Chicago, he told the House Un-American Activities Committee, was a "hotbed" of foreign spies as well as the cource of neutrality "propaganda" being sent in huge quantities to all areas of the United States. "The organized Nazis in Chicago," Dies explained, were "flooding Congress with mimeographed letters" opposing any change in the Neutrality Laws; his hearings would expose the source of the un-American influence behind that propaganda.[4]

The first witness Dies called was Otto Willumeit, a physician and leader of the Chicago branch of the German-American Bund. He testified behind closed doors and acknowledged his support of Nazi racial policies. Willumeit told the Committee, however, that the only intent of the Bund was to "counteract any anti-German propaganda" and to defend German-Americans

in the United States. The doctor estimated that six to seven thousand
Chicagoans belonged to his group and supported its goals. Among these was
a quota system for solving racial problems in the United States. "I would
allow them Government positions, professional jobs, and so on, according
to their numerical strength," he told Chairman Dies when asked what methods
he would adopt in dealing with "the Jewish question." German-Americans and
other "minorities" would be granted positions on the same basis. German-
Americans were being persecuted in the United States, Willumeit continued,
because of their "race" and because "of their political viewpoint," by
which he meant their "sympathies with the new Germany." Dies was unable
to link the Bund with the German-American National Alliance in his question
of Willumeit. The Bund was not affiliated with the Alliance, the doctor
testified, and he had resigned as a director of the Alliance when his
affiliation with the Bund was revealed. As to his opposition to American
involvement in another European war, Willumeit explained that he had "lost
two brothers and a father in the last war, and I would not want to see
anything of that sort happen to anybody. I feel sorry for any nation that
is being sacrificed on the battlefield." Willumeit concluded his testimony
by agreeing with Chairman Dies that it would be a very good idea "to disband
the bund" but on the condition that "the English Speaking Union . . . and
the French bund" and other groups with "definite sympathies with their own
home countries" did likewise.[4]

      The Dies Committee heard testimony from several officers of the
German-American National Alliance. Dr. Walter Silge, an optometrist who
had been in the United States since 1914, held the position of Chairman
of the membership committee. The Alliance was formed, Silge told Dies,

to "keep up German culture" and to be "politically active." The Alliance was an American organization dedicated to fighting "anti-German sentiment" being built up in the United States. German-Americans were not foolish enough to think that a government modelled on that of Adolph Hitler would be acceptable in the United States. Some older German-Americans "admire that man . . . but at the same time they would not have him here. You see what I mean. A Hitler would never fit--any kind of naziism or fascism or anything like that would never fit in this country, because of the assimilation of so many different nationalities. I believe a democratic government, such as we have, a representative government, is the only kind of government that would work in this country." Dies pressed the doctor on his loyalty and Silge reiterated that he was loyal to the United States, not Germany. Dies still was not convinced, however.

> Dies: . . . Do you have any feelings in this present war between Germany on the one hand and France and England on the other?

> Mr. Silge: That is a rather ticklish question to ask me. What do you expect me to say? I was born and raised in Germany. I got my education over there.

> The Chairman: Sure.

> Mr. Silge: I have hundreds of friends from school days, everything. How can you expect me to be anything but leaning toward the German side. . . .

The main thing, from Silge's point of view, was to to avoid involving the United States in another war. Then Dies asked if war did come, "whether right or wrong," would the German-American National Alliance and the good doctor "remain loyal to this country?" Dr. Silge answered, "I will tell you, I have two boys. One is 15 and the other one is younger. I would any time, myself or my boys, defend this country against any invader." The problem, Silge insisted was that the United States was once

again "being dragged into another mess over there where we have no business.
They dragged us in the last time. We should disregard their propaganda . .
Why should we fight their battles over there?"[5] Silge reiterated his views
in many columns he wrote for the Abendpost and in the many speeches he
made at club meetings and society dinners in German areas of Chicago and
the mid-west. The Dies Committee hearings left open the question of whether
German-American opponents of American involvement in the European war were
actually supporters of Adolph Hitler and his racial policies, or whether
they were simply traditional American isolationists or pacifists. Dies,
upon leaving the city, announced that upwards of 30,000 people in Chicago
were sympathetic to Fascism.[6]

The question of divided loyalty faced Germans again as the Roosevelt
administration began moving toward a change in America's Neutrality Laws.
Repudiation of the homeland would once again become a sign of true
Americanism for German-Americans. That some German-Americans retained a
feeling of loyalty toward the motherland was evident from several public
opinion polls taken in 1938-1939. Shortly after the Munich Conference,
the Gallup Poll asked, "If Germany and Italy go to war against Britain and
France, should the United States do everything possible to help them except
go to war itself?" Fifty-three percent of German-Americans answered that
we should not offer Britain and France any help, compared with twenty-six
percent of "other white Americans" who felt the same way. Forty-one per
cent of German-Americans questioned remained convinced that Hitler posed
no threat to the United States even if he defeated Britain and France.
Only thirty-one per cent of "other white" Americans felt that way.

The outbreak of war did little to change the opinion of German-
Americans polled; fifty percent opposed the sale of war material in Britain

and France in September, 1939. Fewer German-Americans (37%) approved a
change in the Neutrality laws than any other group interviewed. Nationally,
fifty-three percent of Americans approved of the sale of munitions to the
Allies.[7] The course seemed clear for the editors at the Abendpost--the
best way to keep out of war was to provide for strict neutrality. "The
last time it was the Kaiser, now it is Hitler," commented the editor of the
German-American National Alliance Newsletter, which claimed a circulation
of 30,000. "This is becoming stale stuff to us. As Americans we have
nothing to do with Mr. Hitler, and just as little to do with the King of
England. The troubles of the old world are not ours."[8]

Only thirty-five percent of German-Americans interviewed felt the
war had anything to do with "dictatorship and democracy," compared with
forty-four percent of other Americans. For as the Abendpost explained,
England was not a democracy, especially in its colonies. "Only after an
endlessly bloody fight for freedom, which has gone on for centuries, has
Ireland finally been freed from the brutal British yoke; while India today
still groans under the English club."[9] Britain, Paul Warnholtz announced
on the German Hour over radio station W.H.I.P., has "chained natives of
India to the mouths of cannon and blown them into nothing" in their search
for world empire, and now "they have returned" to "our own country,
bribing, lying, and hiring tories to assist them" in efforts to get the
United States into war. German-Americans, he concluded, "should know better
than to become victims of propaganda agian."[10]

Editors of the Abendpost admitted confusion as to the exact causes
of the outbreak of war. Receiving accurate information from Germany was
impossible because of Nazi censorship, so several letters from private
citizens were published in an attempt to avoid propaganda. One letter,

from Pastor Karl Ernst Patzer, a Wisconsin Synod Lutheran missionary who had served in Poland, received prominent attention in the newspaper and was republished in several club newsletters. Pastor Patzer blamed the Poles for starting the war; they were intent "on the extermination of everything German" in an area of Poland that until 1919 had been part of Germany. Polish mobs had slaughtered thousands of Germans in Polish cities before the outbreak of war, and had chased him out of his church only moments before burning it down. Charges of German oppression of Jews were outright lies "almost inconceivable in their outright perversity." Yet the world chose to believe lies and ignore charges of Polish assaults on German lives. The German government had done everything in its power to "solve the problems with Poland, but the Poles had refused negotiations and had chosen aggression" as the way to settle disputes.[11]

A feeling that German-Americans were again under attack led to the establishment of the _Einheitsfront_ (German-American United Front) in Chicago early in 1940. Several prominent German-Americans, including Arthur Lueder, a former postmaster and mayoral candidate, and Dr. Walter Silge of the German-American National Alliance, addressed the opening meeting. "German-Americans have a right," Lueder commented, "to be treated and viewed as American citizens of the first rank," not as dangerous "fifth-columnists." But "that right is again under attack" he continued, "so it was time once again to close ranks." German-Americans, according to Dr. Silge, had obligations not only as Germans, but also as Americans. The "war hysteria" made the fight "for justice and the freeing of America from internationalist influence" that much more important for German-American citizens.[12]

The message from German-American leaders was plain: do not let the United States get propagandized into war again, as in 1917. "Then it was German barbarism" which supposedly threatened civilization, Martin Sprengling, a professor at the University of Chicago, told a meeting of German-Americans. "Now, it is Hitlerism," and both threats were merely constructs of British propaganda.[13] German-Americans of more decidedly pro-Nazi feelings heard a similar message at the German Club's Hitler's Birthday celebration. The German Consul General assured everyone gathered that Germany had only peaceful intentions, and it was "the envious" English who were spreading rumors to the contrary. This time, however, he predicted, they would not be as successful in convincing Americans of the German threat to peace as they had been in 1917.[14]

In May, 1940 Attorney General Robert Jackson asked for the registration of all aliens to combat "fifth columnists."[15] A week later J. Edgar Hoover announced the formation of a "national defense investigation unit" to seek out "fifth columnists."[16] These actions prompted a letter from the German-American National Alliance to all congressmen, senators, and candidates for public office which objected to the growing Germanophobia. "If our country is ever attacked," leaders of the Alliance pledged, "we will fight any enemy, including the Germans, but we won't send our sons to Europe to be killed to get the chestnuts out of the fire for the English." Leaders of the Alliance, which claimed 300,000 dues paying members, denounced the "German-haters." No "fifth column" existed in the United States, Dr. Silge claimed. "They may call us fifth columnists, but they can't prove it because it isn't true." As the presidential election neared, however, the charges of disloyalty and "fifth column" activities would grow louder.[17]

Only two German-American groups publicly championed the battle
against Naziism. The German-American League for Culture, and German-America
for Democracy. The latter group, headed by Dr. Frank Bohn, son-in-law of
former Secretary of Commerce Daniel Roper, would become active in the
campaign to re-elect Franklin Roosevelt. Bohn's group was open to all
"American citizens of German descent who want to join together to fight
Hitlerism."[18] The League for Culture had been in existence for over four
years and had taken a leading role in picketting Bund meetings in Chicago
and New York City. Many of its members, estimated at about 500 to 600 in
Chicago, came for the Workmen's Sick and Benefit Society and had ties
with various German Socialist societies.[19]

Spokesmen for the largest German-Americans organizations in the
city, however, did not reflect the views of these anti-Nazi groups. The
head of the Germania Club of Chicago was now Dr. George Scherger, who had
long been a defender of Adolph Hitler. Scherger, a Lutheran minister, also
served as pastor of the most influential German congregation in the city,
St. Paul's Lutheran Church. The German Club had sponsored a birthday
celebration for the German dictator; the "German Hour" on WHIP carried such
fervent denunciations of the British and praise for Adolph Hitler that the
Federal Communications Commission removed the station's license in the
summer of 1940, and even the Abendpost had published articles and editorials
praising German victories in France and calling for a negotiated peace
between Britain and the Fatherland. Fritz Kuhn had entered Sing Sing in
1939 after being convicted of embezzling funds from his Bund, but the
statements of other German-American leaders indicated that his organization's
efforts to keep America out of war and to defend the homeland were being
continued by more traditional German-American groups and leaders. The

general attitude of traditional German-American leaders was summarized
by Theodore Hoffmann, national president of the Steuben Society, which
claimed to speak for six million German-Americans, when he declared that
any "statement that this war is waged for morality and civilization belongs
to the same category as statements from the last war that it was waged in
the interest of democracy."[20]

The beginnings of the presidential campaign led to an intensification
of charges of subversion and "fifth column" activities. Beginning with
Speaker of the House William Bankhead's denunciation of "the shadow of
Hitler" that stalked the land, in his keynote address to the Democratic
National Convention, through Vice President Henry Wallace's assertion that
a vote for Wendell Willkie was a vote for Adolph Hitler, anti-German
rhetoric had a role in the campaign.[21] Democratic charges of Republican
disloyalty hit German-Americans especially hard; any anti-war statement by
a German-American could be used as evidence in establishing the presence of
a "fifth column."

When Avery Brundage and Henry Regnery, leaders of the Chicago branch
of the "Citizens Keep America Out of War Committee," called for an anti-war
demonstration at Soldier Field, Colonel Fran Knox's Chicago Daily News
smeared the rally as a gathering of "Nazi-minded Bund members." The meeting
"assumes a familiar pattern to those who recall similar defeatist and disloyal fiascoes pulled off here in 1917," the paper concluded.[22] After
the rally, Democratic Senators Claude Pepper of Florida and Scott Lucas of
Illinois, denounced the principal speaker, Charles Lindbergh as "the leading
Fifth Columnist" in America. To readers of the Abendpost, on the other hand,
Lindbergh was a new American hero and a spokesman for the true American
principle of non-involvement in European affairs.[23]

The nomination of Wendell Willkie, a second generation German-American, gave _Abendpost_ editors and readers further cause to hope another war with the homeland could be avoided. Though Willkie repudiated isolationism in his acceptance speech and announced support for giving aid to those countries fighting aggression, the _Abendpost_ still found him more likely to keep the country out of war than Franklin Roosevelt. Willkie, unlike the President, had actually fought in the World War, thus "from personal experience he learned what war represents." Willkie had also promised to protect "civil liberties" in the event of war, a point especially worth remembering for German-Americans. The paper, which had supported Franklin Roosevelt in 1932 and 1936, could not do so in 1940, chiefly for reasons of foreign policy.[24]

Early in the campaign Democrats raised the charge that the German government was spending vast sums of money in order to assure a Republican victory. Late in August, Secretary of War Frank Knox issued a report prepared by Colonel William J. Donovan, which concluded that "the United States possessed the finest Nazi-schooled fifth column in the world, one which in case of war with Germany could be our undoing." A few days later Henry Wallace claimed that the Republicans were "Hitler's party," a charge later reiterated by Governor Herbert Lehman of New York.[25]

The German government did take an interest in the American presidential campaign, but hardly to the extent some Democrats charged. The German Embassy helped pay for the publication and distribution of several pamphlets and contributed $3,000 to help pay the expenses of fifty congressmen who went to Philadelphia to argue for an isolationist plank in the Republican platform. More significant, however, were actions the German government took in negotiations with Japan and Italy. The Tripartitie

Pact, signed on September 19, was written with a direct eye on the American electorate. As Foreign Minister Ribbintrop told Count Ciano, "the isolationists would gain a very powerful argument in the campaign if they explain that under these circumstances," that is, the military alliance of the Axis powers, "the risk of war for America is too great."[26] The Pact seemed to have had the opposite effect as indicated by a poll taken at the end of September. Most Americans apparently saw the uniting of the three Fascist powers as a further reason for involvement in the war. Fifty-one percent of all Americans were now willing to help Britain even at the risk of war. For German-Americans, however, the Axis alliance made little difference, as 70 per cent still felt the most important issue was to keep the United States out of war.[27]

Wendell Willkie did not begin the campaign as a strong anti-war candidate, but as it continued his criticism of Democratic foreign policy became more and more strident. In mid-September he promised that "when I am President, I shall not send one American boy into the shambles of a European war."[28] To support this promise he advocated the sale of arms to England. "We must aid her to the limit of prudence and effectiveness," he announced. Nevertheless, the attack on his loyalty, and by inference the loyalty of all German-Americans, continued.

For Henry Wallace, one thing was certain; "you can be sure that every Nazi, every Hitlerite, and every appeaser:" would support the Republican candidate. A pamphlet issued by the Democratic party pointed to Willkie's German ancestry and pointed out that he had been nominated "with the aid of Harold Stassen--the governor of the German State of the Union--Minnesota." Whispering campaigns in New York City and Chicago also spread rumors that Willkie's German background meant he favored Adolph Hitler.[29]

The Republicans responded with the publication of a speech given
by Hermann Willkie in 1917 in Huntington, Indiana, in which the candidate's
father defended American entry into the war "If Germany is right," Hermann
Willkie had said, "then Valley Forge is a myth."[30] Wendell Willkie also
reminded voters that his two brothers had fought in France and said that
"many who came from foreign lands have a deeper appreciation of their
precious liberties than some who have long lived in this country."[31]

The Dies Committee did its work to keep the question of loyalty
before American voters. Early in October, Committee spokesmen charged
that a recently completed investigation of the Bund had discovered that
over 2,000 Bund sympathizers worked in defense plants and posed a threat
to security. The Committee also released testimony from a Bund informer
which alleged that thousands of Bund members drilled incessantly in anti-
cipation of "THE DAY," when "the overthrow of the government and the
establishment of a government like they have in Nazi Germany . . ." would
become a reality.[32] Publication of this testimony came at a time when
Fritz Kuhn was in jail, and the Bund itself was well on its way to dis-
appearance from the American political scene. In Chicago, despite attempts
at revival, membership hovered at around 300.[33] During a speech in Chicago,
however, Martin Dies asserted that the number of active fifth columnists was
about 300,000. That Dies had an audience and people listened to his charges
is indicated by the fact that 67 per cent of Americans had heard of his
investigation and 65 per cent thought his committee should continue its
work. War propaganda and Nazi activities were considered the most important
areas for investigation.[34]

Willkie hammered away at administration policy in the latter days
of October. "Whether intentionally or not this administration is rapidly

pushing us toward war, and it is also rapidly pushing us toward a totalitarian form of government," he claimed. In Baltimore, he said of Roosevelt that "if you reelect him you may expect war in April, 1941."[35] Henry Wallace concluded the campaign by alleging that "Millions of Americans know from personnal observation the extent of Nazi propaganda and Nazi performance for the election of the Republican candidate. Regimented Nazi organizations are marching in the Republican parade."[36]

For leaders of the German-American community in Chicago, war was the major issue. "We do not want to see our youth become cannon fodder," prominent leaders stated in an advertisement urging support of Willkie. German-American voters in the city had other ideas, however, and gave Franklin Roosevelt over 70 per cent their votes on election day. The German community gave solid support to the Democrats regardless of their class, religion, or socio-economic status. Table I illustrates the homogeneity of the German-American vote in terms of class. As is shown, Germans did cast a higher percentage of their votes for Willkie than did voters in the rest of the city (28.9 per cent compared to 16.7 per cent when non-voters are counted) but that 28.9 per cent fell short of what some German-American leaders had hoped for. After all, here was a German-American candidate soliciting German-American votes who received less than one-third of that vote. Minor differences occurred between wealthy and poor voters unlike the rather wide divergences across class lines in the elections of the 1920s. (If non-voters are excluded, Willkie still only received 38% of the total German vote in the city.)

TABLE 1

GERMAN-AMERICAN VOTING IN 1940 BY WEALTH
OF VOTER

(Number of Voters in Parentheses)

Wealth of Voter	Willkie	Roosevelt	Non-voters
Wealthy			
Total City	22.1%(64)	51.2%(148)	12.5%(36)
Germans	29.8%(14)	55.3 (26)	6.1 (3)
Average			
Total City	17.1 (161)	50.5 (475)	19.6 (184)
Germans	31.5 (46)	51.4 (75)	11.0 (16)
Poor			
Total City	13.4 (106)	46.3 (368)	30.4 (241)
Germans	25.8 (16)	40.3 (25)	25.8 (16)
Total City	16.7 (378)	47.9 (1083)	23.6 (533)
Total Germans	28.9 (85)	48.0 (141)	15.6 (46)

Source: Office of Public Opinion Research, OPOR 814K, South America Survey, April 3-11, 1942, Chicago, Illinois (Roper Public Opinion Research Center: Williamstown, Mass., 1942).

As Table 2 demonstrates, religious affiliation made little difference in the German vote in the city. Three times as many German Catholics voted for Willkie (26 per cent) as did Catholics in general (9.9 per cent), and twice as high a percentage of Germans who belonged to no church voted Republican compared to non-churchgoers in the rest of the city (29.6 per cent to 16.2 per cent). This group contained some of the most ethnically conscious Germans because it is among non-churchgoers that German Turners and club members were most likely to be found. Yet, Willkie received less than one-third of this vote. German Lutherans,

TABLE II

GERMAN-AMERICAN VOTING IN 1940
BY RELIGIOUS AFFILIATION

(Number of Votes in Parentheses)

Religion	Willkie	Roosevelt	Non-voters
Catholics (Total City)	9.9%(N=109)	50.1%(551)	27.1%(298)
German Catholics	26.2 (27)	49.5 (51)	17.5 (18)
Lutherans (Total City)	31.3 (40)	54.7 (70)	8.6 (11)
German Lutherans	29.3 (24)	58.5 (48)	7.3 (6)
No Church (Total City)	16.2 (73)	47.0 (212)	25.3 (114)
German-No Church	29.6 (21)	40.8 (29)	22.5 (16)
Total City	16.7 (378)	47.9 (1083)	23.6 (533)

Source: OPOR 814K; op. cit.

generally considered the most Republican group of German voters by political
observers of the time, gave a higher percentage of their vote to Roosevelt
than did any of the religious groups or socio-economic groups listed.
The Republican attempt to capitalize on any supposed anti-war, isolationist
sentiment failed in Chicago. Counting only those Germans in the city who
voted Willkie did only slightly better (38%) than Alf Landon had done in
1936 when he received 34.6% of the vote of German-Americans.[37]

Ethnicity was not a salient issue in 1940. And, once again, German-
American leaders showed that they were out of touch with their followers.
The threat of a new war with the old homeland failed to unite German-
Americans in the city. German-Americans in the city remained within the
New Deal coalition. Other studies have indicated that in 1940 that

isolationism became an important issue for German-Americans in the United
States. The fact that both candidates made statements in opposition to
American entry into the war seems to vitiate that conclusion. Thus, it
seems, that for German-Americans in Chicago neither ethnicity nor isolationis
were the most important factors in the election of 1940. They had a chance
to vote for a German-American but they did not. They had an opportunity
to vote for a candidate who seemed to be saying he was more of an
isolationist than Franklin Roosevelt, but they did not. Leaders of American-
Germans were the only ones for whom ethnic issues were important. Their
careers, in most cases, depended on the existence of ethnic organizations.
Without a German community there would be no need for German newspapers,
German clubs, or German-run businesses catering to the wants of German-
Americans. Thus, some of these leaders participated in pro-Hitler
activities and ceremonies in Chicago thereby giving all German-Americans an
image difficult to live down. The growth of that pro-Nazi image seemed
to be the only gift of German-American leaders to their followers.[38]

As the Einheitsfront saw the United States moving constantly toward
a closer alliance with England, its spokesmen increased their anti-British
rhetoric until Great Britain became the great symbol of evil in the world.
After Franklin Roosevelt proposed Lend-Lease legislation as a means of
helping Britain continue its fight against Germany, the Front's newspaper
labelled congressional supporters of H.R. 1776 "full-fledged traitors" and
asked all members to continue in the struggle toward "the reawakening of
true Americanism." In an attempt to allay fears that the group was pro-
Hitler and un-American, new officers, all born in the United States, were
elected and an attempt was made to eliminate all associations with anti-
Semitic groups.[40]

The Abendpost urged all German-Americans to join the Citizens
Keep America Out of War Committee headed by Verne Marshall. The Committee's
slogan, "Lest We Forget," had special meaning for German-Americans, the
newspaper proclaimed, because of the attack on all things German in the
United States during the Great War. Such an attack might occur again,
according to the Abendpost, if German-Americans did not unite to prevent
the United States government from making an error similar to the great
mistake of 1917. Americans would be best off if they followed the advice
of Charles Gates Dawes, who had warned against American involvement and who
had long been a friend of German-Americans and Germany. Further involvement by the United States would only lengthen the war, Dawes had told an
audience, and would be "national madness." Lend-Lease, therefore, had to
be defeated, General Dawes maintained, and the Abendpost agreed with that
assessment, urging all Germans in Chicago to write their congressmen on the
issue.[41]

Walter Maier, editor of the Walther League Messenger, waged an
intensive campaign against intervention. The United States could avoid
war by following five principles: first, profit to be taken out of war
since "as long as men can make money by trafficking in munitions and war
supplies, they will be in favor of war." Second, Congress had to act "to
prevent the possibility of any president of the United States declaring war
on his own authority, under the claim that a state of emergency exists."
Maier also favored a nationwide referendum on war to prevent such an abuse
of power. Third, "we must take the lies out of propaganda and lend publicity
to the truth. The power of falsehood, as exhibited in the last war,
requires no further comment." Maier asked for "a self-constituted censorship
that refuses to issue as news anything not documented as a fact" to prevent

a recurrence of 1917. Fourth, Walther Leaguers were asked to keep "the terrifying consequences of twentieth-century bloodshed" in their minds so that "the glamour of war" could be removed. Fifth, Lutherans and other Americans were urged to "use the time during which foreign nations are engaged in war to solve our problems and build up our nation." Following these recommendations would keep the United States out of war, Maier predicted.[42]

The less politically oriented Lutheran Witness joined in the chorus, urging "German" Lutherans to remember their experiences of the past war and work to keep the United States out of another war. "Slurs" against German Lutherans were beginning to be heard again and propaganda was being spread against the Missouri Synod. The Witness objected to the growing "war hysteria" which had led some writers to blame Martin Luther "for anything which is supposed to be done by the German armies." Little continuity existed between Luther and Hitler, the Witness concluded, and any such notion represented the same silly tendencies as that which called sauerkraut "liberty cabbage."[43] The official position of the Synod remained unchanged from that adopted in previous wars. "Although, in a democracy, the citizens may at all times try to influence the government in a lawful manner, it is wrong to identify citizenry and government," one theologian explained. Therefore, "citizens owe allegiance and obedience to the constituted government," no matter "what form this government may be. This includes service in war."[44] Until a declaration of war, however, Lutherans had a right to oppose movement toward war.

Forty-eight percent of German-Americans polled opposed passage of Lend-Lease legislation, while forty-four percent favored passage, a higher percentage of opposition than among any other ethnic group.[45]

During the congressional debates much of the opposition came from German-
American organizations, which flooded the House and the Senate with
petitions and resolutions.[46] When the bill passed, the Einheitsfront
denounced the "international monsters" responsible,"they control everything
but hell itself," was the view of Front leaders.[47] The Abendpost felt
passage was another step toward "national suicide" and approved of the
reaction of University of Chicago President Robert Maynard Hutchins, a
noted pacifist, who said Lend-Lease made war for the United States much
more likely. The paper disagreed, however, with Hutchins' idea that the
American people could still prevent the leap into war; that view, it was
felt, was too optimistic.[48] One voice was missing from the reaction to
Lend-Lease legislation, that of Dr. George Scherger. After a lengthy
illness, the historian, minister, and president of the Germania Club
died on April 1, 1941, at the age of 66. His position and influence in
Chicago and Illinois were reflected in the list of honorary pall-bearers,
which included Governor Dwight Green, Senator C. Wayland Brooks, Mayor
Edward Kelly, and former mayor Carter Harrison II.[49]

After passage of the Lend-Lease bill, German-Americans were urged
to join the America First Committee by the Abendpost, the Einheitsfront,
and leaders of the German Day Association. "Every American who is serious
about his duties as a citizen should join," a petition from the leaders
of several German clubs and societies urged. "There is no better investment
in peace." Leaders of America First were unenthusiastic about having
German-Americans flood into their organization, however, fearing that such
activity would only give the interventionists further ammunition to use
in the assault on their loyalty. In a widely distributed pamphlet, the

interventionist Friends of Democracy labelled America First "The Nazi Transmission Belt" and implied that its members were outright supporters of Hitler. The Friends came to their conclusion after finding out that the German-American National Alliance had given its full support to America First. The National Alliance was "Nazi in origin" and subversive of American freedoms. It should be immediately closed down because the Axis had no better friends in the United States than the German-American National Alliance and the America First Committee.[50] In a nationwide radio broadcast interventionists James P. Warburg and Rex Stout conveyed a similar theme: "It is a fact," Sout opined, "that every fascist and pro-Nazi publication in America . . ." approved of America First and Colonel Charles Lindbergh. As to Lindbergh, whom the Abendpost called "a new American hero who speaks for all German-Americans, Stout held that the American flier "would be acceptable to Hitler as an American Gauleiter, or two and two no longer make four."[51] Secretary of the Interior Harold Ickes adopted similar rhetoric in a speech before the Jewish National Workers Alliance when he asserted that the anti-war movement, led by Lindbergh, contained "very few friends of democracy; most wish Hitler success and glory."[52]

In July Ickes had no qualms about calling the principal spokesman for the America First Committee "a Nazi mouthpiece" and a "Knight of the German Eagle."[53] The Friends of Democracy gathered all the attacks into a pamphlet headlined "Is Lindbergh a Nazi?" a question it answered in the affirmative in the case not only of Colonel Lindbergh but of any other opponents of American intervention. The America First Committee and Lindbergh constituted "a very real threat to our democratic way of life"

and had attracted the support of "scores of pro-Nazi groups." Little
other evidence was needed to show that Colonel Lindbergh indeed was a
Nazi than the fact that the German government applauded his statements.

"How does it feel, Senator Wheeler, to know that you have become a
hero to the Nazis?" the Friends asked another leading opponent of inter-
ventionism.[54] Congressman Samuel Dickstein added his point of view to
the debate by declaring that the American First Committee was preparing
America for fascism and by asking for a congressional investigation into
the source of the group's funds. The Committee replied that it would like
nothing better than to have a member of the government investigate its
books, but no government official ever accepted that challenge.[55]
Allegations of disloyalty served the interventionist cause better than a
possible discovery that America First members were patriotic isolationist
Americans.

The America First Committee, headquartered in Chicago, operated
under constant allegations of disloyalty. The Committee attempted, with
some success, to keep German-Americans out of leadership positions and to
disassociate itself as much as possible from German-American organizations
and activities. German Day, 1941, was the first time in years a non-German,
Father John O'Brien of Notre Dame, a member of the America First Committee
and a popular radio commentator, was asked to give the principal address.
Though widely advertised as the principal speaker, Father O'Brien failed to
attend the festivities, a move which spokesmen for the German Day Association
attributed to fears among America Firsters that O'Brien's apperance would
taint their Committee with pro-Germanism.[56] Spokesmen for German groups,
such as the German-Austrian-Hungarian Club, the Steuben Society, the

German-American Citizens League, and the Einheitsfront decried the anti-
German hysteria evident even in isolationist ranks, but with little effect.

The "German-haters," the president of a large choral society
protested, made "no distinction between Germans." Any organized German-
American group was automatically considered pro-Hitler. German-American
organizations in Chicago were especially upset by a weekly radio program
called "While America Sleeps," aired on Sunday afternoons. The program
dealt with Fascist activities in the United States and their attempts to
overthrow democracy; these attempts always failed, but only because Americans
became alerted to the dangers within their borders.[59] The program continued
despite the protests.

After Charles Lindbergh's Des Moines speech, in which he listed
"the British, the Jewish, and the Roosevelt administration" as "the three
most important groups which have been pressing this country toward war,"
the connection between the America First Committee and Nazi ideology seemed
much clearer to interventionists.[60] It was after this speech that the
German-American Bund reiterated its praise for the Committee and hailed
Lindbergh for his words of truth. Asked to comment on Lindbergh's "anti-
Semitism" and pro-Hitlerism, the Steuben Society quoted Senator Gerald Nye
who said that the interventionists were raising the issue of race prejudice
in "a frantic effort to split the popular front against war." Theodore
Hoffman, Society president, commented that German-Americans wanted "neither
Communism, Fascism, Naxism, or British imperialism--only Americanism."[61]

One group, the newly organized Loyal Americans of German Descent,
headed by Dr. George Schuster, president of Hunter College, and Robert
Wagner, Jr., repudiated Lindbergh's statements and deplored his speech in
Des Moines because, in Dr. Shuster's view, "it seems to me final and

shocking proof what happened to a man who speaks on a subject he does not understand."[62] "We respectfully suggest," the group telegraphed the Colonel, "that when you mention those who do not share your attitude toward Hitler and his program you will be good enough to include us."[63] The Loyal Americans of German Descent, Wagner proclaimed, spoke for the true principles Germanism in the United States. "We are warning our fellow German-Americans," Wagner continued, "not to be misled by sly agents of Hitler, foreign or native, . . . They are only attempting to misuse our love for Germany and to win our support of the temporary Hitler regime." Thus, in a similar fashion to the World War I group, the Friends of German Democracy, the newly organized Loyal Americans found the people of Germany blameless for the activities of their government; it would be against Hitler, not the German people if the United states ever went to war.

Wagner recognized the burden placed upon German-Americans by the Hitler government: "The more the gansters get out of control in Germany," he explained, "the more must we prove our loyalty to our new homeland." Such proof of loyalty ultimately entailed another war against the Old Home-land. The defeat of Hitler represented the best chance for the rebirth of German culture, Elmer Davis, a charter member of the group explained; "when Hitler is defeated the real Germany will be re-born." The war would not be one "between rival imperialisms but a fight to the finish between democracy and Hitlerism."[64]

Amendment of the Neutrality Act in November meant the virtual end of any effort to keep the United States out of war in the view of the Abendpost. "The administration can now arm ships and send them into war zones. . . . That the Axis will sink some ships" and that the United States would soon be in the war was "obvious." The administration was counting

on ship sinkings; "it hopes to arouse the populace and in that fashion
bring war."[65] The Einheitsfront vehemently condemned amendment of the
Neutrality Law and found its weekly meetings better attended than ever.

The attack on Pearl Harbor and Germany's declaration of war against
the United States ended the brief resurgence of interest in the
Einheitsfront's activities. The group disappeared quickly from the city
never to rise again. For the first time in its history the Abendpost
published a front page editorial in English; it supported the war effort
but asked other Americans to remember the peculiar position of German-
Americans so "that the molestations unjustly suffered by many German-
Americans in the last war will not take place again."[63] The German Day
Association purchased a new American flag to demonstrate its loyalty, while
the Steuben Society issued a statement calling on German-Americans "to
loyally support our government." Even the Free American, published by the
German-American Bund, urged members to "conform loyally and unreservedly
with the duties of their citizenship." The fact that Japan attacked
American bases made it easier for the Bund and the Einheitsfront to forget
their isolationism. "Our country, right or wrong, when invaded," the
Free American opined, a feeling also expressed by Paul Warnholtz leader
of the Chicago Einheitsfront. The German Day Association announced plans
for a giant patriotic rally but quickly abandoned the proposal after some
members pointed out that a large gathering of German-Americans might stimulate
talk of "fifth columnist" activity.[67]

Instead of any open meetings leaders of German organizations in
the city, including Walter Silge, Major A. F. Seibel of the German Club,
George Iberle, Joseph Immel, and Ernest Buehler of the Germania Club,
urged their members to buy war bonds, make bandages, and attend

Americanization classes.[69] German areas of the city blossomed with
American flags and with service flags representing relatives in the armed
forces. If Mr. Goebbels ever came to Chicago and visited German areas he
would find "just annuder bunch of damnyankees, ach!"[70] German-Americans had
little choice in becoming "damnyankees"; any emphasis on the German part
of their heritage would make them look like Hitlerites. No longer would even
the image of an abused and ravaged homeland draw German-Americans together,
as it had done in the years following World War I, for Germany was no longer
ravaged and abused. Instead, the old homeland had actually become the
image of everything horrible and murderous in the modern world.

With the coming of war, German-Americans felt they had to show,
once again, that they were truly loyal Americans. The few ethnic organizations still maintaining a German identity acted quickly to dispel any rumors
that they were anything less than 100 per cent American. The _Germania_ Club
helped raise money to buy war bonds, and it closed its doors to all
societies which had been under investigation by government authorities,
such as the German-American Citizens League, and the German-American
Vocational League. The new president of the club, a former Chicago police
captain, refused to approve the membership applications of anyone who had
ever been a member of any pro-Nazi groups. Regular Wednesday night meetings
continued and there was no change in name. The Citizens League itself
remained in existence and celebrated its Twenty-fifth anniversary in 1943.
A good part of the crowd attending that affair, however, were local
politicians, judges, county officials, former officials, and their wives.
Edward J. Kaindl, county recorder, served as master of ceremonies. The
theme of the meeting was expressed by the group's historian who noted that
the League "always stood for the highest ideal of Americanism, the only

Ism this organization has ever known." That so many local politicians
felt obligated to turn out indicated that German-Americans had not become
pariahs. Their votes were still valuable and when the war ended German-
Americans might, once again, want to assert an ethnic identity.[72]

The other major German organization remaining in the city, the
German Day Association, attempted to hold parades in 1942 and 1943, but
both attempts were dismal failures as only a few dozen people turned out
for each event. The group, as one member put it, "could not remove the odor
of the swastika."[73]

Once again, Germany had become the principal enemy of the United
States and Germans were considered the "most dangerous" group in the
country. For the most part, German-Americans had shown only the vaguest
of attachments to the Hitler regime, but the notoriety gained by those who
supported the German government between 1933 and 1941 cast a pall over
German-Americans everywhere. Leaders of the German-American community
would have great difficulty rebuilding an ethnic consciousness, at least
until the air was cleared of "the odor of the swastika," or a greater
evil than Nazi Germany appeared to threaten the United States. Few German-
Americans, however, could defend Hitler's Germany after the war was over
without being considered inhuman. After it was discovered what Hitler and
his followers had done to millions of people in pursuit of "the final
solution," the wisest course for German-Americans was to forget any
attachment to the German half of their heritage.

NOTES

Chapter VIII.

1. <u>Abendpost</u>, Nov. 2, 1938; <u>CT</u>, Oct. 31, 1938, April 1, 2, 5, 1939.

2. National Opinion Research Center, "A Study of the Effect of German and Italian Origin on Certain War Attitudes," May 26, 1942, Survey #107 and #109, question 7; see Hadley Cantril, <u>The Gallup Poll, 1935-1960</u> (Princeton, N.J.: Princeton University Press, 1961), p. 167. In response to the question "What country do you like least?", 58 per cent of Americans selected Germany with only 12 per cent choosing Italy and 8 per cent Russia. This was in July 1939.

3. Frederick Luebke, "The Germans," in John Higham, ed., <u>Ethnic Leadership in America</u> (Baltimore: The Johns Hopkins University Press, 1979), pp. 64-90.

4. U.S., Congress, House, Special Committee on Un-American Activities, <u>Investigation of Un-American Propaganda Activities in the United States, Hearings on H. Res. 282</u>, 76th Cong., 3rd sess., pp. 1553-1554.

5. <u>Ibid.</u>, pp. 1597-1601.

6. <u>Chicago Daily News</u>, Oct. 2, 3, 4, 1939.

7. Alfred Hero, Jr., <u>American Religious Groups View Foreign Policy: Trends in Rank and File Opinion, 1937-1969</u> (Durham, North Carolina: Duke University Press, 1973), pp. 420-24.

8. German-American National Alliance <u>Newsletter</u>, I (January 1940), p. 3. (Hereinafter cited as <u>Newsletter</u>.)

9. <u>Newsletter</u>, June, 1940, p. 5; <u>NYT</u>, June 12, 1940.

10. <u>Abendpost</u>, June 8, 1940.

11. <u>Ibid.</u>

12. <u>Abendpost</u>, April 1, 1940.

13. <u>Abendpost</u>, April 21, 1940.

14. <u>Abendpost</u>, April 23, 1940.

15. <u>NYT</u>, May 24, 1940.

16. <u>NYT</u>, June 2, 1940.

17. <u>Newsletter</u>, June, 1940, p. 1.

18. Abendpost, June 15, 1940.

19. Donald S. Strong, Organized Anti-Semitism in America (Washington, D.C.: American Council on Public Affairs, 1941), pp. 36-37.

20. Abendpost, May 19, 1940.

21. Chicago Daily News, Aug. 3, 1940; NYT, Aug. 4, 1940.

22. Abendpost, Aug. 5, 6, 1940.

23. Abendpost, Aug. 6, 1940.

24. Abendpost, Aug. 20, 1940.

25. NYT, Aug. 23, 1940; Abendpost, Aug. 30, 1940.

26. DGFP, Vol. X, Doc. 129, pp. 127-129; Alton Frye, Nazi Germany and the American Hemisphere, 1933-1941 (New Haven: Yale University Press, 1967), pp. 136-137; Manfred Jonas, "Pro-Axis Sentiment and American Isolationism," The Historian XXIX (Feb. 1967), pp. 221-237.

27. Hero, American Relgious Groups, pp. 425-26.

28. CT, Sept. 14, 1940.

29. Hugh A. Bone, "Smear Politics": An Analysis of 1940 Campaign Literature (Washington, D.C.: American Council on Public Affairs, 1941); Robert A. Divine, Foreign Policy and U.S. Presidential Elections, 1940-1948 (New York: Franklin Watts, Inc., 1974), pp. 36-37.

30. CT, Oct. 20, 1940.

31. CT, Oct. 6, 1940.

32. CT, Oct. 5, 1940.

33. Donald Strong, "Anti-Revolutionary, Anti-Semitic Organizations in the United States," (Ph.D. dissertation, University of Chicago, 1939), pp. 237-38.

34. CT, Oct. 20, 1940; Hero, American Religious Groups, pp. 423-24.

35. CT, Oct. 9, 30, 1940.

36. NYT, Oct. 31, 1940.

37. Edward J. Kelly to Franklin Roosevelt, Sept. 21, 1940, "Observations Resulting from Canvas," Roosevelt Library P.P.F. 3166.

38. Samuel Lubell, The Future of American Politics (New York: Harper & Brothers, 1952), p. 133-34. Lubell sees "the existence of pro-German and anti-British ethnic prejudices" and the "exploiting of these prejudices by an opposition political party" as the primary factors responsible for American isolationism. Lubell's analysis obviously does not apply to Chicago suggesting the importance of the rural-urban influence on ethnic consciousness. Maybe the isolation of rural living simply makes ethnicity something more important in a person's life. Howard Allen, "Isolationism and German-Americans," Journal of the Illinois State Historical Society LVI (Summer 1964), pp. 143-149 also shows the importance of ethnicity and isolationism for rural German-American voters.

39. CT, Nov. 6, 1940.

40. Newsletter, January, 1941; Abendpost, January 14, 1941.

41. Abendpost, Nov. 13, 1940, Jan. 25, 1941.

42. Walther League Messenger, 18 (August 1941), pp. 232-234.

43. Lutheran Witness, October 28, 1941, p. 365.

44. Theological Observer 82 (Summer 1941), pp. 207-208.

45. Alfred Hero, American Religious Groups, p. 424.

46. Abendpost, April 4, 1941.

47. Newsletter, March-April 1941, p. 4.

48. Abendpost, April 1, 1941.

49. CT, April 1, 1941.

50. Friends of Democracy, "The Nazi Transmission Belt," (New York, 1941).

51. Radio Speech by Rex Stout, April 24, 1941, Fight for Freedom Committee Papers, Department of Special Collections, University of Chicago, Box XII, Folder 5.

52. Abendpost, April 14, 1941.

53. CT, April 25, 1941.

54. Friends of Democracy, "Is Lindbergh a Nazi?" Fight for Freedom Committee Papers, University of Chicago, Box XII, Folder 9.

55. Abendpost, Sep. 3, 4, 1941.

56. Abendpost, June 30, July 27, 1941.

57. Abendpost, June 10, 1941.

58. Abendpost, July 28, 1941.

59. Everett Gleason to Albert Perry, undated memorandum, Fight for Freedom Committee Papers, University of Chicago, Box XII, Folder 2.

60. Abendpost, Sept. 11, 1941.

61. New York Herald Tribune, Sept. 20, 22, 1941.

62. Chicago Daily News, Sept. 18, 1941.

63. NYT, Sept. 13, 1941.

64. Abendpost, July 29, 1941; NYT, July 28, Aug. 4, 1941.

65. Abendpost, Nov. 14, 1941.

66. Abendpost, Dec. 11, 1941.

67. Newsletter, December 1941, p. 1.

68. NYT, Dec. 12, 1941.

69. CT, June 1, 1942.

70. Chicago Daily News, Oct. 16, 1942.

71. Chicago Daily News, Oct. 22, 23, 1942.

72. Abendpost, Sept. 11, 1942; Sept. 5, 1943. German-American Citizens League of the United States, Silver Jubilee Program (Chicago; n. p., 1943).

73. Abendpost, Sept. 5, 1943.

CONCLUSION

The effect of two world wars in a generation, along with the memory of Adolf Hitler, was devastating to German-American ethnic consciousness. Unlike the revival of ethnic consciousness experienced by other groups in the United States in the 1960s and 1970s, German-Americans had no such experience. Besides the numerous singing societies and social clubs which continued to meet and attract members, only a few groups remained. Even the attraction of social clubs diminished, however, after the Civil Aeronautics Board ruled in 1975 that airline passengers did not have to belong to a legally organized group in order to take advantage of charter flight rates to Europe. After individuals discovered they did not have to pay dues to a society to get a charter rate, membership in German societies dwindled significantly. The German-American National Congress (D.A.N.K), headquartered in Chicago, has attempted to revive an ethnic consciousness as has the German Day Association. This latter group continues to sponsor an annual Steuben Day parade in September. For the past several years this event has attracted an average of 3,000 participants, which, by Chicago standards in events such as the Columbus Day parade, the St. Patrick's Day parade, the Puerto Rican Day parade, the Mexican Day parade, and the Bud Billiken Day celebration, makes it probably the smallest of all ethnic celebrations. The president of the Association, the vice-president, and most other officers are German-born and emigrated to the United States after 1945. Thus, the group is an association of first generation immigrants and has few ties with older German-Americans.[1]

259

The German-American National Congress prides itself on being
an "ethnic defense group." Every time Germans are depicted as storm-
troopers or Nazis on television (as during the presentation of "Holocaust")
or in the movies, the secretary writes a letter to those in charge of the
production complaining of discrimination against Germans. However, the
Nazi image is very difficult to change, the secretary complains. Thus, the
Congress devotes most of its time towards promoting trade with West Germany.
The fact that most of the officers of the Congress are German-born may also
be one of the reasons this group does not really express the point of view
of German-Americans.[2]

The Carl Schurz Society, headquartered in Philadelphia, filed for
bankruptcy in 1978. By that time the only program it supported was a small
effort to promote the teaching of German in American high schools. The
Germania Club of Chicago has sought to attract Americans of German extraction
but with little success. The Club filed for landmark status for its 100-year
old building in 1976, but, amidst charges that the building had been used by
Nazis before World War II and had been an open house for pro-Hitlerites, the
City Council refused to consider the proposal. The German Club of Chicago
continues to hold meetings but its membership is dwindling and it has little
interest in politics.[3] The Turnvereine have turned almost completely to
sports and gymnastics, with a special interest in training children for
Olympic competition. Little of a German identity remains, though several
Chicago Turnvereine leaders would like the United States to emulate East
Germany in its method of training athletes and holding giant rallies to
celebrate amateur competition.[4]

German-Americans have not experienced an ethnic revival similar
to those of other ethnic groups such as the Poles, Italians, and Czechs

because the building-blocks of an ethnic consciousness, language and
loyalty to the old homeland, were lost between 1914 and 1941. The crusade
against anything German in the United States during World War I led many
German-Americans to reject their ethnic past. But the image of a defeated,
devastated homeland gave some German-American leaders an issue for
revitalizing the German-American spirit. In politics, the continuing
prominence of William Hale Thompson in Chicago during the 1920s gave German
leaders a candidate to rally around; and the efforts of various German
Republicans like Arthur Lueder and Arthur Albert served to keep a ethnic
consciousness alive. In national politics, the Republican Party sought and
received the votes of German-American votes in 1920 and 1924, while in 1928
the issue of Herbert Hoover's treatment of Germany in 1919 became an
important factor in the campaign appeals to German-American political groups.
In 1932 and 1936 relations with the old country lost their salience as an
issue because of the depression, but in 1940, these leaders hoped the issue
would return to prominence in the consciousness of German-Americans.
Analysis of the results of that election indicate that German-Americans in
Chicago did not support a candidate with a German-American background and
name, however. Franklin D. Roosevelt managed to win 62% of the votes cast
by German-Americans. Not even loyalty to the old homeland was significant
enough anymore to hold the German-American community together.[5]

Whatever remained of the ties to Germany became even more deeply
submerged with the entrance of the United States into the war against Adolf
Hitler. The new image of Germans which arose during and after World War II,
that of the greatest mass-murderers in history, made any reassertion of a
German-American ethnic consciousness difficult, if not impossible. The
principal factor which made a rebirth of consciousness possible after the
First World War, the image of an abused homeland, was still there for some, but

it was no longer a permissible political concern for the German-Americans.
Germany was devastated and occupied, but few German-Americans cared anymore.
Twenty four per cent of Americans with one parent born in Germany supported
the idea, as early as 1942, of dividing up Germany at the end of the war and
completely destroying it as a nation. In that view they differed only by 2
cent with Americans in general, 26 per cent of whom wanted the total destruc
of Germany. Thirty three per cent of the group with one German-born parent
supported the idea of stationing troops on German soil after the war, while
per cent wished to do nothing to the Germans to punish them. The fact that
per cent of German-Americans were willing to take some action against the ol
homeland, whether by destroying it or by stationing troops there, clearly
demonstrated the hostility against Hitler's Germany on the part of that grou

German-Americans lived through two wars against their old homeland.
During the first they were associated with Huns, spies, and disloyal element
Congressional investigations raised doubts about the patriotism of their
leaders while reports from the American Protective League implicated German-
Americans in thousands of pro-German plots, bomb-throwings, and subversive
activities. German-Americans were victimized by similar charges with the co
of the war with Hitler. When asked which group should be considered the mos
dangerous of "alien groups" in the United States, 46 per cent of Americans
interviewed in 1942 named the Germans, while 35 per cent chose the Japanese,
and only 2 per cent selected the Italians.[5] No other American ethnic group
had its loyalty challenged so frontally twice in a single generation. The
effects on the German-American community were disastrous.

All of these factors--the association of everything German with Naz
the image of the Hun and the storm-trooper, the accusations of disloyalty an
Americanism, and the well-publicized support many German-Americans leaders g
to Adolf Hitler--made a revival of ethnic consciousness impossible. German
Americans continue to be caught between two stereotypes: one the super-effic

Nazi killer, the other the funny, little beer-drinker who likes his schnapps
and obeys his orders.

The World War I experience did not totally destroy the German-American
ethnic consciousness in Chicago, but the challenges of the next two decades
proved fatal to that consciousness. The rearguard efforts of German-American
leaders to preserve a distinct culture in Chicago may be divided into a pre-
and post-Hitler phase.

Concerns of local politicians, such as William Hale Thompson, who openly appealed to the "German vote," and wartime memories, served to maintain an
ethnic consciousness. German-American leaders, through appeals for aid to the
old country and reminders of the antiGerman crusade in the United States during
the war, also kept a spirit of ethnicity alive. In the pre-Hitler era, up to
1933, a small group of German-American leaders continued to teach accomodation
with American political principles and the involvement of German-Americans in
American politics as a distinct group, while also reminding their followers
that complete assimilation into American life would mean a victory for the civilization of England. Thus, these leaders endorsed a policy of cultural
pluralism.

With the coming to power of Adolf Hitler, leaders of German-American
groups at first reacted with glowing tributes to the rebirth of German power
and pride, and as long as he remained at peace with the United States these
leaders declared that Hitler's internal policies were his own business. During
this period, however, rising fears of "fifth columnists" and pro-Fascist
activities in the United States led to a renewed image of German-Americans as
a dangerous alien group and made any ethnic consciousness appear, once again,
as a sign of disloyalty. Once again the image of a barbarous homeland led
many German-Americans into a denial of their ethnic roots. When war came

German-Americans were again asked to fight against their old homeland, and
they did. Forty two per cent of German-Americans surveyed felt Germany was
the "the number one enemy" of the United States even after Pearl Harbor.
That figure demonstrates the depth of rejection of ties to Hitler's Germany.
Only one per cent more of the German-Americans named the Japanese in that
category.[6]

After the second war, what with the new meaning the word "German" ha
acquired, an ethnic consciousness appeared as something to consign to
oblivion, and most German-Americans did just that, as several studies have
shown.[7] Wounded in World War I, battered by the events of the interwar
years, German-American ethnic consciousness ultimately became a casualty of
World War II, one more victim--however inadvertently and ironically--of the
forces which sought to create a 1000-year Reich enshrining their variant of
Germanic culture.

NOTES

Conclusion.

1. Interview with Karl Laschett, President of the German Day Association of Chicago, July 29, 1977; interview with Martin Kaste, Archivist, Northern Illinois District of the Lutheran Church--Missouri Synod, June 15, 1977.

2. Interview with Willie Kanies, Office Manager of the German-American National Alliance, Chicago, May 3, 1977.

3. Interview with George Felbinger, President of the Germania Club of Chicago, July 15, 1977.

4. Interview with Ed Cotter, Turner Camp of Illinois, Algonquin, Illinois, May 24, 1978; interview with Erwin Schrader, Turner Club member, Berwyn, Illinois, June 7, 1978.

5. National Opinion Research Center, "A Study of the Effect of German and Italian Origin on Certain War Attitudes," May 26, 1942, Survey #107 and #109, questions 5, 9, 10, 11, 17.

6. Ibid., question 7.

7. Nathan Glazer and Daniel P. Moynihan, Beyond the Melting Pot: The Negroes, Puerto Ricans, Jews, Italians and Irish of New York City (Cambridge, Mass., The M.I.T. Press, 1963); Joseph Hraba, American Ethnicity (Itasca, Ill., F. E. Peacock Publishers, Inc., 1979).

SOURCES CONSULTED

1. Primary Sources

A. Manuscripts

Chicago, Illinois, Chicago Historical Society. William Dever Scrapbooks and Papers.

Chicago, Illinois. Chicago Historical Society. Germania Club Records and Papers.

Chicago, Illinois. Chicago Historical Society. Otto Schmidt Papers.

Chicago, Illinois. Chicago Historical Society. George F. Schulte Scrapbooks. These three scrapbooks and the Schmidt Papers contain the most information on the German community in Chicago. Unfortunately, Dr. Schmidt died in 1933. The Schulte scrapebooks contain many newspaper items though they fall heavily to sports items in the last volume.

Chicago, Illinois. University of Chicago. Charles E. Merriam Papers. Contain little on German-Americans.

Chicago, Illinois. University of Chicago. Fight for Freedom Committee-Chicago Branch Papers, 1941-1942.

Chicago, Illinois. University of Illinois at Chicago Circle. Jane Addams Papers.

Chicago, Illinois. University of Illinois at Chicago Circle. German Aid Society Papers.

Chicago, Illinois. University of Illinois at Chicago Circle. Immigrant Protective League Papers.

Chicago, Illinois. Newberry Library. Germania Club Scrapbook, 1914-1933.

Evanston, Illinois. Northwestern University. Charles G. Dawes Papers.

Urbana, Illinois. University of Illinois. Historical Survey, Cole Notes, Illinois in World War I.

West Branch, Iowa. Herbert Hoover Library. Herbert Hoover Papers. Campaign and Transition Papers.

Columbus, Ohio. Ohio State Historical Society. Warren G. Harding
    Papers, Reels 143-144, 194-196. (Microfilm Edition.)

Washington, D.C. Library of Congress. Calvin Coolidge Papers.
    (Microfilm Edition.)

Madison, Wisconsin. State Historical Society of Wisconsin. Alexander
    Hohlfield Papers.
    Contains some information on anti-German activity during World War I.

B. Government Proceedings.

U.S. Department of Commerce and Labor. Bureau of the Census, Special
    Reports: Occupations at the Twelfth Census, 1900. Washington:
    Government Printing Office, 1904.

U.S. Department of Commerce, Bureau of the Census. Fourteenth Census of the
    United States, 1920: Population. Washington: Government Printing Office,
    1921.

U.S. Department of Commerce, Bureau of the Census. Fifteenth Census of the
    United States, 1930: Population. Washington: Government Printing
    Office, 1931.

U.S. Congress. House. Special Committee on Un-American Activities.
    Investigation of Nazi Propaganda Activities and Investigation of Certain
    Other Propaganda Activities, Public Hearings. 73rd Cong., 2nd sess.,
    1934.

U.S. Congress. House. Special Committee on Un-American Activities,
    Investigation of Un-American Propaganda Activities in the United
    States, Hearings on H. Res. 282, 76th Cong., 3rd sess.; 78th Cong.,
    2nd sess., 17 vols., 1938-1944.

U.S. Congress. Senate. Committee on the Judiciary. Hearings on the National
    German-American Alliance, 65th Cong., 2nd sess., 1918.

U.S. Congress. Senate. Committee on the Judiciary. Hearings on Brewing
    and Liquor Interests and German Propaganda, 65th Cong., 2nd sess.,
    1918, 3 vols.

U.S. Department of State. Documents on German Foreign Policy: 1918-1945.
    Series D, 8, 9, 10. Washington: Government Printing Office, 1956-57.

C. Interviews.

Cotter, Edward C. Turner Campgrounds, Algonquin, Illinois. Interview, May
    24, 1978.

Felbinger, George. Germania Club, Chicago, Illinois. Interview, July 15, 1977.

Hoellen, John H. Hoellen Insurance Company, Chicago, Illinois. Interview, July 20, 1977.

Kanies, Willie G. German-American National Alliance, Chicago. Interview, May 3, 1977.

Kaste, Martin H. Northern Illinois District, Lutheran Church-Missouri Synod, Chicago, Illinois. Interview, June 15, 1977.

Kretzmann, Adalbert J. St. Luke's Lutheran Church, Chicago, Illinois. Interview, July 15, 1977.

Kurz, Carl L. Chicago, Illinois. Interview, April 18, 1978.

Laschett, Karl L. German Day Association, Chicago, Illinois. Interview, July 29, 1977.

Manz, James. St. Paul's Lutheran Church, Chicago, Illinois. Interview, June 22, 1977.

Martini, Joseph. German Aid Society, Chicago, Illinois. Interview, August 11, 1977.

Schrader, Erwin S. American Turner's Association, Chicago, Illinois. June 7, 1978.

Shied, Frederick. Chicago, Illinois. Interview, June 9, 1978.

Vogel, Clara. Chicago, Illinois. Interview, June 10, 1977.

Wittmer, Frank. Arlington Heights, Illinois. Interview, May 13, 1978.

D. Newspapers.

Chicago Abendpost. 1914-1941.
    The principal source for the period.

Chicago Daily News. 1917-1941.

Chicago Tribune. 1914-1941.

Illinois Staats-Zeitung. 1914-1918.

New York Times. 1914-1941.

Chicago Foreign Language Press Survey. (68 reels of microfilm at the University of Illinois at Chicago Circle Library and the Chicago Public Library.)

Contains translations of stories and editorials from many foreign language newspapers, including almost 12 reels of German translations. Most of the translations in this dissertation, however, are newly done. The Foreign Language Press Survey simply ignored much that was occurring in the German community, and ended in 1936.

E. Periodicals.

American Monthly (Viereck's). 1914-1933. (Fatherland from 1916-1918.)

Fortnightly Review. 1918-1933.

Literary Digest. 1914-1938.

Lutheran Witness. 1914-1941.

Newsletter, German-American National Alliance, 1940-41.

Walther League Messenger. 1921-1941.

F. Articles.

Brooks, William E. "One Way to Cure Hyphenism." Outlook, December 18, 1918.

Creel, George. "Our Aliens-Were They Loyal or Disloyal?" Everybody's, March, 1919.

"Living Down the Hyphen." Dial. April 19, 1919.

Francke, Kuno. "The German Character and the German-American." Atlantic, April 1926.

"Germans are People Too." Colliers, October 14, 1939.

Griffiths, Sanford. "Occupying the Rhineland." New Republic, January 7, 1920.

Hanighen, Frank C. "Foreign Political Movements in the U.S." Foreign Affairs, Oct. 1937.

High, Stanley. "Star-Spangled Fascists." Saturday Evening Post, May 27, 1939.

_____. "Alien Poison." Saturday Evening Post, August 31, 1940.

"Hitlerism Comes to America." Harper's Monthly, November, 1933.

Kramer, David. "American Fascists." Harper's Monthly, September, 1940.

Lewis, Sinclair. "An American Views the Huns." The Nation, July 1, 1925.

Lore, Ludwig. "Nazi Politics in America." Nation, November 29, 1933.

Mencken, Henry L. "Hitlerismus." American Mercury, December, 1933.

"Must America Go Fascist." Harper's Monthly, June, 1934.

Padover, Saul K. "Unser Amerika." Forum, March-June 1939.

Park, Clyde. "Strategic Retreat of the German Language Press." North American Review, May 1918.

Seabrook, William. "America: Ueber Alles." American Magazine, October, 1937

_____. "Try to Make Nazis Out of Us! German Americans Answer to Hitler." Current History, June, 1939.

Smith, A. J. "I Went to a Nazi Rally." Christian Century, March 8, 1939.

"What Is the Fifth Column?" Survey Graphic, October, 1940.

Ward, Henry F. "The Development of Fascism in the United States." Annals of the American Academy of Political Science, July, 1935.

"War of Nerves: U.S. Front; Nazi Agents in the United States." Fortune, October, 1940.

II. SECONDARY SOURCES

A. Periodical Articles.

Adler, Selig. "The War-Guilt Question and American Disillusionment, 1918-1928." Journal of Modern History 23 (March 1951): 1-28.

Allan, Howard W. "Isolationism and German-Americans." Journal of the Illinois State Historical Society LVI (Summer 1964): 143-149. Finds that rural German-Americans remained staunchly isolationist in 1940

Allen, Leola. "Anti-German Sentiment in Iowa during World War I." Annals of Iowa 42 (June 1974): 418-429. Discusses pressure on German-Americans to buy war bonds.

Anonymous. "Chicago and the First World War." Chicago History 7 (Fall 1964): 129-144. Covers events of 1914.

App, Austin. "German-Americans and Wilson's Peace Making." Social Justice Review 56 (June 1963); 93-96; 107; 126-130; 166-171. Filiopietistic.

Bonadio, Felice. "The Failure of German Propaganda in the United States, 1914-1917." Mid-America 41 (April, 1959): 40-57. Nothing on the peace meetings held in Chicago.

Burner, David. "Breakup of the Wilson Coalition of 1916." Mid-America
    45 (January 1963): 18-35.

Carleton, William G. "Isolationism and the Middle West." Mississippi
    Valley Historical Review XXXIII (January 1946); 377-390.
    Ignores the difference between urban and rural Germans.

_____. "The Popish Plot of 1928: The Smith-Hoover Presidental
    Campaign." The Forum CXII (September 1949): 141-47.

Carter, Paul A. "The Campaign of 1928 Re-examined." Wisconsin Magazine of
    History XLVI (Summer 1963): 262-72.
    Finds some basis for Protestant fears of a "papist in the White House."

Cary, Lorin Lee. "Wisconsin Patriots Combat Disloyalty: The Wisconsin
    Loyalty Legion and Politics, 1917-1918." Wisconsin Magazine of
    History XLVIII (Summer 1965): 121-135.

Cole, Wayne S. "American Entry into World War II: An Historiographical
    Appraisal." Mississippi Valley Historical Review XLIII (March 1951):
    613-25.

Conners, Michael. "Development of Germanophobia." Social Justice Review
    53 (January 1961): 328-31.
    Sees Germans as the new scapegoats for the world's evils.

Cuddy, Edward. "Pro-Germanism and American Catholicism." Catholic
    Historical Review 54 (June 1968): 427-54.
    Finds little pro-Germanism among American Catholics.

Dobbert, Guido A. "German-Americans Between New and Old Fatherland,
    1870-1914." American Quarterly XIX (Winter 1967): 663-680.
    Discusses Cincinatti Germans and finds a high degree of German
    nationalism.

Duff, John B. "German-Americans and the Peace, 1918-1920." American Jewish
    Historical Quarterly 59 (January 1970): 424-44.

Eichoff, Juergen. "Wisconsin's German-Americans: From Ethnic Identity to
    Assimilation." German-American Studies 2 (June 1970): 44-54.
    Based on a linguistic analysis.

Esslinger, Dean. "American-German and Irish Attitudes Toward Neutrality:
    A Study of Catholic Minorities." Catholic Historical Review 53
    (January 1968): 194-216.
    Finds both groups hostile to President Wilson after studying the
    German and Irish press in Illinois and Indiana.

Etzold, Thomas H. "The Futility Factor: German Information Gathering in
    the United States, 1933-41." Military Affairs XXXIX (September 1975):
    77-82.

Ewen, David. "German Music in America and the First World War." Decision 3 (Summer 1942): 47-53.

Fensterwald, Bernard J. "The Anatomy of American Isolationism and Expansionism." Journal of Conflict Resolution 11 (June and December 1958): 111-139, 280-309.
A psychological interpretation which ignores the ethnic factor.

Girmarc, Jerry Dell. "Illinois Catholic Editorial Opinion During World War I." Historical Records and Studies, U.S. Catholic Historical Society XLVIII (1960): 167-184.
Contains little on German Catholic views.

Gordon, Milton M. "Assimilation in America: Theory and Reality." Daedelus XC (Spring 1961): 263-285.

Gosnell, Harold F. "An Analysis of the 1932 Presidential Vote in Chicago." American Political Science Review 29 (December 1935): 967-984.
Finds prohibition the predominant factor in Roosevelt's election.

_____. "Factorial and Correlational Analysis of the 1934 Vote in Chicago." Journal of the American Statistical Association (September 1936): 618-625.
Does not discuss ethnic factors.

_____. "Relation of the Press to Voting in Chicago." Journalism Quarterly 13 (June 1936): 129-48.
Nothing on foreign language newspapers.

Gottlieb, Moshe. "The First of April Boycott and the Reaction of the American Jewish Community." American Jewish Historical Quarterly 57 (September 1968): 516-56.

Handlin, Oscar. "Historical Perspectives on the American Ethnic Group." Daedelus. XC (Spring 1961): 220-232.

Hendrickson, Kenneth. "The Socialists of Reading, Pennsylvania and World War I: A Question of Loyalty." Pennsylvania Magazine of History and Biography 36 (June 1969): 430-50.
Socialists destroyed because of opposition to war.

Hickey, Donald R. "The Prager Affair: A Study in Wartime Hysteria." Journal of the Illinois State Historical Society 62 (Winter 1969): 117-134.

Johnson, Hildegarde B. "The Location of German Immigrants in the Middlewest." Annals of the Association of American Geographers 41 (March 1951): 1-51.
Excellent maps tracing the dispersion of German settlers during the 19th century.

Jonas, Manfred. "Pro-Axis Sentiment and American Isolationism." The Historian XXIX (February 1967): 221-37.
Finds little pro-Hitler sentiment among American isolationists.

_____. "Prophet Without Honor: Hans Heinrich Dieckhoff's Reports from Washington." Mid-America XLVII (July 1965): 221-235. Dieckhoff saw little chance for a revival of German nationalism among German-Americans.

Kerr, Thomas. "German-Americans and Neutrality in the 1916 Election." Mid-America 43 (April 1961): 95-105.

Kimball, Warren F. "Dieckhoff and America: A German's View of German-American Relations." The Historian XXVII (February 1965): 218-43.

Leopold, Richard W. "The Mississippi Valley and American Foreign Policy, 1890-1941: An Assessment and an Appeal." Mississippi Valley Historical Review 37 (December 1950): 625-42. Part of the appeal is for a discussion of German-American attitudes towards the coming of both world wars.

Luebke, Frederick. "The Immigrant Church as a Factor Contributing to the Conservatism of the Lutheran Church-Missouri Synod." Concordia Historical Institute Quarterly (Spring 1965): 19-28. One of the best discussions of the Missouri Synod ideology.

Mann, Georg. "Furor Teutonicus: Upper Mississippi Abteilung." Yale Review 60 (Fall 1970): 306-320.

Maurer, Heinrich H. "Studies in the Sociology of Religion." American Journal of Sociology XXX and XXXI (November 1924--January 1926): 408-38; 534-550; 665-682; 39-57; 485-506.

_____. "The Political Attitudes of the Lutheran Parish in America: A Study in Religious Sectionalism." American Journal of Sociology XXXIII (January 1928): 568-85.

_____. "The Lutheran Community and American Society: A Study in Religion as a Condition of Social Accomodation." American Journal of Sociology XXXIV (September 1928): 282-295. Classic studies of the Missouri Synod which point to its extreme alienation from American values and its predilection to follow strong leaders.

May, Ernest. "Nazi Germany and the United States: A Review Essay." Journal of Modern History 41 (July 1969): 207-14.

McMillen, Neil R. "Pro-Nazi Sentiment in the United States, March 1933--March 1934." Southern Quarterly (October 1963): 48-70. Concerned largely with New York City.

Miller, Robert M. "A Footnote to the Role of Protestant Churches in the Election of 1928." Church History XXV (June 1956): 145-59.

Nelson, Keith L. "The 'Black Horror on the Rhine': Race as a Factor in Post-World War I Diplomacy." Journal of Modern History 42 (December 1970): 614-619.

Nichols, Jeannete. "The Middle West and the Coming of World War II."
    Ohio State Archeological and Historical Quarterly LXII (Summer 1953):
    122-45.
    Ignores the ethnic factor.

Norman, John. "Pro-Fascist Activities in Western Pennsylvania during the
    Ethiopian War." The Western Pennsylvania History Magazine XXV
    (September 1942): 143-48.
    Concerns Italian Fascist groups.

Ogburn, William F. "A Measurement of the Factors in the Presidential
    Election of 1928." Social Forces 8 (December 1929): 14-24.

Reinders, Robert C. "Racialism on the Left: E.D. Morel and the 'Black
    Horror on the Rhine." International Review of Social History 12
    (January 1968): 1-28.

Remak, Joachim. "Friends of the New Germany: The Bund and German-American
    Relations." Journal of Modern History 29 (January 1957): 38-41.

Ribuffo, Leo. "Fascists, Nazis and American Minds: Perceptions and
    Preconceptions." American Quarterly 26 (Winter 1974): 417-32.

Russett, Bruce. "Demography, Salience, and Isolationist Behavior."
    Public Opinion Quarterly XXIV (December 1960): 658-664.
    Finds little basis for an ethnic interpretation of isolationism.

Schottenhamel, George. "How Big Bill Thompson Won Control of Chicago."
    Journal of the Illinois Labor History Society 45 (January 1952): 30-50.

Shenton, James P. "Fascism and Father Coughlin." Wisconsin Magazine of
    History XLIV (Autumn 1960): 6-11.

Shideler, James H. "The La Follette Progressive Party Campaign of 1924."
    Wisconsin Magazine of History XXXIII (June 1950): 444-57.

Smuckler, Ralph. "The Region of Isolationism." American Political Science
    Review XLVII (June 1953): 386-401.
    Ignores ethnic factor.

Smith, Arthur. "The Kameradschaft-USA." Journal of Modern History 34
    (December 1962): 398-408.
    Study of a group of American Nazis who returned to Germany.

Stange, Doughlas C. "Al Smith and the Republican Party at Prayer: The
    Lutheran Vote-1928." Review of Politics 32 (July 1970): 347-64.

Strickland, Charles E. "American Aid to Germany, 1919-1921." Wisconsin
    Magazine of History 45 (Summer 1962): 256-70.

Weinberg, Gerhard. "Hitler's Image of the United States." American Historical
    Review LXIX (February 1964): 1006-1021.

Wentz, Frederick. "American Catholic Periodicals React to Nazism." Church History 31 (Winter 1962): 400-20.

_____. "American Protestant Journals and the Nazi Religious Assault." 23 (Summer 1954): 321-38.

Wilkins, Robert P. "Middle Western Isolationism: A Re-Examination." North Dakota Quarterly XXV (January 1957): 69-76.

_____. "The Non-Ethnic Roots of North Dakota Isolationism." Nebraska History XLIV (April 1963): 205-211.

Wittke, Carl. "American Germans in Two World Wars." Wisconsin Magazine of History 27 (Spring 1943): 6-16.

B. General Works

Allswang, John. A House for All Peoples: Ethnic Politics in Chicago, 1890-1936. Lexington: University of Kentucky Press, 1971.

Bagby, Wesley M. The Road to Normalcy. Baltimore: Johns Hopkins University Press, 1962.

Bailey, Thomas A. The Man in the Street: The Impact of American Public Opinion on Foreign Policy. New York: The Macmillan Company, 1948.
Contains some information on the 1920 election and German-Americans.

_____., and Ryan, Paul. The Lusitania Disaster: An Episode in Modern Warfare and Diplomacy. New York: The Free Press, 1975.

Bane, Suda L., and Lutz, Ralph. The Blockade of Germany after the Armistice, Selected Documents of the Supreme Economic Council, Blockade Council. American Relief Administration, and Other Wartime Organizations. Hoover Library on War, Revolution, and Peace, publication no. 16. Palo Alto: Stanford University Press, 1942.

Barry, Colman A. The Catholic Church and German-Americans. Washington, D.C.: Catholic University Press of America, 1953.

Beck, Earl. Germany Rediscovers America, 1920-1931. Tallahassee: Florida State University Press, 1968.
The German view of the United States in the Weimar years.

Beck, Walter. Lutheran Elementary Schools in the United States. St. Louis: Concordia Publishing House, 1939.

Bennett, David H. Demagogues in the Depression: American Radicals and the Union Party, 1932-1936. New Brunswick, N.J.:   1969.

Bell, Leland V. In Hitler's Shadow: The Anatomy of American Nazism. Port Washington, New York: Kennikat Press, 1974.

Billigmeier, Robert H. Americans from Germany: A Study in Cultural Diversity. Belmont, California: Wadsworth Publishing Company, Inc., 1974.

Brooks, Sidney. America and Germany, 1918-1925. New York: The Macmillan Co., 1925.

Burgess, Ernest W., and Newcomb, Charles. Census Data of the City of Chicago, 1920. Chicago: University of Chicago Press, 1931.

_____. Census Data of the City of Chicago, 1930. Chicago: University of Chicago Press, 1933.

Burner, David. The Politics of Provincialism: The Democratic Party in Transition, 1916-1932. New York: W. W. Norton Co., 1968.

Cazden, Robert E. German Exile Literature in America, 1933-1950: A History of the Free German Press and Book Trade. Chicago: American Library Association, 1970.

Child, Clifton. The German-American in Politics, 1914-1917. Madison: University of Wisconsin Press, 1939.
    A study limited to the German-American National Alliance.

Cole, Arthur C. "Illinois and the Great War." In The Modern Commonwealth, pp. 454-471. Edited by Ernest L. Bogart. Springfield: Illinois State Historical Society, 1920.

Cole, Wayne S. America First: The Battle Against Intervention, 1940-41. Madison: University of Wisconsin Press, 1953.

_____. Charles A. Lindbergh and the Battle Against Intervention in World War II. New York: Harcourt Brace Jovanovich, 1974.
    Contains an excellent chapter on Lindbergh and the Nazis.

Compton, James V. The Swastika and the Eagle: Hitler, the United States and the Origins of World War II. Boston: Houghton Mifflin, 1967.
    Finds that Hitler did have a plan to take over the United States.

Cooper, John M. Jr., The Vanity of Power: American Isolationism and the First World War, 1914-1917. Westport, Conn., Greenwood Press, 1969.
    A study of the congressional debate which finds only slight relation between an ethnic constituency and isolationist voting in Congress.

Counts, George S. School and Society in Chicago. New York: Columbia University Press, 1928.

Cunz, Dieter. The Maryland Germans: A History. Port Washington, New York: Kennikat Press, 1972.
    Finds the beginning of a revival of German culture towards the late 1920s.

_____. They Came From Germany: The Stories of Famous German Americans. New York: Dodd, Mead, Inc., 1966.

_____. "The German-Americans." In One America, pp. 104-20. Edited by Frederick Brown. New York: Prentice-Hall Inc., 1952.

DeJong Louis. The German Fifth Column in the Second World War. Chicago: University of Chicago Press, 1956.
    Concludes that the existence of a "fifth column" was largely a myth.

Diamond, Sandor. The Nazi Movement in the United States, 1924-1941. Ithica: Cornell University Press, 1974.

Divine, Robert. American Immigration Policy, 1924-1952. New Haven: Yale University Press, 1957.

Doenecke, Justus. The Literature of Isolationism: A Guide to Non-Interventionist Scholarship, 1930-1972. Colorado Springs: Ralph Miles Publishers, 1972.

_____. "Isolationists of the 1930s and 1940s: A Historiographical Essay." In American Diplomatic History: Issues and Methods, pp. 5-39. Edited by Robert W. Sellen and Thomas A. Bryson. Carollton, Georgia: West Georgia College Studies in the Social Sciences, 1974.

Drummond, Donald F. The Passing of American Neutrality, 1938-1941. Ann Arbor, Michigan: University of Michigan Press, 1955.

Flanagan, John T. "The German in American Fiction." In In the Trek of the Immigrants, pp. 95-113. Edited by Fritrof Anders. Rock Island, Ill.: Augustana Press, 1964.
    All too brief a discussion of an important topic.

Flynn, George L. American Catholics and the Roosevelt Presidency, 1932-1936. Lexington: University of Kentucky Press, 1968.

_____. Roosevelt and Romanism: Catholics and American Diplomacy, 1937-1941. Westport, Conn.: Greenwood Press, 1976.
    Contains little on German-American Catholic opinion.

Friedlander, Saul. Prelude to Downfall: Hitler and the United States, 1939-1941. New York: Alfred A. Knopf, 1967.
    Discounts German-American influence in United States politics.

Frye, Alton. Nazi Germany and the American Hemisphere, 1933-1941. New Haven: Yale University Press, 1967.

Gerson, Louis L. The Hyphenate in Recent American Politics and Diplomacy. Lawrence: University of Kansas Press, 1964.
    Decries "other country loyalty" among American ethnic groups. Includes discussion of 1936 and 1940 elections.

278

Gleason, Philip. The Conservative Reformers: American Catholics and the Social Order. South Bend: University of Notre Dame Press, 1968.

Gordon, Milton M. Assimilation in American Life: The Role of Race, Religion, and National Origins. New York: Oxford University Press, 1964.

Gosnell, Harold F. Machine Politics: Chicago Model. Chicago: University of Chicago Press, 1937.

Gottfried, Alex. Boss Cermak of Chicago: A Study of Political Leadership. Seattle: University of Washington Press, 1962.

Graebner, Alan. Uncertain Saints: A History of the Lutheran Laymen's League. Westport, Conn., Greenwood Press, 1978.

Grassmuck, George L. Sectional Biases in Congress on Foreign Policy. Baltimore: John Hopkins University Press, 1951.

Harbaugh, William H. Lawyer's Lawyer: The Life of John W. Davis. New York: Oxford University Press, 1973.

Hartmann, Edward. The Movement ot Americanize the Immigrant. New York: Columbia University Press, 1948.

Hawgood, John A. The Tragedy of German-America: the Germans in the United States of America during the Nineteenth Century-and After. New York Putnam, 1940.

Hildebrand, Klaus. The Foreign Policy of the Third Reich. Berkeley: University of California Press, 1974.

Hofman, John E. "The Language Transition in Some Lutheran Denominations." In Readings in the Sociology of Language, pp. 621-642. Edited by Joshua A. Fishman. The Hague: Mouton, 1968.

Hofmeister, Rudolph. The Germans of Chicago. Champaign, Ill.: Stipes Publishing Compnay, 1976.

Hutchinson, Edward P. Immigrants and their Children. New York: Oxford University Press, 1956.

Iverson, Noel. Germania, U.S.A.: Social Change in New Ulm, Minnesota. Minneapolis: University of Minnesota Press, 1966.

Jensen, Joan. The Price of Vigilence. Chicago: Rand, McNally Inc.: 1968.

Jensen, Richard. Illinois: A Bicentennial History. New York: W.W. Norton, Inc., 1978.

Johnson, Neil. George Sylvestor Viereck: German-American Propagandist. Urbana: University of Illinois Press, 1972.

Johnson, Walter. The Battle Against Isolation. Chicago: University of Chicago Press, 1944.

Keller, Phyllis. States of Belonging: German-American Intellectuals and the First World War. Cambridge, Mass.: Harvard University Press, 1979.

Kersten, Lawrence K. The Lutheran Ethnic: The Impact of Religion on Laymen and Clergy. Detroit: Wayne State University Press, 1970.

Kinzer, Donald A. An Episode in Anti-Catholicism: The American Protective Association. Seattle: University of Washington Press, 1964.

Kloss, Heinz. Um die Einigung des Deutsch-amerikanerstums: Die Geschichte einer unvollendenten Volksgruppe. Berlin: Volk and Reich Verlag, 1937.

_____., ed. The German Language in America: A Symposium. Austin: University of Texas Press, 1970.

Korman, Gerd. Industrialization, Immigrants, and Americanization: The View From Milwaukee. Madison: State Historical Society of Wisconsin, 1967.

Langer, William L., and Gleason, S. Everett. The Undeclared War, 1940-41. New York: Harper and Bros., 1953.

Livermore, Seward. Woodrow Wilson and the War Congress. Seattle: University of Washington Press, 1968.

Lubell, Samuel. The Future of American Politics. 2nd ed., New York: Harper and Bros., 1965.

Luebke, Frederick. "The Germans." In Ethnic Leadership in America, pp. 64-90. Edited by John Higham. Baltimore: Johns Hopkins University Press, 1978.

_____. Bonds of Loyalty: German-Americans and World War I. DeKalb, Ill.: Northern Illinois University Press, 1974.

McKale, Donald M. The Swastika Outside Germany. Kent, Ohio: The Kent State University Press, 1977.

McKay, Kenneth. The Progressive Movement of 1924. New York: Columbia University Press, 1947.

McKay, Seth S. Texas Politics, 1906-1944: With Special Reference to German Counties. Lubbock, Texas: Texas Tech University Press, 1952.

Meyer, Carol S. ed., Moving Frontiers: Readings in the History of the Lutheran Church-Missouri Synod. St. Louis: Concordia Publishing House, 1964.

Mundinger, Carl L. Government in the Missouri Synod. St. Louis: Concordia Publishing House, 1947.

National Lutheran Council. Chicago Lutheran Planning Study. Chicago: National Lutheran Council, 1965.

Nelson, Clifford L. German-American Political Behavior in Nebraska and Wisconsin, 1916-1920. Lincoln: University of Nebraska Press, 1972.

Nelson, Keith L. Victors Divided: American and the Allies in Germany, 1918-1923. Berkeley: University of California Press, 1975.

Norman, John. "Influence of Pro-Fascist Propaganda on American Neutrality, 1935-1936." In Essays in History and International Relations, pp. 193-98. Edited by Dwight Lee and George McReynolds. Worcester, Penn., 1949.
    Discusses Italian propaganda.

Offner, Arnold A. American Appeasement: United States Policy and Germany, 1933-1938. Cambridge, Mass.: Harvard University Press, 1969.
    Says little about German-American interest in relations with Germany.

Peterson, Horace, and Fite, Gilbert. Opponents of War, 1917-1918. Madison: University of Wisconsin Press, 1957.

Pochmann, Henry A. Bibliography of German Culture in America to 1940. Madison: State historical Society of Wisconsin, 1953.

Rippley, LaVern. Of German Ways. Minneapolis: Dillon Publishing Co., 1970.

Rogge, O. John. The Official German Report. New York: Thomas Yoseloff, 1961.

Schieber, Clara E. The Transformation of American Sentiment toward Germany, 1870-1914. Boston: Cornhill Publishing Co., 1923.

Schwartzkopf, Louis J. The Lutheran Trail: A History of the Synodical Conference Lutheran Churches in Northern Illinois. St. Louis: Concordia Publishing House, 1950.

Smith, Arthur. The Deutschtum of Nazi Germany and the United States. The Hague: Martinus Nyjhof, 1965.

Smith, Geoffrey S. To Save a Nation: American Countersubversives, the New Deal and the Coming of World War II. New York: Basic Books, Inc., 1973.

Strong, Donald S. Organized Anti-Semitism in America. Washington, D.C.: American Council on Public Affairs, 1941.

Tolzmann, Don H. German-Americana: A Bibliography. Metuchen, New Jersey: Scarecrow Press, 1975.

Townsend, Andrew J. The Germans of Chicago. Chicago: University of Chicago Press, 1932.

Trefousse, Hans L. Germany and American Neutrality, 1939-1941. New York: Columbia University Press, 1951.

Von Hagen, Wolfgang V. The Germanic People in America. Normal: University
    of Oklahoma Press, 1976.

Wendt, Lloyd., and Kogan, Herman. Big Bill of Chicago. Indianapolis:
    Bobbs-Merrill Co., 1953.

Wittke, Carl. The German Language Press in America. Lexington: University
    of Kentucky Press, 1957.

_____. German-Americans in the World War. Columbus: Ohio State
    Archeological and Historical Society, 1936.

C. UNPUBLISHED WORKS AND MONOGRAPHS

Bullard, Thomas. "The Distribution of Chicago's Germans, 1850-1914." M.A.
    thesis, Roosevelt University, 1969.

Cressey, Paul F. "The Succession of Cultural Groups in Chicago." Ph.D.
    dissertation, University of Chicago, 1930.

Dobbert, Guido A. "The Disinigration of an Immigrant Community: The
    Cincinnati Germans, 1870-1920." Ph.D. dissertation, University of
    Chicago, 1966.

Ferkiss, Victor C. "The Political and Economic Philosophy of American
    Fascism." Ph.D. dissertation, University of Chicago, 1954.

Graebner, Alan N. "The Acculturation of an Immigration Lutheran Church:
    The Lutheran Church-Missouri Synod, 1917-1929." Ph.D. dissertation,
    Columbia University, 1965.

Hess, Leland E. "Lutheranism in Chicago, 1893-1918." M.A. thesis,
    University of Chicago, 1940.

Holbo, Paul S. "They Voted Against War." Ph.D. dissertation, University
    of Chicago, 1961.

Kohlhoff, Dean. "The Missouri Synod and the Image of Germany, 1914-1941."
    Ph.D. dissertation, University of Chicago, 1975.

Nathan, Meyer J. "The Presidential Election of 1916 in the Middle West."
    Ph.D. dissertation, Princeton University, 1966.

Rogers, William C. "Isolationist Propaganda (September 1939-December 7,
    1941)." Ph.D. dissertation, University of Chicago, 1943.

Schoenthal, Klaus F. "American Attitudes toward Germany, 1918-1932."
    Ph.D. dissertation, Ohio State University, 1959.

Small, Melvin. "The American Image of Germany, 1906-1914." Ph.D.
    dissertation, University of Michigan, 1965.

Thurner, Arthur W. "The Impact of Ethnic Groups on the Democratic Party
    in Chicago, 1920-1928." Ph.D. dissertation, University of Chicago,
    1966.

Umbeck, Sharvy G. "The Social Adaptation of A Select Group of German
    Background Protestant Churches in Chicago." Ph.D. dissertation,
    University of Chicago, 1940.